AMY

MY DAUGHTER

MITCH WINEHOUSE

AMY

MY DAUGHTER

*it*books

AN IMPRINT OF HARPERCOLLINS PUBLISHERS

*it**books***

Also published in Great Britain in 2012 by HarperCollins Publishers.

HarperCollins books may be purchased for educational, business, or sales promotional use. For information please write: Special Markets Department, HarperCollins Publishers, 10 East 53rd Street, New York, NY 10022.

FIRST U.S. EDITION

Library of Congress Cataloging-in-Publication Data is available upon request.

ISBN 978-0-06-219138-0
ISBN 978-0-06-221835-3 (International Edition)

12   13   14   15   16   ID/RRD   10   9   8   7   6   5   4   3   2   1

This book is dedicated to my father Alec, my mother Cynthia and my daughter Amy. They showed me that love is the most powerful force in the universe.
Love transcends even death.
They will live in my heart forever.

CONTENTS

BEFORE WE START

You'll understand if I tell you this is not the book I wanted to write. I had been working on one about my family's history with my friend Paul Sassienie and his writing partner Howard Ricklow. It was due to be published this year.

I needed to write this book instead. I needed to tell you the real story of Amy's life. I'm a plain-talking guy and I'll be telling it like it was. Amy's too-short life was a roller-coaster ride; I'm going to tell you about all of it. Apart from being her father, I was also her friend, confidant and adviser – not that she always took my advice, but she always heard me out. For Amy, I was the port in the storm; for me, she – along with her brother Alex – was the light of my life.

I hope, through reading this book, that you will gain a better understanding of and a new perspective on my darling daughter Amy.

THANKS, AND A NOTE

A huge thank-you to my wife Jane, for being my rock during the most difficult time of my life and for her continuing dedication and support; Alex, my son, for his love and understanding; Janis, for being a fantastic mother to our children; my sister Melody and all my wonderful family and friends, for always being there; my manager Trenton; my PA Megan; Raye and everyone at Metropolis; my agents Maggie Hanbury and Robin Straus, and the lovely people at HarperCollins on both sides of the Atlantic. And special thanks to Paul Sassienie, Howard Ricklow and Humphrey Price for helping me write this book.

I am donating all of my proceeds as author from this book to the Amy Winehouse Foundation, which we, Amy's family, established to help children and young adults facing difficulty and adversity in their lives. I intend to spend the rest of my life raising money for the Foundation.

I believe that through her music, the Foundation's work and this book, Amy will be with us for ever.

PROLOGUE

I'd like to say that the first time I cuddled my new-born baby daughter, on 14 September 1983, was a moment that will live with me always, but it wasn't nearly as straightforward as that.

Some days time drags, and others the hours just fly. That day was one of those, when everything seemed to happen at once. Unlike our son Alex, who'd been born three and a half years earlier, our daughter came into the world quickly, popping out in something of a rush, like a cork from a bottle. She arrived in typical Amy fashion – kicking and screaming. I swear she had the loudest cry of any baby I've ever heard. I'd like to tell you that it was tuneful but it wasn't – just loud. Amy was four days late, and nothing ever changed: for the whole of her life she was always late.

Amy was born at the Chase Farm Hospital in Enfield, north London, not far from where we lived in Southgate. And because the moment itself was quickly over, her family – grandparents, great-aunts, uncles and cousins – soon crowded in, much as they did for almost every event in our family, good or bad, filling the spaces around Janis's bed to greet the new arrival.

I'm a very emotional guy, especially when it comes to my family, and, holding Amy in my arms, I thought, I'm the luckiest man in the world. I was so pleased to have a daughter: after Alex was born, we'd hoped our next child might be a girl, so he could have a sister. Janis and I had already decided what to call her. Following a Jewish tradition, we gave our children names that began with the same initial as a deceased relative, so Alex was named after my father, Alec, who'd died when I was sixteen. I'd thought that if we had another boy he'd be called Ames. A jazzy kind of name. 'Amy,' I said, thinking that didn't sound quite as jazzy. How wrong I was. So Amy Jade Winehouse – Jade after my stepfather Larry's father Jack – she became.

Amy was beautiful, and the spitting image of her older brother. Looking at pictures of the two of them at that age, I find it difficult to tell them apart. The day after she was born I took Alex to see his new little sister, and we took some lovely pictures of the two of them, Alex cuddling Amy.

I hadn't seen those photographs for almost twenty-eight years, until one day in July 2011, the day before I was due to go to New York, I got a call from Amy. I could tell right away that she was very excited.

'Dad, Dad, you've got to come round,' she said.

'I can't, darling,' I told her. 'You know I've got a gig tonight and I'm flying off early in the morning.'

She was insistent. 'Dad, I've found the photographs. You've got to come round.' Suddenly I knew why she was so excited. At some point during Amy's numerous moves, a box of family photographs had been lost, and she had clearly come across it that morning. 'You've *got* to come over.'

In the end I drove over in my taxi to Camden Square and parked outside her house. 'I'm just popping in,' I said, knowing full well how hard it was to say no to her. 'You know I'm busy today.'

'Oh, you're always going too quick,' she responded. 'Dad, stay.'

I followed her in, and she had the photographs she'd found spread out on a table. I looked down at them. I had better ones but these obviously meant a lot to her. There was Alex holding new-born Amy, and there was Amy as a teenager – but all the rest were of family and friends.

She picked up a photo of my mum. 'Wasn't Nan beautiful?' she said. Then she held up the picture of Alex and herself. 'Oh, look at him,' she added, a mixture of pride and sibling rivalry in her voice.

She went through the collection, picking up one after another, talking to me about each one, and I thought, This girl, famous all over the world, someone who's brought joy to millions of people – she's just a normal girl who loves her family. I'm really proud of her. She's a great kid, my daughter.

It was easy to be with her that day: she was a lot of fun. Eventually, after an hour or so, it was time for me to go, and we hugged. As I held her I could feel that she was her old self: she was becoming strong again – she'd been working with weights in the gym she'd put into her house.

'When you're back, we'll go into the studio to do that duet,' she said, as we walked to the door. We had two favourite songs, 'Fly Me To The Moon' and 'Autumn Leaves', and Amy wanted us to record one or other of them together. 'We're going to rehearse properly,' she added.

'I'll believe it when I see it,' I said, laughing. We'd had this conversation many times over the years. It was nice to hear her talking like that again. I waved goodbye out of the cab.

I never saw my darling daughter alive again.

*　　*　　*

I arrived in New York on the Friday, and had a quiet evening alone. The following day I went to see my cousin Michael and his wife Alison at their apartment on 59th Street – Michael had immigrated to the US a few years earlier when he'd married Alison. They now had three-month-old twins, Henry and Lucy, and I was dying to meet them. The kids were great and I had Henry sitting on my lap when Michael got a call from his father, my uncle Percy, who lives in London. Michael passed the phone to me. There was the usual stuff: 'Hello, Mitch, how are you? How's Amy?' I told him I'd seen Amy just before I'd flown out and she was fine.

My mobile rang. The caller ID said, 'Andrew – Security'. Amy often rang me using the phone of her security guard Andrew so I told my uncle, 'I think that's Amy now,' and passed the house phone back to Michael. I still had Henry on my lap as I answered my phone.

'Hello, darling,' I said. But it wasn't Amy, it was Andrew. I could barely make out what he was saying.

All I could decipher was: 'You gotta come home, you gotta come home.'

'What? What are you talking about?'

'You've got to come home,' he repeated.

My world drained away from me. 'Is she dead?' I asked.

And he said, 'Yes.'

1

ALONG CAME AMY

From the start I was besotted with my new daughter, and not much else mattered to me. In the days before Amy was born, I'd been fired from my job, supposedly because I'd asked to take four days off for my daughter's birth. But with Amy in the world those concerns seemed to disappear. Even though I had no job, I went out and bought a JVC video camera, which cost nearly a grand. Janis wasn't best pleased, but I didn't care. I took hours of video of Amy and Alex, which I've still got.

Alex sat guard by her cot for hours at a time. I went into her bedroom late one night and found Amy wide awake and Alex fast asleep on the floor. Great guard he made. I was a nervous dad, and I'd often peer into her cot to check she was okay. When she was a very young baby I'd find her panting, and shout, 'She's not breathing properly!' Janis had to explain that all babies made noises like that. I still wasn't happy, though, so I'd pick Amy up – and then we couldn't get her back to sleep. She was an easy baby, though, and it wasn't long before she was sleeping through the night, so soundly sometimes that Janis had to wake her up to feed her.

Amy learned to walk on her first birthday, and from then on she was a bit of a handful. She was very inquisitive, and if you didn't watch her all the time, she'd be off exploring. At least we had some help: my mother and stepfather, along with most of the rest of my family, seemed to be there every day. Sometimes I'd come home late from work and Janis would tell me they'd eaten my dinner.

Janis was a wonderful mother, and still is. Alex and Amy could both read and write before they went to school, thanks to her. When I came home I'd hear them upstairs, walk up quietly and stand outside their bedroom door to watch them. The kids would be tucked in either side of Janis as she read to them, their eyes wide, wondering what was coming next. This was their time together and I wished I was part of it.

On the nights that I didn't get home until ten or eleven o'clock, I'd sometimes wake them up to say goodnight. I'd go into their room, kick the cot or bed, say, 'Oh, they're awake,' and pick them up for a cuddle. Janis used to go mad and quite right too.

I was a hands-on father but more for rough-and-tumble than reading stories. Alex and I would play football and cricket in the garden, and Amy would want to join in – 'Dad! Dad! Give *me* the ball.' I'd prod it towards her, then she'd pick it up and throw it over the fence.

Amy loved dancing and, as most dads did with their young daughters, I'd hold her hands and balance her feet on mine. We'd sway like that around the room, but Amy liked it best when I twirled her round and round, enjoying the feeling of disorientation it gave her. She became fearless physically, climbing higher than I liked, or rolling over the bars of a climbing frame in the park. She also liked playing at home: she loved her Cabbage Patch dolls, and we had to send off the 'adoption certificates' the dolls came with to keep her happy. If Alex wanted to torment her, he'd tie the dolls up.

When I did come home early I read to the children, always Enid Blyton's Noddy books. Amy and Alex were Noddy experts. Amy loved the 'Noddy quiz'.

She would say, 'Daddy, what was Noddy wearing the day he met Big Ears?'

I'd pretend to think for a minute. 'Was he wearing his red shirt?'

Amy would say, 'No.'

I'd tell her that was a very hard question and I needed to think. 'Was he wearing his blue hat with the bell on the end?' Another no. Then I'd click my fingers. 'I know! He was wearing his blue shorts and his yellow scarf with red spots.'

'No, Daddy, he wasn't.'

At that point I'd give in and ask Amy to tell me what he was wearing. Before she could get the words out, she was already giggling. 'He wasn't wearing anything, he was … naked!'

And then she'd put her hand over her mouth to stifle her hysterical laughing. No matter how many times we played that game it never varied.

We weren't one of those families that had the TV on for the sake of it. There was always music playing and I sang around the house. We used to get the kids to put on little shows for us. I'd introduce them and Janis would clap and they'd start singing – well, I say singing … Alex couldn't sing but would give it a go, and Amy's only goal was to sing louder than her brother. Clearly she liked the limelight. If Alex got bored and went off to do something else, Amy would carry on singing – even after we'd told her to stop.

She loved a little game I used to play with her – we did it a lot in the car. I'd start a song or nursery rhyme and she'd sing the last word.

'Humpty Dumpty sat on the …'

'… WALL …'

'… Humpty Dumpty had a great …'

'… FALL.' It kept us amused for ages.

One year Amy was given a little turntable that played nursery rhymes. It was all you heard from her room. Then she had a xylophone and taught herself – slowly and painfully – to play 'Home On The Range'. The noise would carry through the house, *plink, plink, plink*, and I'd will her to hit the right notes on time – it was agonizing to have to listen to it.

Despite her charm, 'Be quiet, Amy!' was probably the most-heard sentence in our house during her early years. She just didn't know when to stop. Once she started singing that was it. And if she wasn't the centre of attention, she'd find a way of becoming it – occasionally at Alex's expense. At his sixth birthday party Amy, aged three, put on an impromptu show of singing and dancing. Naturally, Alex wasn't best pleased and, before we could stop him, he poured a drink over her. Amy burst into tears and ran out of the room crying. I shouted at Alex so loudly that he ran out crying too. After the party, Amy sat on the kitchen floor sulking, and Alex wouldn't come out of his room.

Despite such scenes, Alex and Amy were extremely close and remained so, even when they got older and made their own circles of friends.

Amy would do anything for attention. She was mischievous, bold and daring. Not long after Alex's birthday party, Janis took Amy to Broomfield Park, near our home, and lost her. A panic-stricken Janis phoned me at work to tell me that Amy was missing and I raced to the park, beside myself with anxiety. By the time I arrived, the police were there and I was preparing myself for the worst: in my mind, she wasn't lost, she'd been abducted. My mum and my auntie Lorna were also there – everybody was looking for Amy. Clearly, Amy was no longer in the park and the police told us to go home, which we did. Five hours later, Janis and I were crying our eyes out when the phone rang. It was Ros, one of my sister Melody's friends. Amy was with her. Thank God.

What had happened was just typical of Amy. Ros had been in the park with her kids when Amy had seen her and run over to her. Naturally, Ros had asked where her mummy was, and mischievous Amy had told her that her mummy had gone home. So Ros took Amy home with her, but instead of phoning us, she phoned Melody, who was a teacher. She didn't speak to her but left a message at the school that Amy was with her. When Melody heard that Ros was looking after Amy, she didn't think too much about it because she had no idea that Amy was missing. When she got home and heard what had happened, she put two and two together. Fifteen minutes later, Melody walked in with Amy and I burst into tears.

'Don't cry, Daddy, I'm home now,' I remember her saying.

Unfortunately, Amy didn't seem to learn from that experience. Several months later I took the kids to the Brent Cross shopping centre in north-west London. We were in the John Lewis department store and suddenly Amy was gone. One second she was there and the next she'd disappeared. Alex and I searched the immediate area – how far could she have got? – but there was no sign of her. Here we go again, I thought. And this time she'd definitely been kidnapped.

We widened the search. Just as we were walking past a rack of long coats, out she popped. 'Boo!' I was furious, but the more I told her off, the more she laughed. A few weeks later she tried it again. This time I headed straight for the long coats. She wasn't there. I searched all of the racks. No Amy. I was really beginning to worry when a voice said over the Tannoy, 'We've got a little girl called Amy here. If you've lost her, please come to Customer Services.' She'd hidden somewhere else, got really lost and someone had taken her to a member of staff. I told her there was to be no more hiding or running away when we're out. She promised she wouldn't do it again and she didn't, but the next series of practical jokes was played out to a bigger audience.

When I was a little boy I had choked on a bit of apple and my father had panicked. So, when Alex choked on his dinner, I panicked too, forcing my fingers down his throat to remove whatever was obstructing him. It didn't take Amy long to start the choking game. One Saturday afternoon we were shopping in Selfridges, in London's Oxford Street. The store was packed. Suddenly Amy threw herself on to the floor, coughing and holding her throat. I knew she wasn't really choking but she was creating such a scene that I threw her over my shoulder and we left in a hurry. After that she was 'choking' everywhere, friends' houses, on the bus, in the cinema. Eventually, we just ignored it and it stopped.

*   *   *

Although I was born in north London, I've always considered myself to be an East Ender: I spent a lot of my childhood with my grand-parents, Ben and Fanny Winehouse, at their flat above Ben the Barber, his business, in Commercial Street, or with my other grandmother,

Celie Gordon, at her house in Albert Gardens, both in the heart of the East End. I even went to school in the East End. My father was a barber and my mother was a ladies' hairdresser, both working in my grandfather's shop, and, on their way there, they'd drop me off at Deal Street School.

Amy and Alex were fascinated by the East End so I took them there often. They loved me to tell them stories about our family, and seeing where they had lived brought the stories to life. Amy liked hearing about my weekends in the East End when I was a little boy. Every Friday I went with my mum and dad to Albert Gardens where we'd stay until Sunday night. The house was packed to the rafters. There was Grandma Celie, Great-grandma Sarah, Great-uncle Alec, Uncle Wally, Uncle Nat, and my mum's twin, Auntie Lorna. If that wasn't enough, a Holocaust survivor named Izzi Hammer lived on the top floor; he passed away in January 2012.

The weekends at Albert Gardens started with the traditional Jewish Friday night dinner: chicken soup, then roast chicken, roast potatoes, peas and carrots. Dessert was lokshen pudding, made with baked noodles and raisins. Where all those people slept I really can't remember, but we all had a magical time, with singing, dancing, card games, and loads of food and drink. And the occasional loud argument mixed in with the laughter and joy of a big happy Jewish family. We continued the Friday-night tradition for most of Amy's life. It was always a special time for us, and in later years, an interesting test of Amy's friendships – who was close enough to her to be invited on a Friday night.

I spent a lot of time with the kids at weekends. In February 1982, when Alex was nearly three, I started taking him to watch football – in those days you could take young kids and sit them on your lap: Spurs v. West Bromwich Albion. It was freezing cold, so cold that I didn't want to go, but Janis dressed Alex in his one-piece padded snowsuit, which made him look twice his size – he could hardly move. When we got there I asked him if he was okay. He said he was. About five minutes after kick-off he wanted to go to the Gents. Getting him out of that padded suit was quite an operation, and then it took another ten minutes to get him into it again. When we got back to the seat, he needed to go again so we had an action replay. At half-time, he said, 'Daddy I want to go home – I'm home-sick.'

When Amy was about seven, I took her to a match. When we got home Janis asked her if she'd enjoyed it. Amy said she'd hated it. When Janis asked why she hadn't asked me to bring her home, she said, 'Daddy was enjoying it and I didn't want to upset him.' That was typical of the young Amy, always thinking of other people.

At five Amy started at Osidge Primary School, where Alex was already a pupil. There she met Juliette Ashby, who quickly became her best friend. Those two were inseparable and remained close for most of Amy's life. Her other great friend at Osidge was Lauren Gilbert: Amy already knew her because Uncle Harold, my dad's brother, was Lauren's step-grandfather.

Amy had to wear a light-blue shirt and a tie, with a sweater and a grey skirt. She was happy to join her big brother at school, but she was soon in trouble. Every day she was there could easily have been her last. She didn't do anything terrible but she was disruptive and attention-seeking, which led to regular complaints about her behaviour. She wouldn't be quiet in lessons, she doodled in her books and she played practical jokes. Once she hid under the teacher's desk. When he asked the class where Amy was, she was laughing so much that she bumped her head on his desk and had to be brought home.

Amy left a lasting impression on her Year Two teacher, Miss Cutter (now Jane Worthington), who wrote to me shortly after Amy passed away:

Amy was a vivacious child who grew into a beautiful and gifted woman. My lasting memories of Amy are of a child who wore her heart on her sleeve. When she was happy the world knew about it, when upset or unhappy you'd know that too. It was clear that Amy came from a loving and supportive family.

Amy was a clever girl, and if she'd been interested she would have done well at school. Somehow, though, she was never that interested. She was good at things like maths, but not in the sense that she did well at school. Janis was really good at maths and used to teach the kids. Amy loved doing calculus and quadratic equations when she was still at primary school. No wonder she found maths lessons boring.

She was always interested, though, in music. I always had it playing at home and in the car, and Amy sang along with everything. Although she loved big-band and jazz songs, she also liked R&B and hip-hop, especially the US R&B/hip-hop bands TLC and Salt-n-Pepa. She and Juliette used to dress up like Wham!'s backing singers, Pepsi & Shirlie, and sing their songs. When Amy was about ten she and Juliette formed a short-lived rap act, Sweet 'n' Sour – Juliette was Sweet and Amy was Sour. There were a lot of rehearsals but, sadly, no public performances.

I was devoted to my family, but as Amy and Alex got older, I was changing. In 1993, Janis and I split up. A few years earlier, a close friend of mine, who was married, confided in me that he was seeing someone else. I couldn't understand how he could do it. I remember telling him that he had a lovely wife and a fantastic son: why on earth would he want to jeopardize everything for a fling? He said, 'It's not a fling. When you find that special someone you just know it's right. If it ever happens to you, you'll understand.'

Unbelievably I found myself in a similar situation. Back in 1984 I had appointed a new marketing manager, Jane, and we had hit it off from the start. There was nothing romantic: Jane had a boyfriend and I was happily married. But there was definitely a spark between us. Nothing happened for ages and then eventually it did. Jane had been coming to my house since Amy was eighteen months old and had met Janis and the kids loads of times. She was adamant that she didn't want to come between me and my family.

I was in love with Jane but still married to Janis. That's a situation which just can't work indefinitely. It was a terrible dilemma. I wanted to be with Janis and the kids but I also wanted to be with Jane. I was never unhappy with Janis and we had a good marriage. Some men who stray hate their wives but I loved mine. You couldn't have an argument with her if you tried: she's such a sweet, good-natured person. I didn't know what to do. I really didn't want to hurt anybody. In the end I just wanted to be with Jane more.

Finally, in 1992, I made up my mind to leave Janis. I would wait until after Alex had had his Bar Mitzvah the following year, and leave shortly afterwards. Telling Alex and Amy was the hardest thing; I explained that we both loved them and that what was happening was nothing to do with anything they'd done or not done. Alex took it very badly – who can blame him? – but Amy seemed to accept it.

I felt awful as I drove away to live with Melody in Barnet. I stayed with her for six months before I moved in with Jane. Looking back now, I was a coward for allowing the situation to go on for so long, but I wanted to keep everybody happy.

Strangely, after I left I started seeing more of the kids than I had before. My friends thought that Amy didn't seem much affected by the divorce, and when I asked her if she wanted to talk about it, she said, 'You're still my dad and Mum's still my mum. What's to talk about?'

Probably through guilt, I over-indulged them. I'd buy them presents for no reason, take them to expensive places and give them money. Sometimes, when I was starting a new business and things were tight, we'd go and eat at the Chelsea Kitchen in the King's Road where I could buy meals for no more than two pounds. Years later, the kids told me they'd liked going there better than the more expensive places, mostly because they knew it wasn't costing me a lot.

Two things never changed: my love for them and theirs for me.

Amy in a contemplative mood. My birthday card in 1992.

2

TAKING TO THE STAGE

Wherever I was living, Amy and Alex always had a bedroom there. Amy would often stay for the weekend and I'd try to make it special for her. She loved ghost stories: when I lived in Hatfield Heath, Essex, the house was a bit remote and quite close to a graveyard. If we were driving home on a dark winter's night I used to park near the graveyard, turn the car lights off and frighten the life out of her with a couple of grisly stories. It wasn't long before she started making up ghost stories of her own, and I had to pretend to be scared.

On one occasion Amy had to write an essay about the life of someone who was important to her. She decided to write about me and asked me to help her. It had to be exciting, I decided, so I made up some stories about myself but Amy believed them all. I told her I'd been the youngest person to climb Mount Everest, and that when I was ten I'd played for Spurs and scored the winning goal in the 1961 Cup Final against Leicester City. I also told her I'd performed the world's first heart transplant with my assistant Dr Christiaan Barnard. I might also have told her I'd been a racing driver and a jockey.

Amy took notes, wrote the essay and handed it in. I was expecting some nice remarks about her imagination and sense of humour, but instead the teacher sent me a note, saying, 'Your daughter is deluded and needs help.' Not long before Amy passed away, she reminded me about that homework and the trouble it had caused – and she remembered another of my little stories, which I'd forgotten: I'd told her and Alex that when I was seven I'd been playing near Tower Bridge, fallen into the Thames and nearly drowned. I even drove them to the spot to show them where it had supposedly happened and told them there used to be a plaque there commemorating the event but they had taken it down to clean it.

During school holidays we had to find things for Amy to do. If I was in a meeting, Jane would take her out for lunch and Amy would always order the same thing: a prawn salad. The first time Jane took her out, when Amy was still small, she asked, 'Would you like some chocolate for pudding?'

'No, I have a dairy intolerance,' said Amy, proudly. She'd then wolfed down bag after bag of boiled sweets and chews – she always had a sweet tooth.

Jane used to work as a volunteer on the radio at Whipps Cross Hospital, and had her own show. Amy would go in with her to help. She was too young to go round the wards when Jane was interviewing the patients, so instead she would choose the records that were going to be played. Once Jane interviewed Amy, and I've still got the tapes of that conversation somewhere. Jane edited out her questions so that Amy was speaking directly to the listeners – her first broadcast.

One link I never lost with Amy when I left home was music. She learned to love the music I had been taught to love by my mother when I was younger. My mum had always adored jazz, and before she met my father she had dated the great jazz musician Ronnie Scott. At a gig in 1943, Ronnie introduced her to the legendary band leader Glenn Miller, who tried to nick her off Ronnie. And while my mum fell in love with Glenn Miller's music, Ronnie fell in love with her. He was devastated when she ended the relationship. He begged her not to and even proposed to her. She said no, but they remained close friends right up until he died in 1996. He wrote about my mum in his autobiography.

When she was a little girl, Amy loved hearing my mother recount her stories about Ronnie, the jazz scene and all the things they'd got up to. As she grew up she started to get into jazz in a big way; Ella Fitzgerald and Sarah Vaughan were her early favourites.

Amy loved one particular story I told her about Sarah Vaughan and Ronnie Scott. Whenever Ronnie had a big name on at his club, he would always invite my mum, my auntie Lorna, my sister, me and whoever else we wanted to bring. We saw some fantastic acts there – Ella Fitzgerald, Tony Bennett and a whole host of others – but for me, the most memorable was Sarah Vaughan. She was just wonderful. We went backstage afterwards and there was a line of about six people waiting to be introduced to her. When it was Mum's turn, Ronnie said, 'Sarah, this is Cynthia. She was my childhood sweetheart and we're still very close.'

Then it was my turn. Ronnie said, 'This is Mitch, Cynthia's son.'

And Sarah said, 'What do you do?'

I told her about my job in a casino and we carried on chatting for a couple of minutes about one thing and another.

Then Ronnie said, 'Sarah, this is Matt Monro.'

And Sarah said, 'What do you do, Matt?'

She really had no idea who he was. American singers are often very insular. A lot of them don't know what's happening outside New York or LA, let alone what's going on in the UK. I felt a bit sorry for Matt because he was, in my opinion, the greatest British male singer of all time – and he wasn't best pleased either. He walked out of the club and never spoke to Ronnie Scott again.

Amy also started watching musicals on TV – Fred Astaire and Gene Kelly films. She preferred Astaire, whom she thought more artistic than the athletic Kelly; she enjoyed *Broadway Melody of 1940*, when Astaire danced with Eleanor Powell. 'Look at this, Dad,' she said. 'How do they do it?' That sequence gave her a love of tap-dancing.

Amy would regularly sing to my mum, and my mum's face would light up when she did. As Amy's number-one adoring fan, who always thought Amy was going to be a star, my mum came up with the idea of sending nine-year-old Amy to the Susi Earnshaw Theatre School, in Barnet, north London, not far from where we lived. It offered part-time classes in the performing arts for five- to sixteen-year-olds. Amy used to go on Saturdays and this was where she first learned to sing and tap-dance.

Amy looked forward to those lessons and, unlike at Osidge, we never received a complaint about her behaviour from Susi Earnshaw's. Susi told us how hard Amy always worked. Amy was taught how to develop her voice, which she wanted to do as she learned more and more about the singers she listened to at home and with my mum. Amy was fascinated by the way Sarah Vaughan used her voice like an instrument and wanted to know how she could do it too.

As soon as she started at Susi Earnshaw's, Amy was going for auditions. When she was ten she went to one for the musical *Annie*; Susi sent quite a few girls for that. She told me that Amy wouldn't get the part, but it would be good for her to gain experience in auditioning – and get used to rejection.

I explained all of that to Amy but she was still happy to go along and give it a go. The big mistake I made was in telling my mum about it. For whatever reason, neither Janis nor I could take Amy to the audition and my mum was only too pleased to step in. As Amy's biggest fan, she thought this was it, that the audition was a formality – that her granddaughter was going to be the new Annie. I think she even bought a new frock for the opening night, that was how sure she was.

When I saw Amy that night, the first thing she said to me was, 'Dad, never send Nan with me for an audition *ever again.*'

It had started on the train, my mum piling on the pressure: how to sing her song, how to talk to the director, 'Don't do this, don't do that, look the director in the eye …' Amy had been taught all of this at Susi Earnshaw's but, of course, my mum knew better. They finally got to the theatre where, according to Amy, there were a thousand or so mums, dads and grandmothers, each of whom, like my mum, thought that their little prodigy was going to be the new Annie.

Finally it was Amy's turn to do her bit and she gave the audition pianist her music. He wouldn't play it: it was in the wrong key for the show. Amy struggled through the song in a key that was far too high for her. After just a few bars she was told to stop. The director was very nice and thanked her but told her that her voice wasn't suitable for the part. My mum lost it. She marched up to the director, screaming at him that he didn't know what he was talking about. There was a terrible row.

On the train going home my mum had a go at Amy, all the usual stuff: 'You don't listen to me. You think you know better …' Amy couldn't have cared less about not getting the part, but my mum was so aggravated that she put herself to bed for the rest of the day. When Amy told me the story, I thought it was absolutely hysterical. My mum and Amy were like two peas in a pod, probably shouting at each other all the way home on the train.

It would have been a great scene to see.

Amy and my mum had a lively relationship but they did love each other, and my mum would sometimes let the kids get away with murder. When we visited her, Amy would often blow-wave my mum's hair while Alex sat at her feet and gave her a pedicure. Later my mum, hair all over the place, would show us what Amy had done and we'd have a good laugh.

*   *   *

In the spring of 1994, when Amy was ten, I went with her to an interview for her next school, Ashmole in Southgate. I had gone there some twenty-five years earlier and Alex was there so it was a natural choice for Amy. Incredibly, my old form master Mr Edwards was still going strong and was to be Amy's house master. He interviewed Amy and me when I took her to look round the school. We walked into his office and he recognized me immediately. In his beautiful Welsh accent, he said, 'Oh, my God, not another Winehouse! I bet this one doesn't play football.' I had made a bit of a name for myself playing for the school, and Alex was following in my footsteps.

Amy started at Ashmole in September 1994. From the start she was disruptive. Her friend Juliette had also transferred there. They were bad enough alone, but together they were ten times worse, so it wasn't long before they were split up and put into different classes.

Alex had a guitar he'd taught himself to play, and when Amy decided to try it out he taught her too. He was very patient with her, even though they argued a lot. They could both read music, which surprised me. 'When did you learn to do this?' I asked. They stared at me as if I was speaking a foreign language. Amy soon started writing her own songs, some good, some awful. One of the good ones was called 'I Need More Time'. She played it for me just a few months before she passed away. Believe me, it's good enough to go on one of her albums, and it's a great pity that she never recorded it.

I often collected the kids from school. In those days I had a convertible, and Amy would insist I put the top down. As we drove along, Alex in the front alongside me, she'd sing at the top of her voice. When we stopped at traffic lights she would stand up and perform. 'Sit down, Amy!' we'd say, but people on the street laughed with her as she sang.

Once she was in a car with a friend of mine named Phil and sang 'The Deadwood Stage' from the Doris Day film *Calamity Jane*. 'You know,' Phil said to me, when they got back, his ears probably still ringing, 'your daughter has a really *powerful* voice.'

Amy's wild streak went far beyond car rides. At some point, she took to riding Alex's bike, which terrified me: she was reckless whenever she was on it. She had no road sense and she raced along as fast as she could. She loved speed and came off a couple of times. It was the same story when I took her skating – didn't matter if it was ice-skating or roller-skating, she loved both. She was really fast on the rink, and the passion for it never left her. After her first album came out she told me that her ambition was to open a chain of hamburger joints with roller-skating waitresses.

She was wild, but I indulged her; I couldn't help myself. I know I over-compensated my children for the divorce, but they were growing up and needed things. I took Amy shopping to buy her some clothes, now that she was nearly a teenager and going to a new school.

'Look, Dad,' she said excitedly, as she came out of the changing room in a pair of leopard-print jeans. 'These are fantastic! D'you think they look nice on me?'

*　　*　　*

Whenever she was staying with Jane and me, Amy always kept a notebook with her to scribble down lines for songs. Halfway through a conversation, she'd suddenly say, 'Oh, just a sec,' and disappear to note something that had just come to her. The lines looked like something from a poem and later she would use those lines in a song, alongside ones written on totally different occasions.

Amy continued to be good at maths because of the lessons she'd done with her mother. Janis would set Amy some pretty complicated problems, which she really enjoyed doing. Amy would do mathematical problems for hours on end just for fun. She was brilliant at the most complex Sudoku puzzles and could finish one in a flash.

The pity was that she wouldn't do it at school. We received notes complaining regularly about her behaviour or lack of interest. Clearly Amy was bored – she just didn't take to formal schooling. (I had been the same. I was always playing hooky but, unlike my friends, who would be out on the streets, I'd be in the local library, reading.) Amy had a terrific thirst for knowledge but hated school. She didn't want to go so she wouldn't get up in the mornings. Or, if she did go, she'd come home at lunchtime and not go back.

Though Amy had been a terrific sleeper as a baby and young child, when she got to about eleven she wouldn't go to bed: she'd be up all night reading, doing puzzles, watching television, listening to music, anything not to go to sleep. So, naturally, it was a battle every morning to get her up. Janis got fed up with it and would ring me: 'Your daughter won't get out of bed.' I had to drive all the way from Chingford, where I was living with Jane, and drag her out.

Over time Amy got worse in the classroom. Janis and I were called to the school for meetings about her behaviour on numerous occasions. I hope the head of year didn't see me trying not to laugh as he told us, 'Mr and Mrs Winehouse, Amy has already been sent to see me once today and, as always, I knew it was her before she got to my office …' I knew if I looked at Janis I'd crack up. 'How did I know?' the head of year continued. 'She was singing "Fly Me To The Moon" loudly enough for the whole school to hear.'

I knew I shouldn't laugh, but it was so typically Amy. She told me later that she'd sung it to calm herself down whenever she knew she was in trouble.

Just about the only thing she seemed to enjoy about school was performance. However, one year when Amy sang in a show she wasn't very good. I don't know what went wrong – perhaps it was the wrong key for her again – but I was disappointed. The following year things were different. 'Dad, will you both come to see me at Ashmole?' she asked. 'I'm singing again.' To be honest, my heart sank a bit, with the memory of the previous year's performance, but of course we went. She sang the Alanis Morissette song 'Ironic', and she was as terrific as I knew she could be. What I wasn't expecting was everyone else's reaction: the whole room sat up. Wow, where did this come from?

By now Amy was twelve and she wanted to go to a drama school full time. Janis and I were against it but Amy applied to the Sylvia Young Theatre School in central London without telling us. How she even knew about it we never figured out as Sylvia Young only advertised in *The Stage*. Amy eventually broke the news to us when she was invited to audition. She decided to sing 'The Sunny Side Of The Street', which I coached her through, helping with her breath control, and won a half-scholarship for her singing, acting and dancing. Her success was reported in *The Stage*, with a photograph of her above the column.

As part of her application, Amy had been asked to write something about herself. Here's what she wrote:

All my life I have been loud, to the point of being told to shut up. The only reason I have had to be this loud is because you have to scream to be heard in my family.

My family? Yes, you read it right. My mum's side is perfectly fine, my dad's family are the singing, dancing, all-nutty musical extravaganza.

I've been told I was gifted with a lovely voice and I guess my dad's to blame for that. Although unlike my dad, and his background and ancestors, I want to do something with the talents I've been 'blessed' with. My dad is content to sing loudly in his office and sell windows.

My mother, however, is a chemist. She is quiet, reserved.

I would say that my school life and school reports are filled with 'could do betters' and 'does not work to her full potential'.

I want to go somewhere where I am stretched right to my limits and perhaps even beyond.

To sing in lessons without being told to shut up (provided they are singing lessons).

But mostly I have this dream to be very famous. To work on stage. It's a lifelong ambition.

I want people to hear my voice and just forget their troubles for five minutes.

I want to be remembered for being an actress, a singer, for sell-out concerts and sell-out West End and Broadway shows.

I think it was to the school's relief when Amy left Ashmole. She started at the Sylvia Young Theatre School when she was about twelve and a half and stayed there for three years – but what a three years it was. It was still school, which meant she was always being told off, but I think they put up with her because they recognized that she had a special talent. Sylvia Young herself said that Amy had a 'wild spirit and was amazingly clever'. But there were regular 'incidents' – for example, Amy's nose-ring. Jewellery wasn't allowed, a rule Amy disregarded. She would be told to take the nose-ring out, which she would do, and ten minutes later it was back in.

The school accepted that Amy was her own person and gave her a degree of leeway. Occasionally they turned a blind eye when she broke the rules. But there were times when she took it too far, especially with the jewellery. She was sent home one day when she'd turned up wearing earrings, her nose-ring, bracelets and a belly-button piercing. To me, though, Amy wasn't being rebellious, which she certainly could be; this was her expressing herself.

And punctuality was a problem. Amy was late most days. She would get the bus to school, fall asleep, go three miles past her stop, then have to catch another back. So, although this was where Amy wanted to be, it wasn't a bed of roses for anyone.

Amy's main problem at Sylvia Young's was that, as well being taught stagecraft, which included ballet, tap, other dance, acting and singing, she had to put up with the academic side or, as Amy referred to it, 'all the boring stuff'. About half of the time was allocated to 'normal' subjects and she just wasn't interested. She would fall asleep in lessons, doodle, talk and generally make a nuisance of herself.

Amy really got into tap-dancing. She was pretty good at it when she started at the school but now she was learning more advanced techniques. When we were at my mother's flat for dinner on Friday nights, Amy loved to tap-dance on the kitchen floor because it gave a really good clicking sound. The clicks it gave were great. I told her she was as good a dancer as Ginger Rogers, but my mother wouldn't have that: she said Amy was better.

Amy would put her tap shoes on and say, 'Nan, can I tap-dance?'

'Go downstairs and ask Mrs Cohen if it's all right,' my mum would reply, 'because you know what she's like. She'll only complain to me about the noise.'

So Amy would go and ask Mrs Cohen if it was all right and Mrs Cohen would say, 'Of course it's all right, darling. You go and dance as much as you like.' And then the next day Mrs Cohen would complain to my mum about the noise.

After dinner on a Friday night, we'd play games. Trivial Pursuit and Pictionary were two of our favourites. Amy and I played together, my mum and Melody made up the second team, with Jane and Alex as the third. They were the 'quiet' ones, thoughtful and studious, my mum and Melody were the 'loud' pair, with a lot of screaming and shouting, while Amy and I were the 'cheats'. We'd try to win no matter what.

Another lovely birthday card from Amy, aged twelve. This came just after
yet another meeting with Amy's teacher about her behaviour.

When she wasn't playing games or tap-dancing, Amy would borrow my mum's scarves and tops. She had a way of making them seem not like her nan's things but stylish, tying shirts across her middle and that sort of thing. She also started wearing a bit of makeup – never too much, always understated. She had a beautiful complexion so she didn't use foundation, but I'd spot she was wearing eyeliner and lipstick – 'Yeah, Dad, but don't tell Mum.'

But while my mum indulged Amy's experiments with makeup and clothes, she hated Amy's piercings. Later on when Amy began getting tattoos, she'd have a go at her about all of it. Amy's 'Cynthia' tattoo came after my mum had passed away – she would have loathed it.

* * *

Along with other pupils from Sylvia Young's, Amy started getting paid work around the time she became a teenager. She appeared in a sketch on BBC2's series *The Fast Show*; she stood precariously on a ladder for half an hour in *Don Quixote* at the Coliseum in St Martin's Lane (she was paid eleven pounds per performance, which I'd look after for her as she always wanted to spend it on sweets); and in a really boring play about Mormons at Hampstead Theatre where her contribution was a ten-minute monologue at the end. Amy loved doing the little bits of work the school found for her, but she couldn't accept that she was still a schoolgirl and needed to study.

Eventually Janis and I were called in to see the head teacher of the school's academic side, who told us he was very disappointed with Amy's attitude to her work. He said that he constantly had to pressure her to buckle down and get some work done. He accepted that she was bored and they even tried moving her up a year to challenge her more, but she became more distracted than ever.

The real blow came when the academic head teacher phoned Janis, behind Sylvia Young's back, and told her that if Amy stayed at the school she was likely to fail her GCSEs. When Sylvia heard about this she was very upset and the head teacher left shortly afterwards.

Contrary to what some people have said, including Amy, Amy was not expelled from Sylvia Young's. In fact, Janis and I decided to remove her as we believed that she had a better chance with her exams at a 'normal' school. If you're told that your daughter is going to fail her GCSEs, then you have to send her somewhere else. Amy didn't want to leave Sylvia Young's and cried when we told her that we were taking her away. Sylvia was also upset and tried to persuade us to change our minds, but we believed we were doing the right thing. She stayed in touch with Amy after she'd left, which surprised Amy, given all the rows they'd had over school rules. (Our relationship with Sylvia and her school continues to this day. From September 2012, Amy's Foundation will be awarding the Amy Winehouse Scholarship, whereby one student will be sponsored for their entire five years at the school.)

Amy had to finish studying for her GCSEs somewhere, though, and the next school to get the Amy treatment was the all-girls Mount School in Mill Hill, north-west London. The Mount was a very nice, 'proper' school where the students were decked out in beautiful brown school uniforms – a huge change from leg warmers and nose-rings. Music was strong there and, in Amy's words, kept her going. The music teacher took a particular interest in her talent and helped her settle in. I use that term loosely. She was still wearing her jewellery, still turning up late and constantly rowing with teachers about her piercings, which she delighted in showing to everybody. When I remember where some of those piercings were, I'm not surprised the teachers got upset. But, one way or another, Amy got five GCSEs before she left the Mount and yet another set of breathless teachers behind her.

There was no question of her staying on for A levels. She had had enough of formal education and begged us to send her to another performing-arts school. Once Amy had made up her mind, that was it: there was no chance of persuading her otherwise.

When Amy was sixteen she went to the BRIT School in Croydon, south London, to study musical theatre. It was an awful journey to get there – from the north of London right down to the south, which took her at least three hours every day – but she stuck at it. She made lots of friends and impressed the teachers with her talent and personality. She also did better academically: one teacher told her she was 'a naturally expressive writer'. At the BRIT School Amy was allowed to express herself. She was there for less than a year but her time was well spent and the school made a big impact on her, as did she on it and its students. In 2008, despite the personal problems she was having, she went back to do a concert for the school by way of a thank-you.

3

'WENN' SHE FELL IN LOVE

As it turned out, it was a good thing that Sylvia Young stayed in touch with Amy after she left the school, because it was Sylvia who inadvertently sent Amy's career in a whole new direction.

Towards the end of 1999, when Amy was sixteen, Sylvia called Bill Ashton, the founder, MD and life president of the National Youth Jazz Orchestra (NYJO), to try to arrange an audition for Amy. Bill told Sylvia that they didn't audition. 'Just send her along,' he said. 'She can join in if she wants to.'

So Amy went along, and after a few weeks, she was asked to sing with the orchestra. One Sunday morning a month or so later, they asked Amy to sing four songs with the orchestra that night because one of their singers couldn't make it. She didn't know the songs very well but that didn't faze her – water off a duck's back for Amy. One quick rehearsal and she'd nailed them all.

Amy sang with the NYJO for a while, and did one of her first real recordings with them. They put together a CD and Amy sang on it. When Jane and I heard it, I nearly fainted – I couldn't believe how fantastic she sounded. My favourite song on that CD has always been 'The Nearness Of You'. I've heard Sinatra sing it, I've heard Ella Fitzgerald sing it, I've heard Sarah Vaughan sing it, I've heard Billie Holiday sing it, I've heard Dinah Washington sing it and I've heard Tony Bennett sing it. But I have never heard it sung the way Amy sang it. It was and remains beautiful.

There was no doubt that the NYJO and Amy's other performances pushed her voice further, but it was a friend of Amy's, Tyler James, who really set the ball rolling for her. Amy and Tyler had met at Sylvia Young's and they remained best friends to the end of Amy's life. At Sylvia Young's, Amy was in the academic year below Tyler, so when they were doing academic work they were in different classes. But on the singing and dancing days they were in the same class, as Amy had been promoted a year, so they rehearsed and did auditions together. They met when their singing teacher, Ray Lamb, asked four students to sing 'Happy Birthday' on a tape he was making for his grandma's birthday. Tyler was knocked out when he heard this little girl singing 'like some jazz queen'. His voice hadn't broken and he was singing like a young Michael Jackson. Tyler says he recognized the type of person Amy was as soon as he spotted her nose-ring and heard that she'd pierced it herself, using a piece of ice to numb the pain.

They grew closer after Amy had left Sylvia Young, when Tyler would meet up regularly with her, Juliette and their other girlfriends. Tyler and Amy talked a lot about the downs that most teenagers have. Every Friday night they would speak on the phone and every conversation ended with Amy singing to him or him to her. They were incredibly close, but Tyler and Amy weren't boyfriend and girlfriend, more like brother and sister; he was one of the few boys Amy ever brought along to my mum's Friday-night dinners.

After leaving Sylvia Young's, Tyler had become a soul singer, and while Amy was singing with the NYJO, Tyler was singing in pubs, clubs and bars. He'd started working with a guy named Nick Shymansky, who was with a PR agency called Brilliant!. Tyler was Nick's first artist, and he was soon hounding Amy for a tape of her singing that he could give to Nick. Eventually Amy gave him a tape of jazz standards she had sung with the NYJO. Tyler was blown away by it, and encouraged her to record a few more tracks before he sent the tape to Nick.

Now Tyler had been talking about Amy to Nick for months, but Nick, who was only a couple of years older than Tyler and used to hearing exaggerated talk about singers, wasn't expecting anything life-changing. But that, of course, was what he got.

Amy sent her tape to him in a bag covered in stickers of hearts and stars. Initially Nick thought that Amy had just taped someone else's old record because the voice didn't sound like that of a sixteen-year-old. But as the production was so poor he soon realized that she couldn't have done any such thing. (She had in fact recorded it with her music teacher at Sylvia Young's.) Nick got Amy's number from Tyler but when he called she wasn't the slightest bit impressed. He kept calling her, and finally she agreed to meet him when she was due to rehearse in a pub just off Hanger Lane, in west London.

It was nine o'clock on a Sunday morning – Amy could get up early when she really wanted to (at this time she was working at weekends, selling fetish wear at a stall in Camden market, north London). As Nick approached the pub he could hear the sound of a 'big band' – not what you expect to hear floating out of a pub at that hour on a Sunday morning. He walked in and was stunned by what he saw: a band of sixty-to-seventy-year-old men and a kid of sixteen or seventeen, with an extraordinary voice. Straight away Nick struck up a rapport with Amy. She was smoking Marlboro Reds, when most kids of her age smoked Lights, which he says told him Amy always had to go one step further than anyone else.

As Nick was talking to her in the pub car park, a car reversed and Amy screamed that it had driven over her foot. Nick was concerned and sympathetic, checking that she was all right. In fact, the car hadn't driven over Amy's foot and she had staged the whole thing to find out how he would react. It was the choking game all over again – she never outgrew that sort of thing. I've no idea what in Amy's mind the test was intended to achieve, but after that Amy and Nick really hit it off and he remained a close friend for the rest of her life.

Nick introduced Amy to his boss at Brilliant!, Nick Godwyn, who told her they wanted her to sign a contract. He invited Janis, Amy and me out for dinner, Amy wearing a bobble hat and cargos, with her hair in pigtails. She seemed to take it in her stride, but I could barely sit still.

Nick told us how talented he thought Amy was as a writer, as well as a singer. I knew how good she was as a singer, but it was great hearing an industry professional say it. I'd known she was writing songs, but I'd had no idea if she was any good because I'd never heard any of them. Afterwards, on the way back to Janis's to drop her and Amy off, I tried to be realistic about the deal – a lot of the time these things come to nothing – and said to Amy, 'I'd like to hear some of your songs, darling.'

I wasn't sure she was even listening to me.

'Okay, Dad.'

I didn't get to hear any of them though – at least, not yet.

As Amy was only seventeen she was unable to sign a legal contract, so Janis and I agreed to. With Amy, we formed a company to represent her. Amy owned 100 per cent of it, but it was second nature to her to ask us to be involved in her career. As a family, we'd always stuck together. When I'd run my double-glazing business, my stepfather had worked for me, driving round London collecting the customer satisfaction forms we needed to see every day in head office. When he died my mum took over.

By now Amy had a day job. She was learning to write showbiz stories at WENN (World Entertainment News Network), an online media news agency. Juliette had got her the job – her father, Jonathan Ashby, was the company's founder and one of its owners. It was at WENN that Amy met Chris Taylor, a journalist working there. They started going out and quickly became inseparable. I noticed a change in her as soon as they got together: she had a bounce in her step and was clearly very happy. But it was obvious who was the boss in the relationship – Amy. That's probably why it didn't work out. Amy liked strong men and Chris, while a lovely guy, didn't fall into that category.

The relationship lasted about nine months, it was her first serious relationship, and when it finished, Amy was miserable – but painful though the break-up was, her relationship with Chris had motivated her creatively, and ultimately formed the basis of the lyrics for her first album, *Frank*.

*   *   *

Excited as Amy was about her management contract, music-business reality soon intruded: only a few months later Brilliant! closed down. While usually this is a bad sign for an artist, Amy wasn't lost in the

Dearest Daddy,

May everything
about your birthday
add up
to a happy day

I love you sooooo much. Thanks
for passing your sense of style
onto me, cos I'd look like Alex
if I took after Mum. Don't tell
either of them I said that.
Amy
x xxx

Every year Amy's birthday cards made me laugh.

shuffle. Simon Fuller, founder of 19 Management, who managed the Spice Girls among others, bought part of Brilliant!, including Nick Shymansky and Nick Godwyn.

As before, with Amy still under eighteen, Janis and I signed the management contract with 19 on Amy's behalf. To my surprise, 19 were going to pay Amy £250 a week. Naturally this was recoupable against future earnings but it gave her the opportunity to concentrate on her music without having to worry about money. It was a pretty standard management contract, by which 19 would take 20 per cent of Amy's earnings. Well, I thought, it looks like she's going to be bringing out an album – which was great. But, I wondered, who the hell's going to buy it? I still didn't know what her own music sounded like. I'd nagged, but she still hadn't played me anything she'd written. I was beginning to understand that she was reluctant to let me hear anything until it was finished, so I let it go. Amy seemed to be enjoying what she was doing and that was good enough for me.

Along with the management contract, Amy became a regular singer at the Cobden Club in west London, singing jazz standards. Word soon spread about her voice, and before long industry people were dropping in to see her. It was always boiling hot in the Cobden Club, and on one hotter than usual night in August 2002 I'd decided I couldn't stand it any longer and was about to leave when I saw Annie Lennox walk in to listen to Amy. We started talking and she said, 'Your daughter's going to be great, a big star.'

It was thrilling to hear those words from someone as talented as Annie Lennox, and when Amy came down from the stage I waved her over and introduced them to each other. Amy got on very well with Annie and I saw for the first time how natural she was around a big star. It's as if she's already fitting in, I thought.

It wasn't just the crowds at the Cobden Club who were impressed with Amy. After she had signed with 19, Nick Godwyn told Janis and me that there had been a lot of interest in her from publishers, who wanted to handle her song writing, and from record companies, who wanted to handle her singing career. This was standard industry practice, and Nick recommended the deals be made with separate music companies so neither had a monopoly on Amy.

Amy signed the music-publishing deal with EMI, where a very senior A&R, Guy Moot, took responsibility for her. He set her up to work with the producers Commissioner Gordon and Salaam Remi.

On the day that Amy signed her publishing deal, a meeting was arranged with Guy Moot and everyone at EMI. Amy had already missed one meeting – probably because she'd overslept again – so they'd rescheduled. Nick Shymansky called Amy and told her that she must be at the meeting, but she was in a foul mood. He went to pick her up and was furious because, as usual, she wasn't ready, which meant they'd be late.

'I've had enough of this,' he told her, and they ended up having a screaming row.

Eventually he got her into the car and drove her into London's West End. He parked and they got out. They were walking down Charing Cross Road, towards EMI's offices, when Amy stopped and said, 'I'm not going to the fucking meeting.'

Nick replied, 'You've already missed one and there's too much at stake to miss another.'

'I don't care about being in a room full of men in suits,' Amy snapped. The business side of things never interested her.

'I'm putting you in that dumpster until you say you're going to the meeting,' he told her.

Amy started to laugh because she thought Nick wouldn't do it, but he picked her up, put her in the dumpster and closed the lid. 'I'm not letting you out until you say you're coming to the meeting.'

She was banging on the side of the dumpster and shouting her head off. But it was only after she'd agreed to go to the meeting that Nick let her out.

She immediately screamed, 'KIDNAP! RAPE!'

They were still arguing as they walked into the meeting.

'Sorry we're late,' Nick said.

Then Amy jumped in: 'Yeah, that's cos Nick just tried to rape me.'

4

FRANK –
GIVING A DAMN

In the autumn of 2002, EMI flew Amy out to Miami Beach to start working with the producer Salaam Remi. By coincidence, or maybe it was intentional, Tyler James was also in Miami, working on another project; Nick Shymansky made up the trio. They were put up at the fantastic art-deco Raleigh Hotel, where they had a ball for about six weeks. The Raleigh featured in the film *The Birdcage*, starring Robin Williams, which Amy loved. Although she and Tyler were in the studio all day, they also spent a lot of time sitting on the beach, Amy doing crosswords, and danced the night away at hip-hop clubs.

Because she had gone to the US to record the album, I wasn't all that involved in Amy's rehearsals and studio work, but I know she adored Salaam Remi, who co-produced *Frank* with the equally brilliant Commissioner Gordon. Salaam was already big, having produced a number of tracks for the Fugees, and Amy loved his stuff. His hip-hop and reggae influences can be clearly heard on the album. They soon became good friends and wrote a number of songs together.

In Miami Amy met Ryan Toby, who had starred in *Sister Act 2* when he was still a kid and was now in the R&B/hip-hop trio City High. He'd heard of Amy and Tyler through a friend at EMI in Miami and wanted to work with them. He had a beautiful house in the city where Amy and Tyler became regular guests. As well as working on her own songs, Amy was collaborating with Tyler. One night in Ryan's garden, they wrote the fabulous 'Best For Me'. The track appears on Tyler's first album, *The Unlikely Lad*, where you can hear him and Amy together on vocals. Amy also wrote 'Long Day' and 'Procrastination' for him and allowed him to change them for his recording.

Dear Daddy....
I love you SO much + I can't wait to see you again in a few weeks.
Everything's fine, I'm working hard + I haven't spent a penny. A few thousand dollars have gone, but no pennies as such. I'm joking.
Amy
xxxxxxx

Amy sent me this Valentine's Day card from Miami,
while recording tracks for *Frank* in 2003.

By the time Amy had returned from Miami *Frank* was almost in the can but, oddly, though she'd signed with EMI for publishing nearly a year earlier, she still hadn't signed with a record label. I kept asking anyone who'd listen to let me hear Amy's songs, and eventually 19 gave me a sampler of six tracks from *Frank*.

I put the CD on, not knowing what to expect. Was it going to be jazz? Rap? Or hip-hop? The drum beat started, then Amy's voice – as if she was in the room with me. To be honest, the first few times I played that CD I couldn't have told you anything about the music. All I heard was my daughter's voice, strong and clear and powerful.

I turned to Jane. 'This is really good – but isn't it too adult? The kids aren't going to buy it.'

Jane disagreed.

I rang Amy, and told her how much we we'd loved the sampler. 'Your voice just blew me away,' I said.

'Ah, thanks, Dad,' Amy replied.

Apart from the sampler, though, I still hadn't heard the songs that were on the short-list for *Frank* and Amy seemed a bit reticent about letting me listen to them. Maybe she thought lyrics like 'the only time I hold your hand is to get the angle right' might shock me or that I'd embarrass her. I teased her after I'd finally heard the song.

'I want to ask you a question,' I said. 'That song "In My Bed" when you sing—'

'Dad! I don't want to talk about it!'

Amy came over to Jane's and my house when she was sorting out the tracks for *Frank*. She had a load of recordings on CDs and I was flicking through them when she snatched one away from me. 'You don't want to listen to that one, Dad,' she said. 'It's about you.'

You'd have thought she'd know better. It was a red rag to a bull and I insisted she played 'What Is It About Men'. When I heard her sing I immediately understood why she'd thought I wouldn't want to listen to it:

> *Understand, once he was a family man*
> *So surely I would never, ever go through it first hand*
> *Emulate all the shit my mother hates*
> *I can't help but demonstrate my Freudian fate.*

I wasn't upset, but it did make me think that perhaps my leaving Janis had had a more profound effect on Amy than I'd previously thought or Amy had demonstrated. I didn't need to ask her how she felt now because she'd laid herself bare in that song. All those times I'd seen Amy scribbling in her notebooks, she'd been writing this stuff down. The lyrics were so well observed, pertinent and, frankly, bang on. Amy was one of life's great observers. She stored her experiences and called upon them when she needed to for a lyric. The opening lines to 'Take The Box' –

> *Your neighbours were screaming,*
> *I don't have a key for downstairs*
> *So I punched all the buzzers...*

– refer to something that had happened when she was a little girl. We were trying to get into my mother's block but I'd forgotten my key. A terrible row, which we could hear from the street, was going on in one of the other flats. My mother wasn't answering her buzzer – it turned out that she wasn't in – so I pressed all of the buzzers hoping someone would open the door.

Of course the song had nothing to do with me buzzing buzzers: it was about her and Chris breaking up. But I was amazed that she could turn something so small that had happened when she was a kid into a brilliant lyric. For all I knew, she'd written it down when it had happened and, eight or ten years later, plucked it out of her notebook. She was a genius at merging ideas that had no obvious connection.

The songs on the record were good – everyone knew it. By 2003, with the record all but done, loads of labels were desperate to sign her. Of all the companies, Nick Godwyn thought Island/Universal was the right one for Amy because they had a reputation for nurturing their artists without putting them under excessive pressure to produce albums in quick succession. Darcus Beese, in A&R at Island, had been excited about Amy for some time, and when he told Nick Gatfield, Island's head, about her, he too wanted to sign her. They'd heard some tracks, they knew what they were getting into, and they were ready to make Amy a star.

Once the record deal had been done with Island/Universal, suddenly it all sunk in. I sat across from Amy, looking at my daughter, and trying to come to terms with the fact that this girl who'd been singing at every opportunity since she was two, was going to be releasing her own music. 'Amy, you're actually going to bring out an album,' I said. 'That's brilliant.'

For once, she seemed genuinely excited. 'I know, Dad! Great, isn't it? Don't tell Nan till Friday. I want to surprise her.'

I promised I wouldn't, but I couldn't keep news like this from my mum and phoned her the minute Amy left.

When I think about it now, I realize I took Amy's talent for granted. At the time I actually thought, Good, looks like she's going to make a few quid out of this.

Amy's record company advance on *Frank* was £250,000, which seemed like a lot of money. But back then some artists were getting £1 million advances and being dropped by their label before they'd even brought out a record. So, although it was a fortune to us, it was a relatively small advance. She had also received a £250,000 advance from EMI for the publishing deal. Amy needed to live on that money until the advances were recouped against royalties from albums sold. Only after that had happened could she be entitled to future royalties. That seemed a long way off: how many records would she need to sell to recoup £500,000? A lot, I thought. I wanted to make sure that we looked after her money so it didn't run out too quickly.

When Amy first got the advance she was living with Janis in Whetstone, north London, with Janis's boyfriend, his two children and Alex. But as soon as Amy's advances came through she moved into a rented flat in East Finchley, north London, with her friend Juliette.

Amy understood very quickly that if her mum and I didn't exert some kind of financial control she'd go through that money like there was no tomorrow. I had no problem with her being generous to her friends – for example, she wouldn't let Juliette pay rent – but she and I knew that I needed to stop her frittering the money away. She was smart enough to understand that she needed help.

Amy and Juliette settled into the flat and enjoyed being grown-up. I would often drop by. I'd left my double-glazing business and had been driving a London black taxi for a couple of years. On my way home from work, I'd go past the end of their road and pop in to say hello, but Amy always insisted I stay, offering to cook me something.

'Eggs on toast, Dad?' she'd ask.

I'd always say yes, but her eggs were terrible.

And we'd sing together, Juliette joining in sometimes.

It was around this time that I first suspected Amy was smoking cannabis. I used to go round to the flat and see the remnants of joints in the ashtray. I confronted her, and she admitted it. We had a big row about it and I was very upset.

'Leave off, Dad,' she said, and in the end I had to, but I'd always been against any kind of drug-taking and it was devastating to know that Amy was smoking joints.

*   *   *

As time progressed, everyone at 19, EMI and Universal was so enthusiastic about *Frank* that I began to believe it was going to sell and that maybe, just maybe, Amy was going to become a big star. On some nights when she had a show, I'd go and stand outside the place where she was playing, like Bush Hall in Uxbridge Road, west London. Her reputation seemed to grow by the minute. I'd listen to what people were saying as they went in, and they seemed excited about seeing her.

Afterwards Amy and I would go out for dinner, to places like Joe Allen's in Covent Garden, and she would be buzzing, talking to other diners, having a laugh with the waiters. In those days she liked performing live – as a virtual unknown she felt no pressure and simply enjoyed herself; she was always happy after a show, and I loved seeing her like that.

Her voice never failed to blow audiences away, but she needed to work on her stagecraft. Sometimes she'd turn her back on the audience – as though she didn't want to face them. But when I asked if she enjoyed performing, she'd always say, 'Dad, I love it,' so I didn't ask anything more.

In the months leading up to *Frank*'s release, Amy did lots of gigs. Playing live meant auditioning a band to perform with her, and 19 introduced her to the bassist Dale Davis, who eventually became her musical director. Dale had already seen Amy singing at the 10 Room in Soho and remembers her flashing eyes – 'They were so bright' – but he didn't know who she was until he went to that audition. Oddly enough, he didn't get the job at that point, but when her bass-player wanted more money, Dale took over.

Amy and her band played the Notting Hill Carnival in 2003. It's always a very hard gig – the crowd is demanding – but when I spoke to Dale later, he said that Amy had carried the whole thing on her own. She didn't need a band. He was knocked out by how great she was, just singing and playing guitar. She might not have been technically the greatest guitarist 'but no one else could play like Amy and fit the singing and playing together'. Her style was loose, but her rhythm was good and the songs were so strong that it all locked together. As Dale says, Mick Jagger and Keith Richards are not great guitarists: it's all soul and conviction. 'You just do it, and throughout the years of doing it you get there.'

Still, Amy's live performances were not without their struggles. One gig I particularly remember was in Cambridge where she was supporting the pianist Jamie Cullum. Amy and Jamie hit it off and became friends, but when you're young and just starting out, it's an unenviable task to be the support act. That night people had come to see Jamie, not her – very few people in the Cambridge audience had even heard of Amy – and initially they weren't very responsive. But when they heard her sing, they started to get into it. One of the most difficult things about being the support act is knowing when to stop and, as that night showed, Amy didn't. I don't blame her because she was inexperienced. Perhaps her management should have clued her up.

Amy ended up doing about fifteen songs, which was probably eight too many. By the end, people were getting restless. I could hear them saying, 'How much longer is she going to be?' and 'What time does Jamie Cullum come on?' Even the people I'd heard say, 'She's good,' were fed up and wanting to see the act they'd paid for – Jamie Cullum. Of course, being me, I ended up shouting at people to shut up and nearly had a fight with someone.

Much to the audience's relief, Amy finished the set, but instead of going backstage, she climbed down and came to stand with us. We all watched Jamie and really enjoyed his performance – Amy cheered, clapped and whistled all the way through. She was always very generous with other performers.

With more gigs, and promotional events linked to the imminent release of *Frank*, Amy wanted to start planning ahead. As the lease on her flat in East Finchley was about to expire, Janis and I sat down with her and asked her what she wanted to do. She said she'd like to buy a place rather than keep renting, and I agreed with her. A flat would be a great investment, particularly if her singing career ever went wrong. Remember those days before the recession? You could buy a flat for £250,000 one day and sell it the next for £275,000 – I exaggerate a bit, but the property market was booming.

Amy loved Camden Town and we soon found a flat there that she liked in Jeffrey's Place. It was small and needed some work, but that didn't matter because all of her favourite places were in walking distance. This was where she wanted to be and the flat had a good feel to it. To get to it, you had to be buzzed through a locked gate, which reassured Janis and me: Amy would be quite safe there. The flat cost £260,000. We put down £100,000 and took out a £160,000 mortgage, which left a good bit of money from the advances. I sat down with Amy and worked out a budget with her. All of the household bills and the mortgage would be paid out of her capital and she would have £250 a week spending money, which she was quite happy with. If she needed something in particular she could always buy it, but that didn't happen too often.

In those days Amy was quite sensible about money. She knew that she had a decent amount to live on and that we were looking after her interests. She also knew that if she developed lavish habits, her funds would soon run out. Although Amy was a signatory on her company's bank account, she wanted a safeguard put in place to ensure that she couldn't squander her money so we agreed that any cheque had to be signed by two of the signatories to the account. The signatories were Amy, Janis, our accountant and myself. It would be an effective brake, we hoped, because Amy was generous to a fault.

When it was time to put the credits together for *Frank* – who had done what on this song, who had written what on that song – in the spring of 2003, her generosity was evident again. Nick Godwyn, Nick Shymansky, Amy and I crowded round her kitchen table to sort it out – there had been a leak in the bathroom the night before and the lounge ceiling had fallen in. So much for the glamorous life. (Mind you, a year on, the place looked like a bomb had hit it.)

Nick Shymansky started off. 'Right. How do you want to divide up the credits for "Stronger Than Me"?'

'Twenty per cent to …' Amy began, and she'd name someone and Nick would ask her why on earth she'd want to give that person 20 per cent when all they'd done was come to the studio for an hour and suggest one word change. While it was certainly important to credit people for what they had done, and ensure that they were paid accordingly, she was giving away percentages to people for almost nothing. Amy was brilliant at maths, but I swear, if she'd had her way, she would have given away more than 100 per cent on a number of songs.

*   *   *

On 6 October 2003, three weeks prior to the release of *Frank*, the lead single, 'Stronger Than Me', hit the shops and peaked, disappointingly, at number seventy-one in the UK charts – it turned out to be the lowest-charting single of Amy's career. When the album came out on 20 October 2003, it sold well, eventually making it to number thirteen in the UK charts in February 2004. It was also critically acclaimed, and sales were boosted later in 2004 when it was short-listed for a Mercury Music Prize, and Amy was nominated for the BRIT Awards for Best British Female Solo Artist and Best British Urban Act.

I devoured all of the reviews, and don't recall anything negative, although the hip-hop/jazz mix confused some at first. The *Guardian* wrote, 'Sounds Afro-American: is British-Jewish. Looks sexy: won't play up to it. Is young: sounds old. Sings sophisticated: talks rough. Musically mellow: lyrically nasty.'

I thought that *Frank*, which is still my favourite Amy album, was fantastic. One of the reasons I love it is because it's about young love and innocence, and it's funny, comical and has brilliantly observed lyrics. It wasn't written out of the depths of despair. I still love listening to *Frank* and play it often. I was so proud of my little girl.

Unfortunately Amy didn't hear things quite as I did. She had mixed feelings about the final cut and complained that the record company had included some mixes that she had told them she didn't like. It was partly her fault: she'd missed a few of the editing sessions, in typical Amy fashion.

We were in the kitchen at her flat in Jeffrey's Place, having a cup of tea, and the window was open. The builders working next door turned their radio up loud and one of the songs from *Frank* was playing.

'Shut the window, Dad, I don't want to hear that,' Amy said.

It had been on my mind for a while to ask her, so I said, 'Were you thinking about anyone in particular when you wrote "Fuck Me Pumps"?' She shook her head. 'There's the line … What is it? Hang on … Let me have a look at the CD. Where is it?'

'I don't even know if I've got one, Dad.'

'What? You haven't got a copy of your own album?'

'No, I'm done with it. It was all about Chris, and that's in the past. I've forgotten about it, Dad. I'm writing other stuff now.'

This was news to me. I'd never seen this side of Amy, the way she could put something so deeply personal and important behind her, as if it didn't matter any more. Nevertheless, she continued to promote *Frank*, and later that year she performed at some very prestigious venues: the Glastonbury Festival, the V Festival and the Montreal International Jazz Festival. No matter what, her music and her family came first. But her other priorities then were like so many other girls of her age – clothes, boys, going out with her friends, her image and style – she was, after all, a woman in her early twenties.

She may have been dismissive about *Frank* but things happened with the album that made her realize it was special, like when 'Stronger Than Me', which she'd written with Salaam Remi, won the Ivor Novello Award for Best Contemporary Song Musically and Lyrically. The Novellos mattered to Amy: her peers, other composers and writers voted to decide the winners. Amy went to the ceremony and rang me to tell me she'd won. I was halfway down Fulham Road, taking someone to Putney in my taxi, when she called.

'Dad! Dad! I won an Ivor Novello!'

I was so excited but I still had to drive this chap home and finish my shift. By then it was late and I had no one to bother so I went and woke up my mum. 'Amy's won an Ivor Novello!'

She was as pleased as I was.

One disappointment we all shared was that *Frank* wasn't initially released in America. 19 felt that Amy wasn't ready for the States. They said that you only get one shot at breaking the States and this wasn't the time, mostly because, in their view, her performance level wasn't strong enough.

Frustrating though it was, they were probably right. At this time Amy was still playing guitar onstage and 19 wanted to get the guitar out of her hands: she was always looking down at it instead of engaging with the audience. Sometimes it was as if they weren't there and she was singing and playing for her own amusement. Her voice was great, but she wasn't delivering a performance: she needed coaching in how to give the best to her audiences. Her act needed refining before she took it to the States.

They told Amy that she had to communicate with the audience and the best way to do that was to show them she was having a good time. This, though, was what she struggled with. She loved singing and playing to family and friends, but as the gigs got bigger, so did the pressure, highlighting the fact that she wasn't a natural performer. As Amy was outwardly so confident, no one imagined that inside she harboured a fear of being onstage, and that as she played in front of ever-increasing crowds, the fear didn't go away. Over time it became worse. But she was so good at concealing it that even I wasn't aware of how hard this was for her. Quite often, during a song, she'd still commit the cardinal sin of turning her back on the audience. I'd be watching and want to shout at her, 'Speak to the audience, they love you. Just say, "Hi, how you doin'? You all havin' a good time?"'

Amy never did figure out how to deal with stage fright. While she wasn't physically sick, as some performers are, she sometimes needed a drink before she went on. Maybe even needed to smoke a little cannabis, but I don't know for sure, because she wouldn't have done that in front of me. What I certainly didn't know and, with hindsight, perhaps I should have seen the warning sign for, was that she was starting to drink a lot more than was good for her, even then.

As a teenage girl she'd suffered from a few self-esteem issues – what teenager doesn't? – but I really don't believe that was at the root of her stage fright; by the time she was performing regularly her self-esteem issues had gone. But 19 were right: she wasn't ready to go to America. Before that Amy needed to work hard on her act and it would take time. Talking to the audience and showing them she was enjoying herself came later, and even when it did, I don't think it was ever natural. To me, she always looked uncomfortable when she was doing it.

It wasn't easy to talk to her about a performance; after maybe a couple of days I could say things about what she was and wasn't doing, but I had to be careful. Amy wasn't so much strong-willed as cement-willed, and she did things her way.

As the promotional gigs continued, her management started to talk about a second album. There were still some good songs that hadn't been included on *Frank*. One in particular was 'Do Me Good'. I told Amy that I thought it should go on the second album because it was fantastic, but she didn't think so and reminded me of something she'd told me once before: 'That was then, Dad. It's not what I'm about now. That was written about Chris and I'm over it.'

All of Amy's songs were about her experiences and by this time Chris was firmly in the past. With him no longer relevant to her life, that made the songs about him even less relevant.

She'd started writing a lot of new material, and there could easily have been an album between *Frank* and *Back to Black* – there were certainly enough songs. But Amy didn't want to bring out an album unless the songs had a personal meaning to her, and the ones she'd written after *Frank* and before *Back to Black* didn't do it for her. She resisted the pressure from 19 to head back into the studio.

Amy and I often talked about her song writing. I asked her if she could write songs the way Cole Porter or Irving Berlin did. Those guys were 'guns for hire' when it came to churning out great songs. Irving Berlin could get up in the morning, look out of the window and ten minutes later he'd have written 'Isn't This A Lovely Day?'. 'Could you do that?' I'd ask Amy.

'Of course I could, Dad. But I don't want to. All of my songs are autobiographical. They have to mean something to *me*.'

It was precisely because her songs were dragged up out of her soul that they were so powerful and passionate. The ones that went into *Back to Black* were about the deepest of emotions. And she went through hell to make it.

5

A PAIN IN SPAIN

During the summer of 2004, in the midst of her first taste of success, Amy's regular drinking habits were worrying me – so many of her stories revolved around something happening to her while she was having a drink. Just how much, I never knew. On one occasion, she had drunk so much that she fell, banged her head and had to go to hospital. Her friend Lauren brought her from the hospital to my house in Kent and they stayed for three or four days. After they arrived, Amy went straight to sleep in her room and I called Nick Godwyn and Nick Shymansky. They came over immediately and we sat down to discuss what they were referring to as 'Amy's drinking problem'.

We had a sense that Amy was using alcohol to loosen up before her gigs, but the others thought it was playing a more frequent role in her life. The subject of rehab came up – the first time that anyone had mentioned it. I was against it. I thought she'd just had one too many this time, and rehab seemed an overreaction.

'I think she's fine,' I told everyone, which she later turned into a line in 'Rehab'.

As we carried on talking, though, I saw the other side – that if she dealt with the problem now, it would be gone. Lauren and the two Nicks had seen her out drinking, and they, with Jane, were in favour of trying rehab, so I shut up.

After a while, Amy came down, and we told her what we'd been discussing. As you'd expect, she said, 'I ain't going,' so we all had a go at changing her mind, first the two Nicks, then Lauren, then Jane and I. Eventually Jane took Amy into the kitchen and gave her a good talking-to. I don't know exactly what was said but Amy came out and said, 'All right, I'll give it a go.'

The next day she packed a bag and the Nicks took her to a rehab facility in Surrey, just outside London. We thought she was going for a week, but three hours later she was back.

'What happened?' I asked.

'Dad, all the counsellor wanted to do was talk about himself,' she said. 'I haven't got time to sit there listening to that rubbish. I'll deal with this my own way.'

The two Nicks, who had driven her home, were still trying to persuade her to go back, but she wasn't having any of it. Amy had made her mind up and that was that.

Initially I agreed with her, since I hadn't been totally convinced she needed to go in the first place. Later it came out that the clinic had told Amy she needed to be there for at least two months – I think that was what had made her leave. She might have stuck it for a week, but a couple of months? No chance. For Amy, being in control was vital and she wouldn't allow someone else to take over. She'd been like that since she was very young; it had been Amy, after all, who'd put in the application to Sylvia Young, Amy who'd got the singing gig with the National Youth Jazz Orchestra, and Amy who'd got the job at WENN. She'd had help, yes, but she'd done it – not Janis, not me.

Amy headed to the kitchen. 'Who wants a drink?' she called over her shoulder. 'I'm making tea.'

*   *   *

Frank sold more than 300,000 copies in the UK when it was first released, going platinum within a matter of weeks. Based on sales, you would have thought Amy's career was in the ascendant, but that wasn't the case.

By the end of 2004 there wasn't much work coming in and I was beginning to think it was all over as quickly as it had started, although Amy wasn't worried and continued being out there and having a good time. The people around her seemed unaware that nothing was happening with her career and carried on treating her as if she was a big star. I guess if enough people tell you you're a big star, you come to believe it.

Only my mother could bring Amy back to earth. She didn't often have a go at her but when she did it was relentless. We were at her flat one Friday night when she told Amy, 'Get in there. If they're finished, get everyone's plates, bring them into the kitchen and do the washing-up.' Amy wasn't happy about that, but when everyone else had left, Mum called Amy to her again: 'Come here, you, I want to talk to you.'

'No, Nan, no.' Amy knew what was coming. She had said something earlier that my mum had considered out of line.

'Never let me hear you say that again. Who do you think you are?'

It did the trick. My mother was a stabilizing influence on Amy and made sure her feet were firmly on the ground. So, it was no surprise that it hit Amy hard when her grandmother fell ill in the winter of 2004. I drove round to Amy's, dreading the moment when I had to say, 'Nan's been diagnosed with lung cancer.' When Amy opened the front door of her flat I choked out the words before we fell into each other's arms, sobbing.

Alex moved into my mum's flat in Barnet for a couple of months to be with her, and when he moved out Jane and I took his place. We wanted to make sure she was never on her own because there had been a mix-up with one of my mum's prescriptions: she had inadvertently been taking ten times the correct dose of one particular drug. It had spaced her out to such an extent that we thought the cancer must have spread to her brain. Once we discovered the mistake and rectified it, she was back to normal within a couple of days.

All of the things that you would normally associate with lung cancer didn't apply in my mum's case. She was a bit breathless so she had an oxygen machine, but other than that she was very comfortable. During the last three months of her life she actually improved – well, outwardly she did. Then one evening in May 2006 I came home to find her on the floor. She'd had a fall. She didn't appear too bad, but I called the paramedics just to be on the safe side. They took her to Barnet General Hospital, and while they were checking her over there, she looked at me and said, 'That's it. I've had enough.'

I asked what she meant.

'I've had enough,' she said.

I told her not to be silly, that after a good night's sleep she'd feel better and I'd be taking her home the following day.

'I've had enough,' she repeated. And those were the last words my mother ever spoke to me. That night she fell into a coma and a day and a half later she passed away peacefully.

I felt awful because my mother had asked me to stay with her, and once she was asleep I'd gone home for a couple of hours' rest.

'Don't be silly, Dad,' Amy said. 'She was in a coma.'

My mother's death had an enormous impact on Amy and Alex. Alex went into a state of depression and withdrew into himself, and Amy was unusually quiet. But the depth of Amy's sorrow didn't surprise me. Five days after my mum died my friend Phil's sister Hilary got married for the first time, aged sixty, to a lovely guy called Claudio. Although we were in mourning, we felt we should go to the wedding. Jane, Amy and I went, but Alex couldn't face it. Weeks before the wedding Amy and I had been asked to sing at the reception. My wedding present to them was a pianist. I'd worked with him before so I didn't need to rehearse with him. That night I got up and sang. It was only a few days after my mum had passed away so it was difficult, but I managed it.

Then Amy got up to sing and just couldn't. She couldn't sing in front of the guests, she was too upset. Instead, she went into another room with the microphone, so the guests couldn't see her, and sang a few songs from there. Although she sounded fantastic, I could hear the pain in her voice.

'Dad, I don't know how you could get up in front of all those people and sing,' she said to me afterwards. 'You've got balls of brass!'

I've always been able to put my emotions to one side, but Amy couldn't. She loved singing, but I've never felt that she really loved performing.

*   *   *

After *Frank* came out, Amy would begin a performance at a gig by walking onstage, clapping and chanting, 'Class-A drugs are for mugs. Class-A drugs are for mugs ...'

She'd get the whole audience to join in until they'd all be clapping and chanting as she launched into her first number. Although Amy was smoking cannabis, she had always been totally against class-A drugs. Blake Fielder-Civil changed that.

Amy first met him early in 2005 at the Good Mixer pub in Camden. None of Amy's friends that I've spoken to over the years can remember exactly what led to this meeting. But after that encounter she talked about him a lot.

'When am I going to meet him, darling?' I asked.

Amy was evasive, which was probably, I learned later, because Blake was in a relationship. Amy knew about this, so initially you could say that Amy was 'the other woman'. And although she knew that he was seeing someone else, it was only about a month after they'd met that she had his name tattooed over her left breast. It was clear that she loved him – that they loved each other – but it was also clear that Blake had his problems. It was a stormy relationship from the start.

A few weeks after they'd met, Blake told Amy that he'd finished with the other girl, and Amy, who never did anything by halves, was now fully obsessed with him.

A couple of months later I saw Blake for the first time, although I didn't actually meet him then, at the Queen's Arms, in Primrose Hill, north-west London, where I'd arranged to meet Amy one Sunday lunchtime. I walked into the busy pub and saw her sitting on some fella's lap. They were kissing passionately. The pub was packed and I thought, This isn't on. I got hold of her, took her outside and gave her a piece of my mind – she shouldn't have been doing that in a public place. We had a bit of a row and Amy told me she had been kissing her boyfriend, Blake. I said I didn't care who he was, and I was about to walk off when I stopped and turned round. 'And another thing,' I said. 'What's with all the big hair and the makeup? Who are you meant to be?'

'Don't you like it, Dad? It's my new look.'

I thought she'd looked nicer when she was a bit smarter, though I had to admit the look suited her, but I didn't say so then.

'Come on, Dad, come and have a drink with us,' she said.

I was still seething so I made some excuse. It was none of my business where and whom my twenty-one-year-old daughter kissed but I've always been a bit hot-headed, especially where my kids are concerned.

*   *   *

Amy's old friend Tyler James says that he noticed a massive change in Amy when she first met Blake. To Tyler, the day Amy met Blake, she fell in love with him, and after that they wouldn't leave each other's side. He became the centre of Amy's world and everything revolved around him. Tyler told me that the first time Blake visited Amy's flat at Jeffrey's Place, he offered Tyler a line of cocaine while they were watching TV – not something that Tyler or Amy would normally have come across. Amy was, as I said, dead against class-A 'chemical' drugs, as she called them, and while Blake was doing cocaine, Amy stuck to smoking cannabis (which led to her lyrics on 'Back to Black', 'you love blow and I love puff'). And she was still drinking.

I found out later that Blake had been dabbling in heroin when Amy had first met him. Tyler, who was staying at the Jeffrey's Place flat at the time, would wake up in the morning and throw up because of passive heroin intake but he didn't know for sure that Blake was a user until Amy told him.

Tyler wasn't the only one who saw a change in Amy. Nick Shymansky remembers a pivotal moment around this time when he called Amy from a ski trip. She sounded 'really different'. 'I've just met this guy,' she told Nick. 'You'll really love him. He's called Blake and we've fallen madly in love.'

Nick came back from his trip and saw immediately that Amy must have lost a stone and a half in weight while he had been away. She started phoning him in the early hours of the morning when she was drunk. One night she called saying she had had a row with Blake and was in a pub in Camden and wanted Nick to pick her up. Nick always felt protective towards Amy so naturally he went to collect her. This was the first time since Chris that Amy had been in love and, according to Nick, it was a terrible two or three weeks. Everyone was worried about her and they all knew something was up.

Amy and Blake's turbulent relationship only got worse. As if the drug use wasn't bad enough, Amy soon found out that Blake was cheating on her with his old girlfriend, a discovery that culminated in the first of their many splits. According to Tyler, Amy ended the relationship because of the heroin and the other woman. Until then, Amy and Blake had been together every day, and then they simply weren't.

She took the break-up hard. Not long afterwards, Amy and I were walking on Primrose Hill – she loved our walks there and, back then, few people recognized her so we weren't mobbed by fans. That afternoon I could tell she was miserable.

'You know, I really want to be with him, Dad, but I can't,' she told me. 'Not while he's still seeing his ex.'

I didn't know whether to be encouraging or realistic. After all, I didn't know anything about Blake at that time. 'You know what's best, darling. I'll support whatever decision you make.'

She squeezed my hand. 'It's me, isn't it, Dad? I always pick the wrong boys, don't I?'

'Tell you what,' I said, wanting to do something, anything, to make her feel better. 'You know Jane and I are off to Spain on holiday? Why not come with us?' I didn't think for a moment she'd agree, but I was delighted when she did.

The three of us stayed at Jane's dad Ted's place in Alicante. It's a lovely old farmhouse, secluded, with a pool. We'd all been there before and had a great time. On that trip we'd gone to a nearby jazz café where Amy had stood up and sung with the band. I felt this holiday would give her a chance to forget about Blake and write some more songs without too many interruptions.

The only problem was that she'd forgotten to bring her guitar. We went into the nearby village of Gata de Gorgos and bought her one from a fantastic workshop owned and run by the brothers Paco and Luis Broseta – we were in there for hours. Amy must have tried out a hundred before she settled on a really nice small one, perfect for someone of her size.

When we got home, Amy went to her room to start writing. I could hear her strumming, then pausing to write down the song. She never brought the guitar out of her room to play any of her songs to us, it all went on privately. This went on for quite a while and then there was quiet. After about an hour, I went to her room and she was on the phone to Blake. When she finished the call, she came outside and happily told me that he wanted to get back with her. After that, they were on the phone for hours – and I do mean hours.

Amy was missing the best parts of the holiday, shutting herself away with the phone. Even dinnertime meant nothing to her. 'Will you come out of your bloody room?' I said to her. 'You're driving us mad.'

So she would leave her room and start walking up and down in the garden – but she'd still be on the phone all the time. It went on and on and on, every day of the holiday.

When we got back to England, Amy and Blake were together for a few weeks until they split up again. And so it began.

It was around that time that Amy met a guy named Alex Clare, and they were together on and off for about a year. Alex was really nice and I got on very well with him. We both loved Jewish food and we'd often go with Amy and Jane to Reubens kosher restaurant in Baker Street in London's West End to eat together.

Shortly after Amy met Alex he moved in with her and, initially, they were very happy. At one point they even talked about getting married. Amy loved cats and dogs, and not long after Alex moved in, she bought a lovely dog called Freddie, but he was like a raving lunatic. One day Amy and Alex were out with him for a walk and Freddie got lost. 'He'd probably had enough of me and ran away,' Amy said. 'I don't blame him!' He was never found.

6

FADE TO BLACK

Looking back on the period between the end of the promotion for *Frank* and the release of *Back to Black*, I realize I had no idea of what was about to happen to Amy musically or in her private life. Her habit of writing highly autobiographical songs meant that when she was happy she didn't turn to her guitar often. There weren't that many gigs, but she didn't seem bothered. I began to wonder if there would ever be a second album. I felt she was drifting.

19 were also wondering about the next album. They'd been ready for her to do something as early as 2004, but with her focus elsewhere, there had been little development. Towards the end of 2005, Amy's contract with them was running out and my impression was that she and 19 were tiring of each other. 19 had set up meetings at restaurants with Nick Gatfield, head of Island Records, and Guy Moot, head of EMI Publishing, and Amy had not shown up. These were big people in the music business, so her no-shows were embarrassing for 19 and they started to lose faith in her.

Amy, in turn, was disappointed that they hadn't broken her into the US market. And, of course, she hadn't been happy with the final cut of *Frank*. When it came time to think about the follow-up, those issues reappeared. Regardless of the problems each side had with the other, the reality was that no money was coming in and I was starting to worry about Amy's finances. Jane and I went to see her play at a pub in east London where the room was thick with smoke (this was before the smoking ban), and she was paid just £250 (I didn't know that she was playing as a favour to a friend).

The next day, I told Amy we might have to think about selling the flat unless the money started coming in.

'Dad, you can't,' she said. 'Don't worry, I'm going to bring out another album.'

I knew she meant it, but those words had been floating around for so long I was beginning to doubt them. All I knew was that she'd written a few songs when we were in Spain, probably not enough for an album; I didn't know how many others she'd worked on previously or since. 'How many songs have you got?' I asked her.

'I'm doing it, Dad,' Amy replied, 'I'm doing it, so don't worry about it.' And that was all she'd say to me. She was never comfortable talking about her writing – especially when she wasn't doing any.

I wasn't seeing Amy as regularly as I used to, although I spoke to her on the phone every day. I put this down to her seeming obsession with Blake, and I noticed she mentioned Alex Clare less and less. But she was a grown-up and it was none of my business, so I kept my mouth shut.

When Amy's management contract with 19 came up for renewal she told Nick Shymansky that she was not sure about carrying on with them. He didn't know what to say because he felt that she still wanted him in the picture but not 19. Amy had issues with Nick Godwyn on a day-to-day level but Nick Shymansky, by his own admission, didn't have enough experience or knowledge to manage her by himself, so he tried to get Amy to work things out with 19.

Around this time Nick took Amy to meet record producer and songwriter Paul O'Duffy. He'd worked with Swing Out Sister and produced the John Barry soundtrack for the James Bond film *The Living Daylights*. The song he and Amy wrote together was 'Wake Up Alone' for *Back to Black*. I was pleased she was getting down to some work but, of course, she wouldn't play me the song.

In the car driving back from Paul's house, Amy said that if Nick wouldn't leave 19 and manage her, then Blake and his mates would take over. Naturally there was no way Nick would allow that to happen – on a few occasions he'd had to pull her out of the pub when she'd been with Blake and his pals to go to meetings. When Nick heard about it he went mad and the two of them got into a huge argument that ended with him telling Amy that, whatever happened, Blake and his mates would not be managing her.

It was then that Nick raised the possibility of Raye Cosbert managing her. Raye was already promoting some of Amy's gigs and she had built up a great relationship with him. Everyone at Island knew and liked Raye too. Amy had known Raye since 2003 and I knew that she liked and trusted him. Importantly, he and Amy shared similar tastes in music.

I'd first heard of Raye in the middle of 2005 when I'd gone to Amy's dressing room after a show and found a bottle of champagne from him. I asked Amy who he was and she told me it was Raye Cosbert of Metropolis Music, who'd been promoting a lot of her gigs. I'd seen a big black guy with dreadlocks hanging around the gigs quite a bit and now I realized he must have been Raye.

One night I introduced myself to him and we got chatting. He told me that, apart from seeing me at some of Amy's gigs, I was vaguely familiar. 'Do you go to the football?' he asked.

'I'm a season ticket holder at White Hart Lane,' I said. He was too.

Then he asked me to turn round with my back to him – I thought he was mad, but I did it anyway.

'That's it!' he said. 'I recognize the back of your head!'

It turned out that my seat was four rows in front of his, just to the left. We're both ardent Spurs fans so we had an immediate rapport. After that we became great friends and always found each other at half-time to have a catch-up.

Once Nick had suggested Raye as a possible manager, Amy, Raye and I had a dinner meeting at the Lock Tavern, a gastro pub in Camden Town, to talk about Amy's management and discuss Raye's experience. I was concerned because I knew him as a promoter, but Amy assured me he was right for her. It was raining that night and Amy came in late, as usual. She arrived wearing a borrowed coat and I suggested she buy one like it because it suited her. She was wearing a dress, her hair was long, and she looked beautiful, smart and stylish.

'Hello, darling. You look lovely tonight,' I told her.

'Aaaah, Dad, thanks.' She beamed at me.

She seemed a bit tipsy so I made a point of not refilling her glass as quickly as she emptied it.

Over dinner Raye outlined his plans for Amy. He impressed us with his forward-thinking ideas, saying that she needed to move on. He suggested it was time to break her in America, and take her to number one there as well as in the UK. He also pushed the idea of a new album and more gigs: if we did this right we were definitely going to crack it. I didn't know it at the time but Amy had already played him some of her new songs and he thought they were fantastic.

Raye speculated that 19 probably felt that doing a second album with Amy might be difficult as Amy wasn't happy with the final cut of *Frank*. They didn't want her to leave them but he thought they wouldn't stand in her way if she decided to go.

After everything Amy and I had heard from Raye, we decided she should sign a management deal with Metropolis. We'd made some marvellous friends at 19, some of whom remained her friends, but it was time for a change. (Amy always accumulated friends rather than dropping them.) 19 had done some great things for her: without them she probably wouldn't have got record and publishing deals, but I think they probably felt they had taken her as far as they could. When it came down to it, I was reminded of Amy's schools: they were quite pleased to see her go.

*   *   *

Leaving 19 was a tough decision but it turned out to be the right one. In the end, Amy's relationship with Raye Cosbert and Metropolis became, in my view, one of the most successful artist/manager partnerings in the music business.

Very quickly, Raye set up meetings with Lucian Grainge at Universal, and Guy Moot at EMI. Raye's energy was just what Amy's career needed – like a kick up the arse. For some time Guy Moot had wanted Amy to get together with the talented young Mark Ronson, a producer/arranger/songwriter/DJ. In March 2006, a few months after she'd signed with Metropolis, Raye encouraged her to meet Mark in New York so the two of them could 'hook up'. She knew very little about him before she walked into his studio on Mercer Street in Greenwich Village, and on first seeing him, she said, 'Oh, the engineer's here.' Later she told him that she'd thought he would be an older Jewish guy with a big beard.

That meeting was a bit like an awkward first date. Amy played Mark some Shangri-Las tracks, which had the real retro sound that she was into, and she told him that was the sort of music she wanted to make for the new album. Mark knew some of the tracks Amy mentioned but otherwise she gave him a crash course in sixties jukebox, girl-group pop music. She'd done the same for me when I'd stumbled over a pile of old vinyl records – the Ronettes, the Chiffons, the Crystals – that she'd bought from a stall in Camden Market. That had been where she'd developed her love of sixties makeup and the beehive hairdo.

They met again the following day, by which time Mark had come up with a piano riff that became the verse chords to 'Back to Black'. Behind the piano, he put a kick drum, a tambourine and 'tons of reverb'. Amy loved it, and it was the first song she recorded for the new album.

Amy was supposed to be flying home a few days later, but she was so taken with Mark that she called me to say she was going to stay in New York to carry on working with him. Her trip lasted another two weeks and proved very fruitful, with Amy and Mark fleshing out five or six songs. Amy would play Mark a song on her guitar, write the chords down for him and leave him to work out the arrangements.

A lot of her songs were to do with Blake, which did not escape Mark's attention. She told Mark that writing songs about him was cathartic and that 'Back to Black' summed up what had happened when their relationship had ended: Blake had gone back to his ex and

Amy to black, or drinking and hard times. It was some of her most inspired writing because, for better or worse, she'd lived it.

Mark and Amy inspired each other musically, each bringing out fresh ideas in the other. One day they decided to take a quick stroll around the neighbourhood because Amy wanted to buy Alex Clare a present. On the way back Amy began telling Mark about being with Blake, then not being with Blake and being with Alex instead. She told him about the time at my house after she'd been in hospital when everyone had been going on at her about her drinking. 'You know they tried to make me go to rehab, and I told them, no, no, no.'

'That's quite gimmicky,' Mark replied. 'It sounds hooky. You should go back to the studio and we should turn that into a song.'

Of course, Amy had written that line in one of her books ages ago. She'd told me before she was planning to write a song about what had happened that day, but that was the moment 'Rehab' came to life.

Amy had also been working on a tune for the 'hook', but when she played it to Mark later that day it started out as a slow blues shuffle – it was like a twelve-bar blues progression. Mark suggested that she should think about doing a sixties girl-group sound, as she liked them so much. He also thought it would be fun to put in the Beatles-style E minor and A minor chords, which would give it a jangly feel. Amy was unaccustomed to this style – most of the songs she was writing were based around jazz chords – but it worked and that day she wrote 'Rehab' in just three hours.

If you had sat Amy down with a pen and paper every day, she wouldn't have written a song. But every now and then, something or someone turned the light on in her head and she wrote something brilliant. During that time it happened over and over again.

The sessions in the studio became very intense and tiring, especially for Mark, who would sometimes work a double shift and then fall asleep. He would wake up with his head in Amy's lap and she would be stroking his hair, as if he was a four-year-old. Mark was a few years older than Amy, but he told me he found her very motherly and kind.

This was a very productive period for Amy. She'd already written 'Wake Up Alone', 'Love Is A Losing Game' and 'You Know I'm No Good' when we were on holiday in Spain, so the new album was taking shape. Before she'd met Mark, Amy had been in Miami, working with Salaam Remi on a few tracks. Her unexpected burst of creativity in New York prompted her to call him. She told him how excited she was about what she was doing with Mark, and Salaam was very encouraging. Jokingly, she said to him, 'So you'd better step up.' Later she went back to Miami to work some more with Salaam, who did a fantastic job on the tracks he produced for the album.

When Amy returned to London she told me excitedly about some of the Hispanic women she'd seen in Miami, and how she wanted to blend their look – thick eyebrows, heavy eye-liner, bright red lipstick – with her passion for the sixties 'beehive'.

By then, Mark had all he needed to cut the music tracks with the band, the Dap-Kings, at the Daptone Recording Studios in Brooklyn.

Shortly after that my mother passed away and Amy, along with the rest of the family, was in pieces. It wasn't until a few weeks later, in June 2006, that Amy added the last touches to 'Back to Black', recording the vocals at the Power House Studios in west London.

I went along that day to see her at work – the first time I'd been with her while she was recording. I hadn't heard anything that she'd been doing for the new album, so it was amazing to listen to it for the first time. The sound was so clear and so basic: they'd stripped every-thing back to produce something so like the records of the early six-ties. Amy did the vocals for 'Back to Black' over the already-recorded band tracks, and I stood in the booth with Raye, Salaam and one or two others while she sang.

It was fascinating to watch her: she was very much in control, and she was a perfectionist, redoing phrases and even words to the nth degree. When she wanted to listen to what she'd sung, she'd get them to put it on a CD, then play it in my taxi outside, because she wanted to know how most people would hear her music, which would not be through professional studio systems. In the end, *Back to Black* was made in just five months.

Amy's CD sleeve for the *Back to Black* sampler. Amy still loved her heart symbol and drew a good self-portrait. She still seemed a schoolgirl at heart.

The album astonished me. I knew my daughter was good, but this sounded like something on another level. Raye carried on telling us that it would be a huge hit all around the world, and I was getting very excited. It was hard to read Amy: I couldn't tell if she expected it to be a triumph, as Raye did, but she was much happier with the final cut than she had been with *Frank*. This had been a much more hands-on process for her.

Back to Black was released in the UK on 27 October 2006, and during its first two weeks it sold more than 70,000 copies. It reached number one on the UK Albums Chart in the week ending 20 January 2007. On 14 December 2007 it was certified six times platinum in the UK in recognition of more than 1.8 million copies sold. By December 2011 *Back to Black* had sold 3.5 million copies in the UK and more than 20 million copies worldwide.

I was blown away, beyond proud. But deep down I never wanted Amy to write another album like it. The songs are amazing but she went through hell to write them. I don't like *Back to Black* as much as I like *Frank*; I never really did. And that's for one reason only: all of the songs on *Back to Black*, apart from 'Rehab', are about Blake. It occurred to me recently that one of the biggest-selling UK albums of the twenty-first century so far is all about the biggest low-life scum-bag that God ever put breath into. Quite ironic, isn't it? Mind you, you don't get albums written about really good people like Gandhi or Nelson Mandela, do you? Good people's places in Heaven may be assured, but nobody's going to have a chart-topping album full of songs about someone's good deeds.

While the album's success altered Amy's career in every way imaginable, it came with a high price tag. The nature of the songs made it hard for her to feel as excited as you might expect about the album's reception and success. Whereas people might walk along the street humming 'Love Is A Losing Game', to Amy it was like a knife in the heart, a reminder of the worst of times.

I knew what the songs meant because she always wrote about her life, and I didn't want to discuss them with her when I knew how painful she found it to listen to them.

Even though Amy was with Alex Clare, Blake wasn't far away. Sometimes with Amy, sometimes not, but an all-important figure to her nonetheless. The fact was, although Amy loved Alex, she was not in love with him. She was in love with Blake.

Alex wasn't stupid and he soon found out that Amy was seeing Blake. He told me that he thought Amy had been smoking heroin with Blake. He said he could smell it on her. I laughed, and told him the 'Class-A drugs are for mugs' story. At that point, Amy was still opposed to hard drugs, and Alex was wrong: Amy wasn't doing heroin then, but Blake was smoking it in front of her, which was why her clothes smelt of it.

Alex wanted to have it out with Blake and I said I'd go with him. I didn't want him to walk on his own into a situation he couldn't handle. Blake used to drink regularly in a pub called the Eagle in Leonard Street, east London, but every time we went to confront him, he was never there; I'm pretty sure Amy rang him to tell him we were on our way.

Eventually, around the start of 2007, Alex and Amy split up. Then Amy was back with Blake full time, and I finally got to meet him at the Jeffrey's Place flat. Despite everything I'd heard from Tyler and Alex, I decided, given how Amy felt about him, that I wanted to make up my own mind about him.

My first impression was that he seemed to be a decent and respectful guy, if a bit scruffy. Amy had talked about him off and on during the Alex Clare period, but I didn't know much about him. I wondered about his age, as his hair seemed to be receding, and he looked like he could do with a good meal. We had a bit of a chat and he told me that he had been born in Lincolnshire and had come to London when he was sixteen. He said he was working as a video production assistant and wanted to get into pop videos. On that occasion Amy and Blake looked very happy together, and he didn't strike me as a drug-user, so I thought that perhaps Alex had been mistaken about him. I couldn't have been more wrong. In the light of what happened later, I'm pretty sure that Amy had started smoking heroin and crack cocaine by then, although at the time I had no idea.

*   *   *

Amy's last time in New York with Mark Ronson was in December 2006. They were talking about Motown Christmas songs, and how all the great soul artists of the sixties and seventies had brought out a Christmas record.

'Why aren't there any great Jewish-holiday records?' Amy wondered. Later that week she went with Mark to the studio where he did his regular radio show and they hosted it together as 'Two Jews and a Christmas Tree'. They decided that that might make a good title for a Jewish-holiday song. By the next day Amy had come up with a whole load more great titles including, 'Heart Of Coal' and 'Alone Under The Mistletoe'. To Mark, everything Amy came up with was an instant classic, even if it was just a throwaway line.

Doing the promotion for *Back to Black* brought Amy back into the public eye, and she appeared in the newspapers regularly. They were all in love with her new look but far less kind about her drinking: she was often pictured going into and coming out of pubs. 'Amy, darling, you've got to do something about your drinking,' I said to her. 'You're not doing yourself any favours.'

I got the usual Amy shrug. 'Yeah, yeah, Dad.'

There were also allusions to drugs, but I didn't believe these for one minute.

In March 2004, as part of the ongoing promotion for *Frank*, Amy had appeared on BBC2's irreverent weekly pop quiz *Never Mind the Buzzcocks*. It had been a pretty good show – Amy was very funny and got quite a few laughs – so in November 2006 when she was promoting *Back to Black* she was invited back. It didn't hurt that her look was so striking that the cameras loved her and – unlike with *Frank* – her beehive image was now everywhere.

Now, there was a long time between Amy arriving at the studio and the recording starting. She got bored and had too much to drink. By the time the recording got going Amy was drunk, and while she was very funny on the show, in hindsight it's clear to me that this was when her reputation for being out of control began to take shape.

Amy was on the comedian Bill Bailey's team. She hit it off with the host, Simon Amstell, when he introduced her: 'Bill's first guest is Amy Winehouse, the Ivor Novello Award-winning "Jazz Jew". Amy's likes include Kelly Osbourne and the smell of petrol. I quite like matches. Let's do lunch.'

Amy got her first big laugh when *GMTV* presenter Penny Smith, who was on the other team, asked Amy if her beehive was her own hair.

'Oh, yeah,' Amy replied. 'Yeah, it's all mine. Cos I bought it, yeah.'

Shortly after that Amy asked Simon if she could have another drink and Simon refused, which led to some friendly banter. Amy said she was seeing Pete Doherty later that night to talk about doing a tune together.

'He wants to sell you drugs,' Simon yelled. 'Don't go near him! Do something with Katie Melua. There you go.'

'I'd rather have cat AIDS, thank you,' Amy replied.

When it came to the 'Intros' round, where two of the panel sing an intro to a tune the other panellist has to name, Amy stood up, saying, '*Pssssh*,' as she did so.

'What's the push-push?' asked Simon Amstell.

'I dunno. It's my new thing,' said Amy.

Quick as a flash, Amstell retorted, 'Is it? I thought that was crack.'

Amy didn't take offence, just gestured towards herself. 'Do I look like Russell Brand?' Then, in mock-horror, she buried her head in her hands when the audience laughed.

Amstell snapped back, 'Yes!'

When she sat down again Amy took a drink of water, then turned and spat over her shoulder.

'This is not a football match,' Simon said to her. 'You come here full of ... crack ... spitting all over things ...'

Amy jokingly pleaded, 'Let it die, please. Let it die ... please.'

'The addiction I'd like to die ...' Simon replied. 'This isn't even a pop quiz any more. It's an intervention, Amy.'

Amy laughed and told me later she'd thought that was the best line on the show. I think Amy liked Simon Amstell. She let him get away with remarks she wouldn't have taken from someone she didn't like.

The following day I went round to see her. 'You know, you really shouldn't drink when you're working,' I lectured. 'Everybody could see you were drunk, and it was embarrassing.'

We had a bit of a row. 'You don't know what you're talking about, Dad,' Amy said. 'Everyone laughed.'

'They were laughing at you, not with you.'

'Watch it again, Dad, and you'll see what I mean,' she insisted.

'But I'm right. Stop bloody drinking.' I stormed off.

7

'RONNIE SPECTOR MEETS THE BRIDE OF FRANKENSTEIN'

By the beginning of 2007 *Back to Black* was at number one in the UK and we had a celebration to mark it. Amy drank more than she should have but everyone was so happy about the success of the album that I let it go. 'Congratulations, darling,' I said.

'Are you proud of me, Dad?'

I couldn't believe my talented daughter needed to ask that. 'Always, darling. I'm always proud of you, whatever you do.'

Back to Black was due to be released in the US in March; so on Tuesday, 16 January Amy did a couple of shows at Joe's Pub, a live showcase venue in Manhattan, New York. It wasn't the best night of the week for an American début but both shows were sell-outs. Amy performed a fifty-minute set in each to enthusiastic audiences. The next day the reviews were pretty good. My favourite, though, which made us both laugh, was from an online blog. It described Amy's look as 'Ronnie Spector meets the Bride of Frankenstein'.

In February Amy was back in the UK, recording the video for 'Back to Black', when she got some exciting news. It was bitterly cold and Amy had forgotten to bring her coat, so during the breaks in filming she was freezing in her trailer. Halfway through the day she called Jane, asking her to bring down a coat for her. As I was out in the cab, I took it to her.

When I arrived she squealed, 'Dad! I'm number one in Norway!'

'That's great,' I said, although I did wonder why she was so keen on making it big in the Norwegian market. She had to explain that to be number one outside the more obvious, if bigger, markets of the US and UK meant she really was on her way to international stardom.

Shortly before the release of the album in the US, I was at the Turkish baths at Porchester Hall, Notting Hill – I used to go there most Wednesday afternoons and there'd usually be a whole crowd of my pals there, having something to eat and playing cards. Above the baths there's a fantastic hall where they put on music events, corporate dinners and weddings. Amy was due to do a concert there for *The BBC Sessions* on the Thursday, but I didn't know she'd be rehearsing there that afternoon. But she was and, boy, could you hear it! There was the constant muffled thump, thump, thump of the bass and Amy's incredible voice over the top. 'Keep your daughter quiet,' one of my pals joked. 'I can't hear myself think.' They were all ribbing me so I went upstairs to see Amy.

She was as surprised and delighted to see me as I was to see her. She came over straight away and gave me a big hug. Blake was with her and came over as well. He was very friendly, but he looked agitated and on edge. He said he was okay when I asked, but then he disappeared. When he returned, he was a different person – full of life and energy. You can make your own mind up as to the reason why. I thought back to what Tyler had told me. But I believed then that Amy would give him what for when she found out he was still taking drugs.

Later that month Amy was back in the US for a tour to promote *Back to Black*. It began in Austin, Texas, at the SXSW Festival, then went on to West Hollywood, California, where she played the Roxy Theater. There were a lot of big names at that gig and they wanted to go to Amy's dressing room to say hello. First Raye told Amy that Courtney Love was outside and wanted to meet her.

'God!' Amy replied. 'What does *she* want?'

Next up was Bruce Willis. It was his birthday and, as Amy put it, 'He had a bit of a wobbly head on.'

Bruce said to Amy, 'Hi, I'm Bruce Willis. Would you like to come to Las Vegas with me to celebrate my birthday?'

Quick as anything, Amy said, 'Only if I can bring my dad!' Bruce was astounded and Amy carried on the joke, 'Shall I call him and see if he wants to come?' Apparently Bruce beat a hasty retreat.

Then Ron Jeremy, the famous porn star, was led into the dressing room. He was accompanied by two women with pneumatic breasts – if you'd stuck a pin in them, Amy said, they might have exploded. Ron was wearing a pair of loose tracksuit bottoms. Amy looked down at them. 'Been working today, Ron?'

'Funnily enough, yes,' Ron said, playing along. They sat down for a good ten minutes and had a drink and a chat, minus the women. Amy was very sharp; her spontaneous wit never failed to make me laugh.

Danny DeVito was at one of the other gigs and Amy kept sidling up to the bar next to him, mouthing to Raye, 'Look, I'm taller than him.' And she was, if not by much.

Amy met a lot of famous people on that tour and they had all come to see her because they loved what she was doing. Some stars get swept away by the conviction that everybody wants to be their friend, but it wasn't like that with Amy. Those people weren't jumping on the Amy Winehouse bandwagon: they just wanted to hear her sing. I witnessed it at first hand when I joined the tour in Canada a few weeks later. I turned up after the gig and found Amy with a man she introduced to me as Michael.

'Very nice to meet you,' I said. 'What do you do, Michael?'

He laughed, as Amy hissed, 'Dad – it's Michael Bublé.'

He was a sweet man – I was a fan of his music – and all he wanted to talk about was how fantastic Amy had been that night.

The following day we walked into a shopping mall and 'Stronger Than Me' was playing. 'Isn't that me, Dad?' Amy asked. 'Isn't that my song?'

'Yes, and you've just earned twenty-eight cents,' I joked, 'so feel free to buy something.'

She stopped and listened. 'It sounds pretty good, doesn't it?'

It was as if somebody else had written and sung the song, as if it didn't belong to her any more. Wait a second, I thought. This is surreal. She doesn't know her own song. But when she did listen to her own records, she always thought she could have done better – not that she could have sung better but that she could have written more powerful lyrics. 'I should have changed that word to this word...' she'd say.

She was never satisfied with what she'd done.

*   *   *

In May 2007 Amy and Blake booked to go on holiday to Miami together. Before they left she called me: she wanted to know how I felt about her and Blake getting married. Since they'd got back together, they'd been virtually inseparable, aside from some of her trips to the US to promote the album. I wasn't too thrilled about the prospect of Amy tying herself to Blake, but I thought I'd have the chance to get to know him better – and for him to get to know the family before they eventually tied the knot.

'I won't stand in your way,' I told her. 'You're both adults. It's for you and Blake to decide.'

The issue of his drug use occurred to me, but I pushed it aside. I was pretty sure by now that Amy's stance on class-A drugs would have rubbed off on Blake: if he hadn't stopped on his own, she would have made him. If I was wrong, I thought, there would be enough time before they got married for me to do something about it.

I wondered then if she planned to marry sooner than we thought. I reminded her what had happened when Janis and I had got married, how upset Janis was that her mother didn't come to our wedding – she had recently left Janis's father and run off with another man. Janis still got upset about that and I didn't want her to miss our daughter's wedding. She deserved to be there. And me? Well, of course I wanted to be at my little girl's wedding – but to Blake? I wasn't sure.

I told Amy that if they were thinking of getting married while they were in Miami I would fly Janis out so she could be part of it. Amy promised me that Janis and I would both be at the wedding. It seemed to me that Blake couldn't have cared less if his mother was at his wedding or not, and I think he was partially to blame that neither Janis nor I was there when they were married in Miami on 18 May 2007.

Just after the ceremony Amy called me, all excited. 'Dad, we've just got married!'

I was stunned into silence.

'Aren't you going to congratulate us?' she carried on, seemingly oblivious to how I felt.

I couldn't bring myself to say the words to her. In fact, I couldn't say anything to her – I pretended I couldn't hear her properly and hung up. I was beside myself with sadness for Janis, and really angry with Amy. After that she called me back several times, but I didn't pick up.

Eventually I phoned her. 'Amy, you know what?' I said. 'Your mum should have been there. Never mind me. *Your mum should have been there.*'

'Yeah,' she said. 'I know that, Dad, but we thought it was the right thing to do at the time …'

'What do you mean *we* thought it was the right thing to do? What's it got to do with Blake about your mother being at your wedding?' I didn't object to Amy marrying him: she'd told me she loved him and that he loved her. But I took great exception to them preventing Janis from being at the wedding. What business was it of Blake's? They'd been married five minutes and he'd already put my back up.

The call ended badly, but I resigned myself to what had happened and made sure that it wouldn't cause a rift between us, even though I was seething about the snub to Janis. I suggested throwing a wedding party later in the year, but although Amy was up for it, it never happened.

8

ATTACK AND THE 'PAPS'

Over the next few months I didn't see much of Amy and Blake – which was not surprising: they were newly married, after all. Amy still found time for me, though, and we met often enough for me to think all was well.

On the evening of Monday, 6 August 2007, at her flat in Jeffrey's Place, Amy had her first seizure. She was alone with Blake. He put her on her side in the recovery position, but instead of calling an ambulance, he phoned Juliette. I doubt very much that he told her the severity of the situation. Had he done so, I'm sure Juliette would have told him to call an ambulance right away. Instead she drove from her home in Barnet to Camden Town, which must have taken at least half an hour, and then, in Juliette's car, they took Amy to University College Hospital in central London, arriving at about one a.m.

By the time they got to the hospital, Amy was unconscious and Juliette called me. I was working in my cab that night and luckily I wasn't too far away. I got to the hospital about fifteen minutes later. By the time I arrived Blake had gone and Amy had had her stomach pumped. It was reported in the press that she was given an adrenalin shot, but that's not true. She was very woozy and I couldn't get much sense out of her. I thought drinking might have caused the seizure.

When I got home, I wanted to get my head down for a couple of hours but I couldn't switch my thoughts off. I had a cup of tea and replayed the events of the night. I tried to remember how Amy's behaviour had changed since she'd got married, and realized I needed to start keeping a daily diary. I wanted a record of events as they happened. Maybe I'd been a bit naïve and missed some obvious signs. How much was she drinking? She was probably still smoking 'puff', as she called it, but was there anything else? What had I not noticed?

The next morning I met Raye and Nick Shymansky at the hospital. Amy was still asleep and I found out that there had been no sign of Blake since the previous day – as far as I knew he hadn't even bothered to phone the hospital. However, in the press, there were pictures of him outside the hospital with a bunch of flowers for Amy – pity he never made it to her bedside while I was there.

We decided when Amy was discharged that she could do with a change of scene so I arranged for us to go and stay at the Four Seasons Hotel in Surrey for a few days. To cheer her up, we also booked a room for her friends Juliette and Lauren. Amy wanted to turn it into a girly thing and I hoped that might keep Blake away.

Amy left hospital the following afternoon and we drove her straight to the hotel, where she settled into her room. Unbeknown to me, though, she had phoned Blake and told him where we were going. At ten o'clock that night he turned up at the hotel.

Amy wasn't her usual self. She'd been talking a lot of nonsense throughout the evening, so I made some calls and arranged for a doctor to see her straight away. At eleven p.m. Dr Marios Pierides, a consultant psychiatrist at the Capio Nightingale Hospital, in north-west London, arrived and examined Amy. He said that she had *just* taken drugs, probably crack cocaine. He warned Amy that if she continued she could have another seizure at any time.

Words cannot describe the depths to which I plummeted. I had to sit down before I fell. This was a bombshell. Amy had always been dead against hard drugs. Why had that changed? What could I do? I couldn't believe that Amy was taking drugs but the evidence was there. Now I knew I'd been wrong in thinking Amy was stronger than Blake and had weaned him off class-A drugs. It appeared to be the opposite. But, even so, how had the drugs got into the hotel? I didn't know what to do, who to turn to. I tried talking to Amy, but she was out of it. I wanted to hear what she had to say for herself. Maybe it had been a one-off. I lay awake all night wondering.

I didn't see much of Amy the following day and neither did her friends. She spent most of it in bed with Blake. Juliette and Lauren were really worried about her too and kept going up to the room, but Amy didn't want to see them because she was with Blake. I was told that Blake, as a result of his 'withdrawal', was having a very bad time. Finally people were acknowledging that he was a drug-user.

Blake and Amy surfaced at about nine p.m. and we sat down to have something to eat, except Blake, who went for a walk in the hotel grounds. I guessed that he'd made arrangements for drugs to be delivered, and when he returned, the look on his face suggested that they had arrived. Later Juliette and I managed to get into the room while Amy and Blake were out. I didn't know what I was looking for but we came across a scorched strip of silver foil in the bin. This confirmed what we had suspected: that one or both of them had been smoking a class-A drug. I now had to accept that Amy, as well as Blake, was using. I looked about for evidence of other drugs but didn't find anything.

I felt sick. Our whole world had been turned upside down. Should I confront Amy here? How should I talk to her about it? Would she listen? I knew Amy had had bad moments with alcohol, but crack? It seemed impossible.

By this time word had got out about Amy's seizure and there were reporters all over the hotel looking for a story, so I decided to leave talking to Amy until we got home. The reporters didn't get anything from any of us, but Blake's mother, Georgette, spoke to the press from her home that day saying we should all leave Amy and Blake alone, and calling Amy's friends, whom Amy had known most of her life, 'hangers-on'.

That Friday it was Jane's birthday, so after work that night she came to the hotel to join us for the weekend. Blake's mother and stepfather, Georgette and Giles, were there too, having travelled from their home in Newark, Lincolnshire. Raye and I had asked them to come so we could discuss what to do about the evidence of drugs we'd found in their room and that had been in Amy's system.

When we sat down together, Georgette did not apologize for her 'hangers-on' remark. This was the first time we'd met and already she had offended me. As we spoke, I realized how little they knew about Blake's drug abuse. They had decided that it had been Amy who had introduced drugs to Blake, which I, and all of Amy's friends, knew wasn't true. It's going to be difficult moving forward, I thought, unless we're all on the same side.

Later that night we sat down to dinner in a private dining room. Amy was at one end of the table and Georgette at the other. Georgette kept waving a designer bag at Amy. 'Ooh, look at the bag you bought me, look at the bag …' she was saying.

What was wrong with her? She'd just learned that her son was a drug addict, but all she could go on about was a handbag. She and her husband were in complete denial about their son's problems, and remained so for the rest of the evening. That was the first time I met the Civils: I thought they were obnoxious.

The next morning Raye arrived and we had breakfast on the terrace. Amy, Jane, Georgette and Giles were at the next table. I went over to them and suggested that we walk along the terrace for some privacy. I told Giles about the silver foil I'd found in Amy and Blake's room; he said he didn't believe me, he didn't think it had anything to do with Blake. I told him he was deluding himself about his stepson, but he was adamant that it was Amy's fault.

The conversation quickly became heated and, forgetting there were reporters in the hotel, I lost my temper. We were both shouting. It was a surreal moment: a wedding was to take place in the hotel that day, and while I was arguing with Giles on the terrace, I could see the guests starting to arrive. Fortunately, Raye came out onto the terrace, put his hand on my shoulder and said quietly, 'Calm down, Mitch, calm down.' And I did. But, believe me, I was so angry with Giles that I was shaking.

Earlier that day, before breakfast, I had called Amy's doctor, Paul Ettlinger, to ask him to come and examine her again. He did so, and suggested that Amy and Blake should spend some time at the Causeway Retreat, an addiction treatment centre on Osea Island in Essex. It's in the Blackwater estuary, not far from the town of Maldon. The island is only accessible for an hour or so a day via a causeway. Once you're on the island, you're stuck there – at least until the next low tide. He told me that the Causeway was almost impenetrable, which was just what we needed, especially after the previous night when Blake had arranged for drugs to be brought to the hotel. I was desperate to get help for Amy and agreed to this right away.

Naturally Amy didn't want to go, but this time, unlike her previous trip to rehab, we weren't taking no for an answer. 'Listen,' I said to her, 'you're going. You're a drug addict now, and that's the end of it.'

I was angry with her, and she knew it. She looked to Blake for support but I told them they were both going.

Later that day Raye and I drove Amy and Blake to Battersea Heliport from where a helicopter took them to the island. But before Blake got into the helicopter, he took me to one side. I was so shocked by what came next that I recorded his exact words in my diary: 'I am going to Osea Island for Amy's sake. I have no intention of getting clean, I like being a drug addict.'

I was dumbfounded. I got back into the car and told Raye, who just shook his head. What chance had Amy got if her husband felt like that? I hoped rehab would work for them.

Amy and Blake were meant to stay at the Causeway Retreat for an indefinite period, but after just three days they came back. I met them at Battersea Heliport, but Amy brushed past me and got into the back of the car. I banged on the window and made her open the door.

'Why'd you leave early, Amy?' I asked, trying hard to sound reasonable.

'I ain't talking to you, Dad. It was you made us go to that place.'

She slammed the door and told the driver to take them home. I was left standing there alone. As I replayed the events in my head, I was sick about it all. I was devastated that Amy had given up on rehab so quickly, but even worse, this was the first time that Amy and

I had fallen out. All I'd been doing was trying to prevent a dangerous problem becoming worse – I hadn't expected gratitude (I'm not that naïve), but I was shocked that she wouldn't speak to me.

The newspapers were all over this story like a rash. I was struggling to know what to think, let alone say about it. The next day the *Daily Mail* ran the following headline: '"I'm proud Amy told me she's a heroin addict," says Winehouse's mother-in-law.' It was a new experience for me to wake up to horrible stories about my daughter, knowing they were on everyone else's breakfast tables.

I couldn't sit and let things just happen. On Wednesday, 15 August, we had a crisis meeting at Matrix Studios, a media centre and recording studios in south-west London, partly owned by Nigel Frieda, who was also a part-owner of the Causeway Retreat. Dr Mike McPhillips, of the Causeway, Dr Ettlinger, Shawn O'Neil and John Knowles, representing Universal, Raye and I were at the meeting, which went ahead with Amy and Blake's agreement. Georgette and Giles were invited to attend and would bring Amy and Blake with them. They never showed up. In their infinite wisdom, Georgette and Giles had decided it would be a better idea to take Amy and Blake to a pub for a drink instead.

The following day there were pictures in the newspapers of Amy and Georgette, arm in arm, coming out of a pub. They had been taken while the rest of us were pulling our hair out, trying to decide the best way to help Amy and Blake. Later, when I confronted Georgette about it, she said the whole situation had been thrust upon her and Giles and they'd needed time to take it in. I thought it was a pity I hadn't thrust harder.

In the absence of Amy, Blake and his parents, the meeting concluded that Amy and Blake should go back to the Causeway Retreat and, after much cajoling, we managed to get them back on Osea Island two days later. As I saw the helicopter leave Battersea Heliport for the second time, I breathed a sigh of relief. I just hoped that this time they would stay and be helped. Sadly, though, it wasn't to be. Somehow or other a friend of Blake's, someone I'll call Geoff for legal reasons, got on to the island and into the Causeway to give Amy and Blake drugs. So much for the impenetrable Osea Island and second-to-none security.

Two days later – again cutting their stay short - Amy and Blake left the Causeway Retreat and checked into a £500-a-night suite at the Sanderson Hotel in London's West End.

*   *   *

On Wednesday, 22 August, my son Alex went to visit Amy and Blake at the Sanderson. They ended up having a big row about drugs. When Alex phoned me, I could tell immediately that he was upset. I calmed him down and arranged for Amy and Blake to meet us in a restaurant in Goodge Street, not far from the hotel, so he and his sister could make up. We had a nice dinner together that night – Amy and Alex could never stay mad at each other for long and, for Amy's sake, I was polite to Blake, but I felt as if we were all walking on egg shells.

We left the restaurant at about nine thirty. Amy and Blake went back to the hotel and Alex and I went home. Then, at about three thirty a.m., all hell broke loose at the Sanderson. Amy and Blake had had a huge bust-up. The first I heard of it was from the next morning's newspapers. The *Daily Mail* ran the story with the headline: 'Bloodied and bruised Amy Winehouse stands by husband…' The pictures that accompanied it showed Amy with cuts on her face, legs and feet. She also had a deep cut on her arm, which needed several stitches.

At some point during the fight Amy had run out of their room, out of the hotel and into the street. This was when the paparazzi had got their shots. Blake had followed – I don't know if he was chasing her to bring her back or to continue the fight. Amy hailed a passing car and jumped in. She was dropped off nearby and walked back to the hotel where she and Blake made up. I raced to the hotel to see Amy. Blake was out and she told me that they'd had a terrible row and she had cut herself. Later she admitted that she had hit and scratched Blake, but she wouldn't tell me if he had hit her.

'What were you fighting about?' I asked, while she climbed back into bed.

'Not now, Dad,' she replied. 'I'm tired.'

Upsetting as it was, I knew she wouldn't tell me any more, but my most pressing concern was that she was okay. 'As long as you're all right now.'

She was drowsy and murmured, 'I'm fine, Dad. Let me sleep.'

There was no doubt in my mind that the fight had been drug-fuelled, even though there was no drug paraphernalia in the room. I wanted to wait for Blake to come back so I could talk to him. How could someone treat my little girl in this way? When Amy fell asleep, I went downstairs and checked into the hotel. I had to keep an eye on them in case there was a repeat of the previous night's events, and I was frightened for her.

That afternoon I found out that Blake's parents had arrived as well; they were staying at the Monmouth Hotel, in nearby Covent Garden. As much as I disliked them, I decided to go and see them. I hoped to persuade them to try to talk some sense into Blake. They were out, so I left a message for them to contact me. They never called.

I went back to the Sanderson and was informed by the concierge that Amy and Blake had left the hotel arm in arm to go for a walk. I felt helpless and, unusually for me, unsure what to do next. Until now, I'd known what to expect from Amy in any given situation, but I was out of my depth. There is no way to describe how it feels to wake up to photos of your daughter covered with blood on the front page of the newspaper. It was unimaginable that we had gone from the excitement of *Back to Black* to this, yet here we were.

The drugs made her behave erratically, and I was living on a knife edge. Anything might happen. In the end I went back to my room and told the front desk to inform me immediately if any trouble was reported from Amy and Blake's room. It was a quiet night.

The following day Georgette, Giles and Blake's younger brothers, then thirteen and fourteen, arrived at the Sanderson. Georgette left the boys with Amy and Blake while we went off for a talk. It was a waste of time: the Civils wouldn't accept that Blake had introduced Amy to class-A drugs and blamed her for Blake's addiction.

The next day the Civils told me they blamed Amy's career and record company for her and Blake's problems. Even now, when I look back, I can't get over their behaviour. For me, they came to epitomize everything I disliked about Blake and what he'd done to Amy.

Later that afternoon I went up to see Amy and Blake and found out they had spontaneously decided to go on holiday to St Lucia. They had been in touch with Juliette to ask her to bring their passports and some money to the hotel. They were planning to leave the next day.

'What are you thinking?' I asked Amy, when I found out. 'Are you mad?' I couldn't believe what I was hearing. 'You two need to go back to rehab, to Osea Island, not swan about on some bloody beach.'

'And you need to mind your own business,' said Amy, laughing – she and I both knew that I never would.

I'd been keeping Jane, Janis, Alex and Raye up to speed with everything that was happening in the hotel, and they laughed too, when I told them what Amy had said. I suppose it was quite funny, really. A couple of hours later Juliette arrived with the passports and three thousand pounds in cash; I overheard Blake on the phone arranging to go to Hackney, east London, to pick up some drugs.

That was it. I'd had enough and told him as much. I didn't care about the consequences, I said, I was going to the police to tell them what I'd heard. That seemed to work: he didn't go to Hackney that afternoon. Instead, out of the blue, he accused Juliette of stealing a hundred pounds from the money she had brought them, which Juliette would never do. There was a horrible row and I tore into Blake – in front of Amy for the first time. And then Juliette left.

The next day Amy and Blake flew to St Lucia. Amy texted that they'd arrived safely and, I have to admit, part of me felt relieved. I wasn't foolish enough to think that all of the problems were over, but at least they were a bit further away; I needed to forget about the past couple of weeks and spend some time with my wife, whom I'd been neglecting. I poured into my diary everything I'd seen and felt to get it out of my mind. I didn't know where else to turn.

The following Tuesday the Civils did an interview with Radio 5 Live and told listeners not to buy Amy's records: if they did, they would be encouraging a drug addict. Giles accused Amy's record company of working her to the bone and implied that we, Amy's family, had a vested interest in them doing just that.

Things were getting out of hand. I felt the only way to protect Amy was to tell the truth, rather than have people listen to strangers' lies about her. I decided to have my say as well. Later that day, on Radio 5 Live, I told Victoria Derbyshire how much worse things had become since Amy and Blake had been married: I was getting no support from the Civils in helping Amy and Blake, and if they had turned up at the Matrix Studios meeting instead of going to the pub, they would have seen for themselves how caring and understanding Amy's record company was.

Over the next few days I did a lot of radio and television interviews, trying to set the record straight about Amy and her problems. It was probably a waste of time but it made me feel a little better.

On 31 August I received a text from Blake:

By the way, if it eases anyone's minds, we are on an island where it is impossible to get heroin – I read that somewhere, look it up! We are on a posh resort where we haven't even been offered a spliff. Don't worry about us, we're doing fine with delicious cocktails instead. Love, Blake & Amy.

'What a load of crap!' I wrote in my diary.

The next day I got another text:

We're ok papa, phone's a little tricky here but texts are ok. Love you to xs, lots of xxx's. Tell me u love me.

It was from Amy's phone, but I knew it must have been from Blake – Amy would never have used words like that in a text to me. Later that day I went to the Jewish Burial Grounds at Rainham, Essex, to visit the graves of my father, my grandparents and my uncle. I was looking for comfort and solace and peace, which I found.

Unfortunately, the news worsened. On 2 September the *News of the World* ran another horrible and shocking story about Amy. They had pictures of her that showed what appeared to be track marks on her arms, which suggested she was now taking drugs intravenously. Devastated, I called Dr Ettlinger straight away. He believed that the marks on Amy's arms were from the cuts she had inflicted on herself and were definitely not track marks. I was relieved for a moment – yes, people around the world might think that my darling daughter was injecting herself, but at least it wasn't true; that was one more problem that I knew I wouldn't be able to deal with.

The same day the *Mail on Sunday* ran a story about the Civils. I hated going to the newsagent's every morning and seeing Amy's face plastered across the front pages of the papers. It was like living in a glass house, with the world picking over every scrap about Amy's life. But this one cheered me up a bit. In May 2007, just days after Amy and Blake had got married, Georgette and Giles had been convicted at Grantham Magistrates' Court in Lincolnshire of disorderly behaviour and using threatening and abusive words likely to cause harassment, alarm or distress. The *Mail on Sunday* reported:

> The couple were found guilty by the magistrates and were given a one-year conditional discharge after headmaster Giles and his wife Georgette were involved in a furious incident on a village school's football pitch.
>
> The court heard how the Civils threatened the assistant manager of their village junior football team, Neil Swaby, and his wife Jane. Mr and Mrs Civil stormed on to the touchline and berated Mr Swaby for telling off their youngest son. Then Georgette hit him across the face with a bunch of car keys. The couple were found

guilty by the magistrates and were given a one-year conditional discharge. Mr Swaby told the *Mail on Sunday*: 'The problem is that Giles and Georgette blame everyone else.'

I can't say that any of this surprised me – I knew they were nasty people and now everybody who read the *Mail on Sunday* did too – but it did make me wonder what else they might be capable of. Sadly, I didn't have to wait long to find out.

On 3 September Amy and Blake came home from St Lucia. I couldn't wait to see Amy but at the same time I was a bit nervous of what I'd find. I went to see them at Blakes Hotel in Kensington, south-west London. Amy looked fine, if a bit thin: I made a mental note to talk to her about it – another thing to worry about. I realized I hadn't seen her eating like she used to recently, and put that down to the drugs. Blake, meanwhile, was slurring and a bit out of it; he looked like he'd taken something.

Seeing them together, I had no illusions that much had changed. I felt plunged straight back into battle. All I could think was that I had to do something: act, act, act, whatever it took to fix my daughter. Clearly whatever I'd tried so far hadn't worked so I had to do something different, even if that meant being nice to Blake and telling Amy I'd altered my opinion of him.

When Georgette arrived we agreed to call a truce. Perhaps as a result, and with Amy and Blake still in holiday mood, we had a more rational conversation in which Amy and Blake said they wanted to get clean. I was delighted when they agreed to embark on daily counselling. It didn't last a day.

That evening we left Blake in the hotel while I took Amy for a full-check up with Dr Ettlinger at his surgery in Upper Devonshire

Place in London's West End. On the way there I had a text from Blake:

> I can't tell you how grateful I am to you personally, that you and my mum made a truce. It's very positive and means a lot to me. Your second son, Blake x

Five minutes later he sent me another:

> I will always do my best for Amy, you have my word. She is my world. Blake x.

I showed the texts to Amy straight away. 'Okay, let's give him another chance,' I lied. 'On the face of it, these texts tell me he's actually a nice guy.'

Dr Ettlinger examined Amy, and said she was okay, but reiterated that she must not take any drugs for fear of another seizure. He also told her that she was very thin and needed to put on some weight. When we got outside, the pavement was swarming with paparazzi.

'Dad, how did they know I was coming here?' Amy asked. I shook my head. I had no idea.

*　　*　　*

In just two months so much had happened. None of us knew how to help Amy – nothing we tried seemed to be working. Raye and I both thought that getting back to work would be the best thing for her as it would break the routine of the last few weeks. We thought it was unlikely she'd be writing any new songs, so there was no reason to push for another album, but she loved having a guitar in her hands and being with her band. I knew those boys weren't drug-users so it would be good for Amy to be around them, and away from Blake, for a while.

Earlier in the year Amy had been nominated for a Mercury Music Prize for *Back to Black*, and on 4 September I went with her to the awards ceremony at Grosvenor House on Park Lane. She was beaten by the Klaxons, but she was on absolutely top form and sounded fantastic when she sang 'Love Is A Losing Game' with just an acoustic guitar, reminding everyone – including me – just how great her voice was. I was pleased that the drugs hadn't changed that. The audience went mad for her and, for a few minutes, I could forget all the recent nastiness.

She came back to our table and I gave her a big hug. It didn't matter that she hadn't won. To me, seeing the expression on her face as she sang the song, and the silent rapture of the fans around the room, had been worth everything. When I looked up at her on the stage that night, I saw my little girl again, possessed by nothing but her incredible music. There was so much love in the room for her. This cheered me up: she was in there somewhere – she wasn't gone, just a little lost. But at the end of it all she still went home to Blake.

To add to my problems, Jane was worried about my health. I hadn't had much time to think about myself lately, but I had noticed I felt nervy and tired all the time. The least little thing would set me off. For example, if I was going to work in the cab and heard on the radio that there was a traffic jam at Trafalgar Square, a busy location in central London, I would just go home. I couldn't take the thought of sitting in traffic. Any excuse, I guess – there's always a traffic jam at Trafalgar Square. It turned out I was suffering from anxiety.

Adding to my worries, Amy's company had had to bear unanticipated expenses, with bills piling in for the recovery treatment, the holiday and the hotel stays Amy and Blake were racking up. If this continued, we would have a short-term cash-flow problem until Amy received her next royalty cheque. Of course, if that happened, I'd find the money somehow to fund Amy's doctor's bills. I was already working all the hours I could spare in the cab just to earn my living but I'd call in a favour or two if I had to. My friends would never let me down.

When I saw Amy's accountants, there was a bill from the Causeway Retreat for £21,000. I wasn't going to pay that one. I was still furious with them about drugs getting into the facility while Amy and Blake were there. I'd lodged a complaint and they had promised me answers; until I got them that bill would remain unpaid. (The Causeway Retreat closed in 2010 after it was refused registration by the Care Quality Commission. In November, Twenty 7 Management, which had run it, pleaded guilty at Chelmsford Magistrates' Court to running an unlicensed hospital and was fined £8,000, plus £30,000 costs. District Judge David Cooper said the firm's standards 'would really shame a third-world country'.)

Nonetheless, that day I wrote out £81,000-worth of cheques. Despite the incredible success of *Back to Black*, that left only £175,000 in the bank until the royalties came in; hardly the millions that the newspapers reported Amy had, but I was told that the next cheque would be a good one.

On Saturday, 8 September, there was nothing about Amy in the newspapers. There hadn't been a day for weeks when there wasn't at least one story about her in the press. It was so unusual I noted it in my diary – I'd even smiled when leaving the newsagent's.

A couple of days later the *News of the World* declared that Amy was pregnant. I only told Amy about the more ridiculous stories and she hardly ever read anything about herself. I spoke to her on the phone that night and we had a good laugh about the *News of the World*'s piece. Then we talked about Alex, who was thinking of doing the Knowledge to become a taxi driver – it had been Amy's idea and she had offered to lend him some money while he did it. She hardly ever talked about money – but then I heard Blake in the background, prompting her with questions.

For the first time ever, she asked me when the next record and publishing royalties were due to be paid. I told her we were expecting £750,000 from Universal. She put her hand over the phone and told Blake what I'd said.

'Dad, I want to go into partnership with Georgette,' she said next. 'I want to open a hairdressing salon for her.'

'You must be joking,' I said. 'After everything that woman's done?'

I could still hear Blake in the background telling her what to say, and she was relaying his words to me.

'Hang on,' I said, 'who's earned this money? You or him? You're out there grafting while he's making plans to spend your money.' We didn't talk for long after that. The last thing I would do was help Blake spend Amy's money, especially if it was to fund a hairdressing salon for Georgette.

'Amy is getting on my nerves,' I wrote in my diary that night. 'I'm fed up with her!'

9

HOOKED

A couple of days later Amy phoned to ask me if there was any truth in the story that I was trying to take control of her money and keep Blake away from it. I was gobsmacked. 'No,' I told her, and reminded her that she owned her company 100 per cent and my job was to keep an eye on things, sign the cheques and protect her interests. But one thing was for sure: if anything happened to Amy, I didn't want Blake or Georgette to get their hands on any of her money.

'Amy asked me if I love Blake,' I wrote in my diary that night. 'Is she out of her mind? I lied and told her I was fond of him but that there was too much shit with his family.' The old saying came to mind: 'Keep your friends close, and your enemies closer.'

It seemed to me that Blake felt threatened by Amy's close relationship with her family. He resented the time she spent with us and was trying to distance her from us. I knew what he was doing, but if you'd asked me to point out the where and when I couldn't have put my finger on it. He was too slippery for that.

On 14 September 2007, it was Amy's twenty-fourth birthday. Birthdays have always been a big deal in our family, so at about five o'clock I went to see her at Blakes Hotel to give her my presents. Blake was still in bed – always a bad sign – but with him in the other room, Amy and I had a lovely time together and toasted her birthday with tea and biscuits. While I was there, Raye called and said he'd arranged for Amy to go to America again at the end of the month to work with Salaam Remi.

'That's great news, Amy,' I said. 'How many new songs have you got to work with?'

Given what'd been going on, it didn't surprise me when she said she hadn't got anything finished, just a few ideas. I knew, though, that she would be inspired when working with Salaam.

'Why don't you come with us, Dad?' she asked.

'What? You, me and Blake? I'll think about it.' I had already made up my mind not to go.

Amy was in a great mood and wanted to go shopping, just the two of us, at Harrods, in Knightsbridge. I bought her a couple more presents – two sweaters that cost £140 each, a big chunk of the money I'd earned that week in the cab – and we had a really lovely time. But somehow I got separated from her. I was searching all over the store, but I couldn't find her. It felt like history repeating itself. Was she playing the old hiding joke on me again? I found out later that she had jumped into a cab and gone back to the hotel. When I arrived there, I found a drug-dealer in Blake and Amy's room. I kicked him out straight away, but one of the hotel's security guards told me he'd been there nearly every other day.

That evening Raye and I had arranged a birthday party for Amy at the Century Club in London's Soho. All of her pals were there, with Alex, Jane, Janis and me. Tyler was meant to be bringing Amy to the party as Blake had decided not to come, which I was very pleased about. And we were enjoying ourselves, although Amy and Tyler were missing. I called her a couple of times, but couldn't get through. I only recently found out why.

Tyler was always with Amy on her birthday, and on this occasion he particularly wanted to be with her because he was concerned otherwise that she would spend it trapped in the hotel room with Blake. She hardly ever went out now – she was constantly worried about the paps outside. It was Tyler's mission on her twenty-fourth birthday to be with her and encourage her to go out. He found her in a great mood, perhaps brought on by the news that she'd be going to the US to record with Salaam, and she was looking forward to going out that night.

It was obvious that Blake did not want her to go out – he wanted to keep her all to himself. Given everything that had been going on, Tyler was keen to get her away from Blake for a night and find out from her exactly what had been going on in their room. He'd been worrying ever since Amy first moved into the hotel with Blake because it was then that she'd admitted to him she was smoking crack cocaine and heroin. She had promised Tyler that she would stop but, considering she spent nearly every waking moment with Blake, it was hard to imagine how that would happen.

More than the fact of her being cooped up in the hotel, it was the phone calls he took from Amy that really worried Tyler. Amy and Tyler always spoke regularly, but since she'd been staying at the hotel she was ringing him two, three or four times a day. They would be in the middle of a deep conversation and she would suddenly put the phone down. He thought she was calling him whenever Blake went out – it sounded almost as though she was trapped. That was when Tyler had become concerned about what Blake was doing.

The cab arrived and Tyler went downstairs to wait for Amy in Reception. When she didn't show he went back up to her room. This time, when she opened the door, she was crying. She had a busted lip and makeup all down her face. She told Tyler she was really sorry but she wasn't going out. Tyler asked her what was wrong with her face but she told him not to worry about it. He tried to force his way into the room, but Amy begged him not to and persuaded him to go.

Had I known what had happened that evening, I would have gone straight over to rescue Amy, but Tyler obviously felt it wasn't his place to call me since that would have been disloyal to Amy.

The next day, Amy and Blake moved back into her flat at Jeffrey's Place. It was a relief to us all.

*   *   *

On Wednesday, 19 September, it was the 2007 MOBO Awards. Amy and I were due to attend together, but that afternoon Tyler called me to say there had been some problems with Blake – Amy was upset and Blake didn't want her to go to the MOBOs. As Tyler was telling me this, my other phone rang. It was Raye: he was with Amy and on the way to the O2 in Greenwich for the MOBOs. He told me Blake had stayed at the flat and surprisingly, instead of staying with him, Amy had agreed to go to the MOBOs. I could only hope this was a good sign.

Amy was nominated in four categories that night: Best UK Female, Best R&B Act, Best Song, for 'Rehab', and Best Video, for 'Back to Black', and performed two songs. Raye was confident that she would win all four, but in the end she won Best UK Female. Amy was thrilled all the same, and so were Raye and I. It was fantastic to see her back onstage enjoying herself, but more than anything I was happy we'd had a great night without Blake. I wrote in my diary: 'Amy's not swallowing Blake's crap as much as she used to. Could this be the beginning of the end? I hope so.'

At the end of that week, Amy, Raye and I met with Lucian Grainge, head of Universal in the UK at the time, to discuss future plans for Amy's career, including her imminent trip to the US to work with Salaam Remi. Blake had wanted to join us at the Universal meeting, but I'd managed to persuade Amy that it wasn't a good idea. It was a positive meeting and it was good to hear about the big plans Universal had to remarket *Frank* internationally on the back of the global success of *Back to Black*. Positive though it was, throughout the meeting Amy's mind was somewhere else.

The following Monday Raye called: Amy was out of it and she was saying she would not go to the US. When I spoke to Amy later she sounded okay, but she was still saying she didn't want to go to America: 'Working with Salaam will be boring, Dad.' I called Raye back and we agreed not to push it and see how she felt in a few days' time.

That night, I wrote in my diary, 'Amy says working with Salaam will be boring – yes, probably for him! She's really losing it, thanks to that idiot she's married to.' I was so disappointed it had come to this. I couldn't believe Amy was throwing away the chance to work with someone she admired so much but, clearly, if I wanted to understand the person my daughter was becoming I had to stop thinking about these things rationally and try to get inside her head.

*   *   *

A few weeks later Amy and Blake moved into a modern apartment up a flight of stairs in a block where her friend and hairdresser Alex Foden lived in Fish Island, Bow, in east London. I popped in to see

Amy a couple of days after she'd moved in and had a nose about. The rooms were nice-sized, and one wall of the main room was all glass. Amy seemed a bit woozy. I asked if Geoff had been to see her and she said yes. It was no good talking to her when she was in that state, so after twenty minutes I left. I sat in my cab, put my head in my hands and wept like a baby. No matter what plans I or anyone else – Raye, her doctors and her clean friends – had for Amy, they disappeared like smoke, thanks to her erratic behaviour.

On 10 October Amy went to a party at Harvey Nichols in Knightsbridge for the launch of the Olsen twins' fashion range. As usual, she was late, and by the time she arrived Blake was ensconced with the supermodel Lily Cole. Amy went mad, screaming at Blake, and they had a big row in public. Blake left the party with Lily Cole, leaving Amy to put on a brave face. Sadly, when Blake returned to the party some three hours later, Amy forgave him. When I spoke to her about it, she tried to play it down, but a friend of mine was at the party, so I knew exactly what had gone on. 'What will it take before Amy sees Blake for what he is? ' I wrote in my diary that night. 'I know if she gets away from him we can start to solve the drug problem. I am at my wit's end.' It seemed to me, as far as Amy was concerned, that Blake could get away with anything.

The next day Raye called and asked if I would go with Amy on her European tour, which was due to start the following week. I was pleased Amy was getting back on the road: at the last group meeting we'd had about her, we'd agreed it would be good for her to focus on music again. When she was on stage Amy always got a lift from her rapport with the fans – if she wasn't high. I told Raye I'd go, but only if Blake didn't. It was obvious to me that Blake was Amy's biggest problem, but I couldn't see a way of stopping him going on the tour. To make matters worse, Raye told me that Blake wanted to take one of his mates as well and put him on wages. We agreed that Blake shouldn't go and we tried to encourage Amy to take Naomi Parry instead – Naomi was Amy's stylist, and one of her sensible friends, and we thought she'd be a good influence. But it was useless. We couldn't persuade Blake to stay at home, so in the end he went, along with Naomi and Alex Foden.

The tour got off to a bad start before Amy and Blake had even left London. On the morning of Sunday, 14 October, Raye arrived at Amy's Bow flat to take her and Blake to the airport, but when he got there they were both high and looked terrible. He couldn't get them out of the flat, so they missed the flight and the band travelled without them. Luckily they caught a later flight to Berlin, and the first gig, the following evening, went well by all accounts.

The second show, in Hamburg, went as well as the first, but I should have known that it was too good to last. The next evening I had a very different call from Raye. Amy and Blake had been arrested in Bergen, Norway. They had been smoking weed in Amy's hotel suite, a security guard had smelt it and the police had been called.

I packed my bag straight away and caught a flight to Norway. When I arrived, the first thing I saw was Amy on the front page of nearly all of the Norwegian newspapers. She and Blake had been held in jail overnight and, after pleading guilty to possessing marijuana and paying fines of approximately £350, they had been released. When I arrived at the hotel, Amy was very pleased to see me but Blake looked worried. He kept going on about how unfair it was – it had been only a tiny bit of weed. 'You've broken the law,' I pointed out to him. 'Therefore you have to be prepared to suffer the consequences.'

I was livid with Amy and made it clear to her how I felt. I was also worried about how this might affect her visa application: she was due to go to America the following February, but that would be difficult with a drug conviction. Now wasn't the time to raise it: I'd discuss it with our lawyers first. For now it was best to get her focus back on the tour.

In spite of everything, the show that night was fantastic and Amy was in her element. I was standing near the mixing desk so I could see everyone on stage at the same time. I watched Dale, Amy's bassist and musical director, doing his normal great job with the band and nodding happily to Amy when she turned to him. I thought his influence on her, on and off stage, was great. He encouraged her performance by anticipating brilliantly her every move. She responded by reacting to the audience's whistles and cheers. I'm sure she didn't do it to please me but they played loads of *Frank* songs. Near the end of the set, Amy put her hand to her forehead and peered out over everyone's heads. 'Where's my dad? Where are you, Dad?'

People turned to look as I waved to her. 'I'm here, Amy,' I shouted.

'That's my dad, everybody!' she cried, and I was applauded by a crowd of bemused Norwegians.

After that morning's events, though, I was stressed out and, for one of the few times in my life, drank too much beer. Well, when I say too much, I don't think it was the volume but the strength. We were travelling overnight on the tour bus to Oslo and, believe me, I had a rough time. I had a terrible cold and by the time we got to Oslo, at about nine thirty a.m., I must still have had alcohol in my system because I slipped and fell down the stairs of the tour bus, hurting my back.

Amy was very concerned about me. She made sure I had plenty to eat and ordered hot water with lemon for me – she'd always hated it when I was ill, and could be very maternal at times. Then, suddenly, out of nowhere, Amy announced that *she* didn't feel well and wasn't going to do the show that night. Ten minutes later Blake went for a walk, came back with who-knew-what, and, hey presto, Amy felt better and the show was back on. In those days I was so naïve about drugs.

The show that night wasn't great. Amy sounded okay, but she kept walking to the back of the stage to give Blake a kiss. He was standing behind the brass section of Amy's band, so anyone who didn't know better probably thought he was part of the show. But it was very unprofessional and I hated seeing Amy behave like that on stage. My back was really hurting, so I decided to fly home the next day, but I had a word with Raye about the kissing, and he said he'd deal with it. I flew home and Amy continued the tour; her next stop was Holland.

*   *   *

When I got back to London I went on *GMTV* and did a piece about Amy's drug addiction. I wasn't specific and didn't mention crack cocaine or heroin, but I felt that airing some of her problems might help not only me and my family but also other families in a similar position. It was an incredibly difficult thing to do, and I knew Amy wouldn't be happy, but after what I'd witnessed on tour I couldn't see any other way forward, and there was a very positive response from viewers.

A few days later I spoke to Amy. She was meant to be coming home the next day, but she had decided to stay in Europe until the end of the week. She'd heard I'd been on *GMTV* and was furious, ranting at me. When she paused for breath, I asked, 'What are you so upset about?'

'Dad, you said it's about a father's struggle to help his daughter or something like that. I don't want you talking about our problems on TV.'

'Too bad,' I said. 'Let me put you straight on something. I'll do whatever I need to do to get you off drugs. Don't you dare lecture me about my family loyalty.'

I was really annoyed, and in the background I could hear Blake whispering to her. The call didn't end well. Amy must have known how upset I was, though, because she called me back a few minutes later in a much more conciliatory tone.

'I'll be honest, darling,' I replied. 'I'm struggling here – we all are. We're just trying to help you. After *GMTV* I got loads of messages from people who called in, parents saying they were in the same boat as us, and how what I said helped them feel less isolated.' Then I told her about something that had happened that morning, which made her laugh. The *Daily Star* had run an 'exclusive': 'Amy Winehouse says she's had her stomach pumped and an adrenalin injection in her chest …' I had phoned the paper and explained to them that yes, Amy had had her stomach pumped – but that was months ago – and she had never had an adrenalin injection. They weren't interested.

'Yeah, Dad, why let the truth get in the way of a good story?' she replied. It was my turn to laugh.

The following week Amy performed at the MTV European Music Awards in Munich, where she won the Artists' Choice award. She sounded great, and the recognition of her peers meant a lot to Amy, so it should have been a special moment, but things were really starting to get on top of me. 'Very good, another award.' I wrote in my diary that night. 'Pity she can't win an award for kicking drugs.' I was trying desperately to find a solution but I kept coming back to the same thought: Blake is the problem, but Amy loves Blake. With him around, I felt there could be no solution.

10

A BROKEN RECORD

Despite the success of *Back to Black*, and the near-constant playing of her songs in clubs, bars, shops and just about everywhere else, 2007 was a bad year for Amy. The papers were savaging her and it seemed there was nothing we could do to stop their regular assaults. Of course, it would end if only she would stop taking drugs. Worse, she was still all-consumed with Blake. Now problems from his past were going to turn Amy's life upside-down.

Back in 2006, Blake and his friend Michael Brown had been drinking in the Macbeth pub in Hoxton, east London. Run by James King, it was a top music venue frequented by celebrities, including Amy, although she wasn't there that night. During the evening King had thrown Brown out of the pub, and after the pub closed Brown had taken his revenge. When King left the pub at around midnight, Brown pounced on him and knocked him to the ground. Blake joined in, repeatedly stamping on King and kicking him in the head and body. King was so badly hurt that he needed twelve hours of surgery, with metal plates and bolts to reconstruct his face. Blake and Brown were arrested and charged with grievous bodily harm (GBH) with intent. They pleaded not guilty and the case was transferred to the Crown Court to be heard at a later date.

Now, more than a year later, in November 2007, Blake was due back in court to face the charges. Amy was terrified that he would go to prison and moved some tour dates so she could be in court. She refused to accept he was guilty and I kept my opinion to myself as, more than ever, I needed to be there for her. And I thought it would be the best thing for Amy if Blake did go to prison. At that time, it felt like the only way we'd be able to separate the two of them and, hopefully, help her see just how bad he really was. At the very least, with him in jail, we could help her with her addiction without any interference.

As Amy prepared to go to court, Raye was focused as ever on the positive, going to the US Embassy to try to get a visa waiver for Amy so that she could travel to the States in a few days' time to appear on some TV talk shows. After some back and forth, he managed to arrange it, on condition that Amy had a drug test the day before she was due to travel. As soon as I heard that, my heart sank. It meant she wouldn't be going: there was no way she'd pass a drug test.

The following Tuesday Amy failed the drug test – one more opportunity had fallen through because of drugs. As luck would have it, the previous day the Writers' Guild of America had gone on strike, which meant that the shows Amy was to appear on were cancelled anyway. For once, the media worked in our favour and the stories that emerged about Amy's cancelled trip attributed it to the writers' strike.

Even though the failed drug test was not headline news, Amy was upset, and the next day she asked me to meet her. I suggested we went out as Blake was always around, telling her what to think, say and do. We went to the Hawley Arms in Camden Town, where I insisted that we stuck to soft drinks. She was really disappointed that she wasn't going to the US, and even the arrival of the royalty cheque for £750,000 from Universal didn't cheer her up.

I felt like a broken record. She didn't want me to lecture her and I didn't want to have to, but I was just so frustrated. 'It's your own fault you can't go to America,' I told her. 'What are you going to do about it?'

She couldn't look at me because she knew I was right and fiddled with a button on her shirt. 'I know, Dad,' she mumbled. Then she looked up and I saw something in her eyes that I hadn't seen for a while. 'I'm going to try, Dad. I'm really going to try.'

She shuffled her chair closer to mine and I put my arm round her. She rested her head against my neck. 'I want to clean up my act, Dad.'

I knew she really meant it.

After a while, she stood up. 'Anyway, Dad, let's not be miserable any more.' When she went to the bar to get more soft drinks, I noticed just how fabulous she looked that day. About half an hour later she got into a row with a very drunk girl and ended up slapping her.

Later we went to Soho to get something to eat, but Amy was mobbed by fans and before we knew it the paps were there. We finally found a quiet little bistro and sat down for lunch, but were interrupted constantly by Blake phoning, wanting to know what we were talking about.

Each time he called, Amy would tell him virtually word for word our conversation. It was very annoying, and I asked Amy why she had to do it. She didn't answer and, to placate me, changed the subject by telling me that it was possible Blake would be willing to sign a post-nuptial agreement. I'd believe that when I saw it. I asked her what she would do if Blake went to prison and she said she'd need to keep busy.

After lunch we were intending to do a little shopping but fans and paps made it impossible so I dropped her back at her flat and went home with mixed feelings. On the one hand, Amy was going to clean up her act. On the other, Blake's continued presence made that seem less likely to happen.

The following day, I went to the Turkish baths at Porchester Hall. I had just come out of the steam room at about five thirty when I got a call from Alex Foden to say that the police were breaking into Amy's flat in Camden. Straight away I assumed two things: first, that the police were looking for drugs, and second, that Amy and Blake were at the Camden flat.

In fact, the police were looking for Blake, not drugs, but neither he nor Amy was there. They were at the flat in Bow. I left in a hurry and drove to Bow where I arrived at about six thirty and found them. Still thinking that the police had raided the Camden flat for drugs, I went on a diatribe about drugs to Amy and Blake, who weren't listening. Unsure of what to do, I called my solicitor, who suggested I bring them to his office and let the police arrest them there.

As we were trying to figure out what to do, we glanced through the window and noticed about five police cars drawing up outside the flat with the paps not far behind. A few seconds later, the police were hammering on the door and I let in eight plain-clothed officers. Blake was cautioned and arrested, though not for anything related to drugs. I'd been wrong about that. They had no interest in Amy.

Blake's charge was on suspicion of perverting the course of justice, which carries a maximum sentence of life imprisonment.

'Baby, I love you. I'll be fine,' Amy called to Blake, as they led him away in handcuffs. She wanted to go with him but the police wouldn't let her. I held on to her as she sobbed, but as the door closed, she pulled away from me and ran out of the flat. From the window, I saw Blake being put into one of the police cars. Amy rushed over to it and hammered on the window, shouting, 'I'll be fine, I love you.'

Shortly afterwards Tyler arrived and the three of us sat down to make sense of what was going on. At this point the details were sketchy because Blake had kept from Amy what he had been doing, but apparently he'd been worried that he would be found guilty of GBH so he had tried to bribe King into not testifying and withdrawing his complaint.

Unfortunately the confusion didn't end there. At about nine thirty that evening Georgette, who had been told about Blake's arrest, arrived with Giles and one of Blake's brothers. As I opened the front door, she barged past me, screaming, 'You grassed Blake!'

I didn't know what to say. Giles joined in, and they accused me of setting up Blake by concocting the bribery story. Within seconds everyone was shouting at once and I felt the room close in.

'Oi, leave my dad alone,' Amy said, defending me.

'Shut up, bitch,' Giles yelled.

That was it. I lost it and hit him. Suddenly we were all fighting, and Georgette and Giles were both landing punches. Then Blake's brother hit me and I fell to the floor. I was being attacked by all three of them.

In the middle of everything Amy was screaming, 'No, no, no, don't hurt my dad!'

Somehow or other I ended up pinning the Civils to the floor. I was shaking as I said to them, 'If you don't stop this, somebody is going to get hurt here tonight and it isn't going to be me.'

While I was trying to keep them on the floor I ended up with my trousers round my ankles. Any minute now, I thought, the paps are going to burst in and photograph me with my trousers down.

After things had calmed down, Georgette continued to accuse me of setting Blake up. It wasn't until the next day that we learned what had really happened. Even then Georgette never apologized to me. The *Daily Mirror* explained that it had informed detectives about Blake's attempt to bribe King. He and Brown had enlisted the help of two friends, Anthony Kelly and James Kennedy, to act as middle-men and pay James King £200,000 to ensure he did not testify. As part of the *Daily Mirror's* investigation, King was filmed withdrawing his allegations about the assault. He was to have been flown out of the country before the hearing in the hope that the case against Blake and Brown would be dropped. Matters were then complicated by Kelly and Kennedy attempting to sell footage of the pay-off to a newspaper reporter. It was one big mess of duplicity.

As the facts rolled out, it didn't take long for press attention to turn to Amy. The *Daily Mirror* said that there was no evidence to suggest she had been involved in the alleged plot, but where would Blake and Brown get such a large sum of money? The speculation was that it could only have come from Amy. I was confident she'd had nothing to do with it because it was impossible for her to get her hands on that kind of money without my knowing, but the general public weren't aware of that and the rumours began to circulate. That Amy and Blake had such a public romance and Amy was so devoted to him added fuel to the flames.

Later that day, Raye and I stopped by the flat at Jeffrey's Place to see the extent of the damage the police had caused during the raid. It had been torn apart. We went on to see Amy at the flat in Bow. She was asleep when we got there and woke up in a foul mood. There was no talking to her and she ended up turning a table over and storming back to her bedroom. Her frustration at the extraordinary events of the last twenty-four hours had boiled over. Raye and I left Tyler to look after her.

That Saturday, Amy and I went to Blake's bail hearing at Thames Magistrates' Court. Before the hearing we spoke to Blake's solicitor, who said it was likely that the GBH case would be dropped as James King was now a co-defendant in the bribery case. The police believed that King had been prepared to accept the bribe not to testify.

As expected, Blake was denied bail and sent to Pentonville Prison, north London, on remand. Our solicitor told us that the police would probably want to interview Amy, and his advice was that we should think about going to see them voluntarily.

When we left the court, Amy and I were mobbed by paps. Amy was a bit tearful but, considering what had happened, she handled it well. I felt desperately sorry for her – I hated to see her so unhappy – but I was secretly delighted that Blake was nowhere near her. His absence meant there was at least a chance Amy could get clean.

That afternoon and evening, Georgette and Giles phoned me a number of times. Suddenly they were my new pals, but all they wanted to talk about was their 'poor' son and what I could do to help him. I think that what they really wanted was for me to persuade Amy to pay for a top barrister, but they didn't say that.

The next day, Sunday, Raye and I took Amy to see Blake's solicitor, who introduced us to another solicitor, Brian Spiro. Brian laid out a case that he thought the police might have against Amy. We agreed that we wanted to avoid a high-profile arrest so we left it to Brian to approach the police and suggest that Amy might be willing to talk to them. That was what we had been told the previous day, but hearing it again made me feel that this was more serious than I had previously thought.

The prospect of speaking to the police worried Amy. Blake's solicitor said the case against Blake looked weak and naturally this cheered her up, but the dark cloud of having to talk to the police still hung over her. She was unresponsive throughout the meeting and looked dreadfully tired. I took her for lunch at the Diner in Curtain Road, east London, and she seemed to buck up for a while, but then she went to the bathroom and threw up.

'What's going on, darling?' I asked. 'Are you all right?'

'It's this drug I'm on, Dad,' she replied. 'No – not that,' as she saw my reaction. She'd seen a doctor who'd prescribed Subutex, a drug-replacement treatment designed to wean the user off heroin. It had made her throw up. I was so relieved and told her how proud I was of her for taking control.

After lunch I took Amy back to my house and spent the afternoon with her and Jane. I didn't wake her the next morning, which I spent researching Subutex and its side-effects.

When she did surface, Amy wanted to go and see Blake in Pentonville Prison. Visits had to be booked in advance and a visiting order (VO) had to be issued. Amy rang the prison and was told that Georgette had booked all of the visits for that week, which made her very, very angry. Eventually Georgette gave her a VO for that Wednesday.

On the Wednesday I picked Amy up and took her to the prison where she was allowed to see Blake. While I was waiting, I went to the appointments office and managed to book a visit for the following Wednesday. I saw that Geoff had booked himself a slot, and it occurred to me that it wasn't beyond the realms of possibility that he would smuggle drugs in for Blake. I didn't tell Amy my thoughts, but wrote in my diary that night: 'Seeing Amy so sad is horrible. But maybe this is the only way she can get clean. Being apart from Blake, and hearing about her taking Subutex, gives me real hope for her future.'

11

BIRMINGHAM 2007

Although Amy and I were very similar, we were quite different in one respect: I've always believed that the show must go on but Amy cancelled several. One show that went ahead when I wish it hadn't was at the Birmingham NIA (National Indoor Arena) on Thursday, 16 November 2007, the first gig of her UK tour.

After seeing Blake in prison the previous day, Amy was in a bit of a state: she had slept badly and looked as if she'd been crying. But she pulled herself together and insisted that she was going to do the tour. I thought long and hard when Raye asked me to go with her to the Birmingham gig. I had a feeling it was going to be bad, and I didn't want to see it – I knew it would upset me. In the end I put my feelings to one side and agreed to go.

On the tour bus, Amy was fine, except she couldn't stop talking about Blake. From her behaviour, it seemed that she hadn't taken any drugs, and she didn't have a drink while we were driving, so things started well. Raye had filled the bus with Amy's friends to boost her morale, and I noticed how different the atmosphere was without Blake.

Before the show I went into Amy's dressing room to wish her good luck and she still seemed fine, apart from her usual pre-gig nerves. Despite the triumphs of the last year, she still hadn't conquered stage fright. Half an hour later when she came out onstage it was a different story. She slurred her way through the songs and staggered around the stage. She was definitely drunk and the audience hated her for it. They booed and jeered, but instead of walking off the stage, Amy responded.

'First of all, if you're booing, you're a mug for buying a ticket,' she told them. 'Second, to all those booing, just wait till my husband gets out of incarceration. And I mean that.'

Standing at the side of the stage, I could hardly believe this was happening. It didn't feel like I was watching Amy. I was sobbing and there was nothing I could do.

Afterwards I told Raye the whole tour should be cancelled. He agreed with me that this had been the worst show he'd seen Amy do, but he waited until she sobered up to ask her what she wanted to do about the rest of the tour. More than fifty thousand tickets had already been sold and the tour was expected to gross more than £1.25 million. If Amy pulled out, she'd be stuck with a big bill.

When I walked into Amy's dressing room, she was giving a friend's mother a £20,000 watch as a present. Why? Because she was drunk. I cleared the dressing room, and the look on Amy's face told me everything. She was in a terrible state. With everyone out of the room she became very tearful, apologizing for her performance and for what she had said to her audience. 'Give me a cuddle, Dad,' she said, like a small child, as if somehow I could make everything right again.

I hugged her tightly, and she said, 'I'm the luckiest girl in the world to have my family, I really am.' I didn't know what to do, what to say. I knew that lecturing her or stating the obvious wouldn't help. I wanted to support her, so I just carried on holding her.

The next day at about four o'clock I got a call from the BBC telling me they'd heard a rumour that Amy's show in Glasgow had been cancelled. I phoned Raye and he said that the show wasn't cancelled but that Amy had been upset because of all of the paps at Glasgow airport. The show went ahead, and Raye called me as the first set ended. He held the phone so that I could hear what was going on. 'Listen to this!'

The audience were going wild for Amy. They were chanting, 'Amy, Amy, Amy,' over and over.

At the end Raye called me again and I could hear the crowd, still cheering Amy. It had been a great show, but what made it even better was that Amy had taken no drugs and drunk no alcohol. The more emotional songs, 'Wake Up Alone', 'Unholy War' and 'Back to Black', had been dropped because Amy found them too difficult to sing while Blake was banged up, which seemed to have helped. I spoke to Amy and told her how proud of her I was, that she was a fighter. Amy's reply? 'Aaah, thanks Dad.'

A few days later, Amy put on another great show, this time in Newcastle, with the audience again chanting her name in between songs. The best news of that day wasn't the show but what happened afterwards: Raye called me to say that Amy had told him she wanted to clean up and go to a clinic as soon as the tour was over. Raye was hoping to work something out so that she could have help during the tour.

When I finally spoke to Amy, she sounded absolutely fine and lucid. It seemed that the good shows had turned her around and given her a new focus. Still she couldn't stop talking about Blake and her belief that he was going to be let out on bail. I humoured her as best I could, but I thought she was deluding herself about his immediate future regarding prison. It didn't seem to me like he was going anywhere.

Part of what made it so difficult to be around Amy at this time was how quickly everything changed. She told me she'd stopped taking Subutex as it was making her throw up. Two days later the lucidity in her voice was gone. She called me from her flat, either high or drunk, saying she needed 'kisses and cuddles', a phrase from her childhood.

*   *   *

Amy's performances were improving, but the police remained interested in what she knew about the possible attempted bribe. They went to our accountants and took bank statements. They were pressing to interview her, and we were advised again to go and see them voluntarily. They also wanted to interview me to find out if it was possible for large sums of money to be taken out of Amy's account without my knowledge, but I wasn't worried about that: I knew it couldn't happen.

I was still driving my cab when I could, and throughout this time, whenever punters recognized me as Amy's dad, I'd be asked, 'How're you doing? How's your daughter?'

I answered as I always did, 'She's fine, thank you, and thanks for asking.'

But the truth was she wasn't fine, and neither was I. Every day was like a ride on a rollercoaster, turning us upside-down and inside-out, so we didn't know where we were from one minute to the next. Amy had never been chaotic before but she was now.

On Friday, 23 November, Blake was refused bail, and Amy was devastated. We were back on board the rollercoaster.

Perhaps I shouldn't have been surprised that Amy's show the following night at the Hammersmith Apollo in west London was a bit of a mess. Whenever I could, I would see Amy before a show, to gee her up and make sure she was okay. Before that one I went to see her in her hotel and the singer Pete Doherty was there. They were both sitting on the bed strumming guitars. Doherty was always in the news over drink and drugs binges so I didn't want Amy anywhere near him. I threw him out. Later, some people said I'd hit him over the head with his guitar. I have no further comment to make on that point, but he did leave the room with his head in his hands.

Amy was half an hour late going onstage that night and there was some booing from the audience. On the whole, she sang very well, but there were a few moments when she looked a bit wobbly. I thought the show was a bit of a shambles, but from what I heard, most people loved it.

Ultimately it didn't matter. A day or two later, Amy called me, saying she wanted to cancel the rest of the tour: she just wasn't up to it emotionally. I spoke to Raye and we concluded that cancelling was the best thing to do. Amy's health was far more important than any tour but cancelling was pointless unless Amy went into rehab. I decided that a gentle approach was called for and went round to see her.

I told her that Raye and I had spoken, and she seemed relieved when I told her that the tour had been cancelled. 'You know why we're doing this, don't you Amy?' I asked. 'It's because we all love you and want you to get better. Your health is more important than any tour. But the only way you're going to get better is with proper help.'

'You mean rehab, Dad,' she said. 'I want to get better but I ain't doing rehab.' She wasn't obstinate, just resigned.

'I understand,' I said. 'I'm going to look at some options for you.

There must be other ways of doing this.' If she could get back to writing again it would help, I thought. Once she threw herself into something there was no stopping my Amy. We hugged each other for a while before I left.

As I got into my taxi I received the first of what would be a series of anonymous texts. It said: 'You're a real prick for the things you've said about Georgette. Sort your daughter out you c***.'

I decided not to mention it to Amy.

*   *   *

I went to the police station and showed them that there was no way a large payment could have been made from Amy's bank account. I'd been a bit nervous going in, but I knew we were innocent of any wrongdoing so I explained how the accounting worked and the measures we had in place to protect Amy. Walking out of there, I felt relieved that neither Amy nor I was implicated.

Feeling optimistic about the outcome, I went to see Amy at her flat in Bow to discuss the rehab options, but she was in bed and I couldn't get her up as she was suffering from the after-effects of drink and/or drugs. Would every day be like this? Although Blake was in prison – and Amy wanted to get clean – she was horribly addicted and might remain so. I resolved to ask the professionals what else I and the rest of her family should be doing to help.

I spent the next hour or so walking around aimlessly, trying to make sense of everything and planning my next move to help Amy. The first step was to book her an appointment with Dr Ettlinger for eleven o'clock the next day.

Raye took Amy to the appointment, but she wasn't particularly communicative and couldn't wait to leave. I phoned Dr Ettlinger and arranged another appointment for the following day. I would be bringing her, I told him, and would like to sit in on the consultation. I also made an appointment for Amy with Dr Pierides, the clinical psychologist; we would see him first, then go on to Dr Ettlinger. She went to both, but neither appointment proved very productive. While she was receptive to Dr Pierides, she shut down when Dr Ettlinger began to talk to her about the harm she was doing to her body. She refused to hear what he had to say.

A few days later, I called Amy's flat in the afternoon. Alex Foden was with her and told me she'd been sleeping all day. While that wasn't particularly unusual at the time, I decided to drive over to make sure she was okay. By the time I got there, Amy was awake, but not very coherent. After a while she came round a bit and we talked more about looking for a rehab place where she would feel comfortable.

It seemed that we were going round in circles. When Amy wasn't high, she wanted to get clean. Then she would get high and forget she wanted to get clean. I felt that the people going in and out of the Bow flat were a bad influence on her as, quite clearly, a lot of drug-taking was going on there.

And there were constant stories in the media. I'd had a call from Alex Foden to say that Georgette had sold a story to the *Daily Mail* for three thousand pounds. I was furious – Amy had enough problems without getting upset about press coverage – but I later found out the story was about Blake and hardly mentioned Amy. Then, in the first week of December, there were pictures of Amy, supposedly running through the streets near her flat dressed only in a red bra and jeans. I was fuming: as usual, there was a big gap between what the pictures implied and the truth.

What had happened was that at about four a.m. Amy had wanted a cup of tea and one of her friends had gone to the all-night garage at the top of the road to buy some milk. The flat was inside a gated community, and when Amy's friend went out he left the front gate open by mistake. There were paps outside it day and night and they wasted no time in taking advantage of the open gate. They banged on Amy's front door and Amy, thinking it was her friend coming back, opened it. Flash, flash, flash, flash, flash – they had pictures of Amy in her bra. So, she was not running through the streets in her underwear, simply opening her front door.

Tuesday, 4 December, was my birthday. My son Alex called me but I didn't hear from Amy and I was too fed up to be upset. Over the next couple of days there were more pictures of Amy in the newspapers, this time with Pete Doherty. One was of them standing outside the flat in Bow, supposedly at four a.m. Just hours later Amy was meant to be visiting Blake in Pentonville; she missed the visit because she overslept. Blake might have been bad, but Doherty wasn't much better – this time I felt sorry for Blake.

When I talked to Amy about the missed visit, she offered no excuses. I was disgusted with her and told her so. 'You can't let someone down like that. I was glad to walk out of there after just half an hour when we went to see him, so what must it be like being stuck in there twenty-four hours a day? You'd want your own wife to understand that and make sure she stuck to her visits.' I couldn't be bothered to tell her I was upset that she'd forgotten my birthday.

Later she phoned and asked me to meet her in the West End. I told her I didn't want to see her because I was still fed up with her. The truth was I now felt that the situation was hopeless and I didn't want to see her when I might end up saying the wrong thing.

Two days later Amy had a VO to see Blake. She made the trip this time, but got there too late and wasn't allowed in. I had a meeting with the Outside Organization, Amy's PR company, to discuss how we could get more positive press for her. Looking back now, it seems we didn't do very well.

Not long after that meeting an open letter to Amy from Janis was published in the *News of the World*. Janis didn't write it, but she approved its contents. In it she virtually begged Amy to get clean. I understood why she said everything she did and it wasn't entirely her fault – she'd been told the day before, possibly erroneously, that the *News of the World* would be publishing an open letter to Amy from Georgette – but it really upset Amy. Janis had Amy's best interests at heart, but this was another reminder that we had to be really careful how we handled the press. It showed how manipulative they could be.

*   *   *

When I next met with Drs Ettlinger and Pierides they were both very concerned about Amy's health. At this stage I was still trying to persuade her to go to rehab but nothing was agreed or accomplished. She was very thin and both doctors commented on it. Amy herself said that during her most recent visit to Blake he'd told her she should try to put on some weight and stop taking drugs.

I went home feeling depressed. Even a call from Raye to say that Amy had been nominated for six Grammy Awards didn't lighten my mood. 'They want her to perform at the ceremony in LA on the tenth of February 2008,' he added.

'What did she say when you told her?' I asked.

'She was really excited, Mitch. She really wants to do it. She couldn't believe she'd been nominated for so many awards. I haven't heard her sound so happy in ages.'

'Hang on a minute, Raye,' I said. 'She's not going to get the visa, is she?'

Raye replied, 'She says she's going to get clean in time.'

'Well, that won't happen.'

I rang Amy to congratulate her. She was really, really happy about the Grammys, and we ended up having quite a long conversation – one of our best in ages.

'Who'd have thought, when you were sitting in your bedroom in Spain playing that little guitar, those songs you were writing then, you'd be going on to win Grammy Awards? It's unbelievable, Amy.'

'I tell you what, Dad …' She went quiet. For once in her life Amy was stuck for words. 'Do you know what, Dad? This is just the beginning. I need to start writing again.'

I got off the phone and thought, Well, let's see, shall we? One step at a time – she's got to get there first.

Shortly after this, though, Amy officially became a suspect in Blake's case. This had come about because Blake had admitted he was going to pay £200,000 to James King so that he wouldn't testify in the GBH case. Blake obviously didn't have that kind of money and the only person it could have come from was Amy. As I've said, Amy couldn't have got that kind of money out of her account without a counter-signature so, although I was worried about this latest development, I knew nothing would come of it.

As Amy was now a suspect in the case, she was not allowed to be physically with Blake any more: their visits had to take place with a sheet of glass between them. Amy was very upset – I had tried to protect her from the details of what was going on, but there was no avoiding this. Amy's solicitor advised again that we should prepare a statement and take it to the police, rather than waiting for her to be arrested, which, in his view, was imminent. A couple of days later he arranged for Amy to attend Shoreditch Police Station in east London where she was arrested. It's common practice, under English law, for a suspect to be arrested before they can be questioned by the police, and Raye, who had accompanied her, was also arrested after an altercation with paps outside the police station. The charges against him were subsequently dropped. After questioning, Amy was released on bail without restrictions, and when I spoke to her later she was coping much better than I'd expected.

I suggested that she should consider going on holiday with some of her friends while we tried to sort everything out. Surprisingly, she agreed and called me later to say that she would like to go to Mustique with Tyler, then rang back to say she'd like to take Juliette and Lauren too. I was delighted and began to make the arrangements.

Tyler was a good influence, and I knew that Juliette and Lauren simply wanted the best for Amy. They had always been close to her, but recently, because they disagreed with the way Amy was dealing with her drug problem, their relationship had suffered. I suppose you could say their solution was tough love. They seemed to think that Amy should be locked up in rehab, but Amy would never have gone along with that – and I'd never thought things were that simple. I'd always favoured the supportive approach, encouraging her in her desire to quit and comforting her through the bad times. Again and again Amy had shown that she'd get drugs if she wanted them.

It didn't matter whether my approach or theirs was right. I just wanted my Amy to get better – and I was happy that she wanted to take her friends on holiday. On 20 December I gave Amy four thousand pounds for her trip to Mustique. She was set to leave on 28 December with Tyler and Juliette; in the end Lauren didn't go.

Christmas Day was soon upon us and we were all due to go to my sister Melody's house for lunch. Alex Foden was supposed to be bringing Amy, but by two o'clock they hadn't arrived and my calls to Amy and Alex Foden went straight to voicemail. I had predicted that Amy wouldn't come to Mel's and assumed she was asleep after, probably, being high the previous night. I tried to put it to the back of my mind but at seven o'clock, when there was still no word, I drove to her flat in Bow.

When I knocked on the door, there was no answer, but I peered through the window and could see her lying on the couch in the living room. I banged on the glass again – nothing. I was on the point of breaking the door down or smashing the window when one of Amy's friends came out of the bedroom. She woke Amy and opened the door. Amy couldn't understand what all of the fuss was about and was a bit tetchy with me. At times like this, it became frighteningly apparent that she had no idea how much worry she caused all of us.

Three days later, Amy, Juliette and Tyler flew to Barbados, where they spent a few days, then travelled on to Mustique. I hoped she would be okay and have a good holiday. I felt relieved that other people now had the responsibility of looking after her. That might sound a horrible thing to say but twenty-four hours a day, seven days a week, was exhausting me when I still had to earn my living and be a husband to Jane and a father to Alex. I began to relax – until I took a call from a 'freight company' to say that Amy had left her bag at the airport and they wanted a forwarding address in Barbados. The lengths the paps will go to for a story...

As the year ended, a number of clinics all over the world contacted me to tell me they could help Amy. Each said they were right for Amy. One even guaranteed that their treatment would rid Amy of her addiction. I gave Dr Ettlinger the details and he told me that, although he was sceptical of so-called guarantees, he would look into it.

Not long ago, I would have dismissed all such claims, but times were getting harder by the day. It was difficult to imagine surviving another year like the last. My diary entry for the last day of 2007 reads: '*Frank* now Platinum, meaningless unless Amy gets better. Please God help me to make 2008 a better year for my darling daughter.'

12

'AGAIN, SHE'S FINE, THANKS FOR ASKING'

I resolved that 2008 would be the year we helped Amy get clean. Heroin and crack cocaine must become a thing of the past. I knew that everyone who cared about Amy's wellbeing felt the same and, with Blake still in prison, we had a fighting chance of making it happen.

New Year's Day started well, with an early-morning call from Amy in Mustique, where she was staying with the singer Bryan Adams, whom she'd met in London some time before. She sounded fine and told me she was having a lovely time. However, Raye had heard a different story. Amy told him she wanted to go back to Barbados, where she could stay with Salaam Remi's father, but Raye dissuaded her – he was convinced she only wanted to go back to score drugs. Amy didn't tell me how much she was suffering. I know she really struggled on Mustique, but she was a fighter and stuck out the terrible pains of withdrawal. Bryan Adams was concerned about her weight – she was being sick a lot.

Her trip lasted about a week. Then Amy decided she wanted to come back to show Blake that she was off heroin, but I didn't believe her. It was more likely that she wanted to come home specifically to get some heroin. When she arrived, I arranged for Dr Ettlinger to examine her, and he told me that, in his opinion, she would go back to drugs the minute she could get hold of them. We were back to square one.

Meanwhile it came to my attention – it doesn't matter how – that Amy owed a certain drug-dealer twelve thousand pounds and this dealer was going to the Bow flat to collect. I made sure I was there when the dealer arrived and I said, in no uncertain terms, that neither I nor Amy would be paying a penny. There was no argument and the dealer left. When Amy found out, she was angry with me because I had cut off one of her lines of supply.

'Too bad,' I said. You've got to be cruel to be kind. The way I saw it, it was one less person Amy could buy from. I took out my frustration with Amy and her behaviour on the people I found hanging about the flat and probably got too much enjoyment from kicking them out forcefully. I thought it would do Amy no harm to see how angry she made me sometimes.

She needed any distraction from drugs that we could give her, so we were all excited by the news that Raye had arranged for Amy to sing the title song for the next Bond film, *Quantum of Solace*. Amy was very excited about it. She'd really liked *Casino Royale*, and immediately started making plans to work with Mark Ronson, who would be writing the music. That was exactly what she needed: to start thinking about music again – a new project for her to work on. I wondered how she'd deal with deadlines and a brief that she had to fulfil.

The hope was that we'd be able to make that distraction last long enough to keep her clean for her drug-test. Dr Ettlinger felt that Amy was improving but he decided to prescribe Valium to help her relax, which she was finding harder and harder to do. However, he explained that there was a problem: after 15 January Amy could not take any drugs at all, including prescription drugs, if she was to pass the drugs test to enable her to get her visa to enter the US to perform at the Grammy Awards the following month. The appointment for the drugs test had been made for 22 January.

Although it was only for a week that Amy couldn't have any medication, it would seem like a lifetime to her. I didn't know if she could do it. The only thing keeping me optimistic was a conversation I'd had with Tyler. He'd been with her through her withdrawal in Mustique and was encouraged by her efforts to quit drugs. He agreed to keep an eye on her.

On the drive home I stopped several times, for Amy to get out of my cab to buy sweets, a mobile phone and finally fish and chips for both of us. She even bought portions for the paps that were following us. Each time she was mobbed by fans. It was great to know that they saw her as herself and not as the Amy the tabloids had created. It was hilarious and Amy was on top form. We had a lot of laughs – at one point I was laughing so much I had to stop the cab. Amy jumped out of the seat next to me and into the back, as if she was a passenger.

'Where to, madam?' I called over my shoulder, playing the game.

'To my flat in Camden Town, my good man, and don't spare the horses.'

'To Jeffrey's Place?'

'It's mine, not Jeffrey's,' she said, and I laughed again. This was my girl, the way she used to be, before drugs. I went home feeling uplifted for the first time in ages. Maybe she could pull it off, after all.

A day or two later I heard from Tyler that Amy had taken drugs. When I confronted her, she admitted it was true and told me Alex

Foden had given them to her. I was furious but kept my temper in check and did nothing about Foden. The next day was meant to be the start of the drug-free week and there was no way round it. If she failed the test, she wouldn't be admitted to the US. My hopes dimmed again when I went to see her at the Bow flat and, lo and behold, Geoff was there again.

The following morning Raye landed me with a bombshell. The *Sun* newspaper had told him they had pictures and videos of Amy taking drugs. Upsetting as this was, I tried to stay calm: this just confirmed what everyone already knew.

On the day we'd scheduled for the US drug test, the *Sun* published the story, complete with pictures of Amy apparently taking crack cocaine. To make matters worse, the video had been set up by two of Blake's friends who had sold it to the *Sun*. I expected Amy to be mortified, but she maintained, in the face of all the evidence, that she hadn't been set up, and said, 'What do I care? Everybody thinks I take drugs anyway, Dad.'

After the story appeared, I was inundated with calls from the press. I naturally wanted to protect my daughter and said that Amy was now in treatment and that we were all proud of her progress.

We postponed the US drugs test until the following week but, drugs test or not, we had to get Amy focused. She was scheduled to perform a concert in Cannes, France, on 24 January; Jane and I were to go with her. However, in the wake of the photos surfacing in the *Sun*, Raye and I met with Lucian Grainge, at Universal Records. He told me he would not allow Amy to perform. Furthermore, unless Amy went into rehab, he would not allow her to perform at the Grammys or the BRIT Awards either. His concern was that Amy would make a laughing stock of herself. She might have been number one in the charts in France, Germany, Spain and Italy, but he was worried about the fallout for Universal.

This was serious. While he was not talking about Universal dropping Amy, he was insistent that she had medical treatment in rehab. It was clear that his intentions were good and that he, like all of us, just wanted to see Amy back to her best so she could use her talent. I had been through so much with her over the last year that I had serious doubts about her agreeing to go to rehab. Lucian, though, was adamant, telling me to bring Amy to a meeting at Universal at one o'clock the following day. If she failed to show up, no excuse would be acceptable.

The next day I went to collect Amy to take her to the meeting. Of course she wasn't ready but after a lot of messing about we eventually left. On our journey Raye called to say that Amy was going to be arrested on drugs charges relating to the *Sun* video. We finally arrived at Universal an hour and a half late. I could feel the tension the moment we walked into the room. Lucian, Raye, Alan Edwards and Chris Goodman from the Outside Organization, Dr Ettlinger and Dr Pierides were all there.

For once, a doctor wasn't leading the discussion, which might have been helpful. Lucian laid down the law, instructing Amy that unless she went into rehab that day he would stop her working. Resistant as she was to the idea, she couldn't ignore the threat to her career. With that, and reinforcement from everyone else in the room, she reluctantly agreed to be admitted to Capio Nightingale, a leading private psychiatric hospital in London's St John's Wood.

That day I drove her there, but it wasn't long into the journey that she started to change her mind, pleading with me to stop the cab and turn round, swearing she'd beat it herself and didn't need to go into hospital. In the end I didn't literally have to drag her in, but it was a struggle. She calmed down a bit but once she was in her own room, she kicked off again and threatened to kill herself. I didn't believe a word of it because I'd heard all this in the car, but the doctors ran in from the corridor, now convinced that she was a threat to herself, and told me they would section her, which meant she would be compelled to remain in hospital if she tried to leave. For someone to be sectioned, their doctor, clinical psychologist and the local area health authority have to agree to it, which, given the state Amy was in, they would have done.

During the initial consultation I broke down several times. What a terrible thing it was to see my baby in that situation, but I knew she was in the best place. It was breaking my heart to see her so distressed and I had to bury my natural instinct to scoop her up and take her away from what was scaring her, and the horrible days ahead. I knew this time I couldn't fix it and that she had to go through each step of the recovery process. On her own.

Later that evening Kelly Osbourne came to see her, and I left them to it while I drove back to Bow to collect some things Amy needed. When I got back to the hospital at about eleven o'clock, she seemed more settled, which was good for everyone. I learned later that if she had left the clinic, she would have been arrested over the *Sun* crack-cocaine video. I stayed until she fell asleep, kissed her goodnight and left.

To stop unwanted calls or callers at the hospital, we devised a password system. The password was 'Gordon', my mother's maiden name. I called the hospital early the next day and spoke to Dr Pierides, who said that Amy had had a comfortable night and they were sedating her so she could rest. He thought it was best that she had no visitors that day.

Rest was a crucial part of the programme for the first few days, and Amy spent quite a bit of time sleeping. At one point, Raye spoke to Blake who surprisingly said he was pleased that Amy was in hospital. As much as I didn't care about his opinion, it would be important for Amy that she had his support in her recovery when she got out.

His mother, though, was anything but supportive. As Amy was trying to get clean, a different drama was unfolding around Blake. Once again he had been refused bail. Before Amy had gone into treatment, Georgette had been hounding her about paying his legal fees. Given Amy's position in relation to Blake's case, no one thought that was a good idea. Numerous solicitors had said as much. While Amy remained a suspect, it could be detrimental to her case to pay Blake's legal fees. Still, Amy wanted to help Blake, and I'd attempted several times to talk her out of it. Eventually she agreed, reluctantly, to wait until she was cleared of charges before she paid for Blake.

Needless to say, Georgette was not happy about any of this. On Sunday, 27 January, an interview with Georgette and Giles was published in the *News of the World*. They referred to me as the Fat Controller, which I thought was quite funny. What was not funny was that they went on to accuse me of taking money from Amy. These stories in the press were anything but helpful, and a lot of the 'facts' published around that time were inaccurate to say the least.

As it turned out, Amy couldn't pay Blake's legal fees anyway. Her accountant, Margaret Cody, informed me that she couldn't afford to. Of course, the money problem was only short term as a lot of royalties were due to be paid later, but our discussion highlighted the fact that Amy wasn't working. The royalties were coming in, but there was no plan for what would happen when they ran out. Something had to change.

* * *

I visited Amy as often as I could at the hospital. When you're dealing with someone who's recovering from drug addiction, you look for small signs of progress wherever you can find them, such as when I saw her eating. That pleased me because she desperately needed to put on some weight.

After only a few days, it was clear there were other positive effects. On one of my visits, Dr Pierides mentioned that he was pleased with Amy's progress, and Amy was also pleased with it. She was beginning to feel a little better and, to my surprise, she said she wanted to stay in the hospital. She also said she wanted to move out of the Bow flat as she felt the people there were a big part of her problem. I thought this was a major turning-point for Amy, and that she'd come to it after so long left me feeling more relieved than I'd been in days, if not weeks.

The following day Dr Ettlinger called me to say that they were transferring Amy to the London Clinic, in the West End, not far from Harley Street, which is stuffed with high-end private medical practitioners. She was admitted for rehydration as she had lost a lot of weight through vomiting. The plan was that she would stay there for three or four days, then go back to Capio Nightingale. I went to visit her at the London Clinic; I knew the place well as I'd dropped punters off there. The entrance was imposing but old-fashioned, in that red-brick London way, but I'd never been inside and was impressed by the clean modern lines. Amy told me she was feeling a lot better and didn't want to go back to Capio Nightingale. I said she had to, and she reluctantly agreed. My worst fear was that she would go back to Capio Nightingale, then just walk out, which would leave her open to arrest over the *Sun* crack-cocaine video. The police were now saying they were willing to drop the drugs charges against Amy – if she was willing to name the people who had taken the video of her so they could be arrested for drug-dealing. Now definitely wasn't the time to put this to Amy though.

Sadly, despite the progress she'd made, her leaving was a very real possibility. And if Amy wanted to leave, no one could stop her because she had improved to the point at which they could no longer section her. Amy was feeling so much better that she thought she was cured. Of course, she was far from that. I knew that if she left Capio Nightingale, it wouldn't be long before she was back on drugs. I really didn't know what to do and it seemed that no one had a solution. It was sending me round the bend. The people I thought would know best what to do, how to help Amy, how to heal her, could only do so much, and then it was down to her.

One day I took Amy out of Capio Nightingale briefly so that she could have a medical examination with a doctor in Knightsbridge for her visa to enter the US. It went well and Amy and I were both pleased that there was still a chance she could attend the Grammys. The US Embassy said they would let us know their decision within forty-eight hours. I held out the hope that the Grammys might work out for her. Amy seemed so much better, and Dr Ettlinger told me he was thrilled with her progress. Amy had an incredible power of recovery. Given the quantity of poisonous substances she had put into her body, it was wonderful to see her getting better so quickly.

A few days later, I had a call from Security at Capio Nightingale, who told me that Geoff had smuggled drugs into the hospital, crudely stuffed inside a teddy bear. Amy's friend Blake Wood, whom I called American Blake, didn't do drugs. He had come to see her shortly afterwards and made sure the drugs were immediately removed. By then, though, Amy had taken some. I rushed to the hospital and stayed with her all night. I was mad with frustration at her weakness, but furious with the awful, awful man who was prepared to risk her wellbeing, even her life, for the sake of a few quid. I banned all visitors who weren't on a list I had given to the hospital.

The next morning I chaperoned Amy to Pentonville for her visit with Blake. The newspaper coverage of the visit was upbeat about Amy's health and there were some nice photographs of her, smiling at the cameras. On the way back in the cab, I asked Amy what Blake had said to her when she had told him about the hospital. In fairness to Blake, around that time he appeared to be supportive of Amy getting clean.

'We didn't talk about me, Dad,' she said. 'We talked about him and then a bit about us, you know, Blake and me.'

I knew then that she hadn't told him.

In spite of the setback with the drugs from the teddy bear, Amy was making progress, and we all felt confident she would continue heading in the right direction. But a question mark still hung over the Grammys. We had still had no word from the US Embassy about Amy's visa and, as time was running out, Raye arranged for her to perform in London on a live link to the Grammys. It was a smart move. Not long after, we learned that the embassy had declined Amy's visa application on the grounds that traces of cocaine had been found in her blood.

Initially Amy was upset: she had wanted more than anything to play in front of her peers at the Grammys. She bucked up when I explained the plans for a live performance to be beamed to Los Angeles, but she was still very disappointed that the visa wasn't forthcoming. She had had enough of Capio Nightingale, she said, and definitely wanted to leave. I was able to keep her there one more day, but that was it. I found her a two-bedroom suite at the Plaza on the River Hotel, Albert Embankment, near the Houses of Parliament. Amy liked the fact that the suites were separate from the hotel, giving her privacy. I arranged for American Blake to stay there with her, which she was very pleased about.

At ten o'clock on Friday, 10 February, Raye, Lucian, Dr Ettlinger, Amy's new consultant psychiatrist Dr Kelleher, Amy and I had a meeting at Capio Nightingale, during which Amy was told that there must be no drugs or the live link to the Grammys would be pulled. Amy was on top form. She agreed to the terms of her leaving, so Raye and I drove her to the Plaza on the River where we discussed the plan for the live link. Amy was going to do a show for invited guests first, then perform two songs for the live link. She was very excited, and I saw the old Amy gradually emerge as we went through the details. Amy assured me that she would not take any drugs before the show. I really wanted to believe her but there was a nagging doubt in the back of my mind.

The next day I took my sister Melody and her husband Elliott to watch Amy rehearse for the following night's show. Her set sent tingles down my spine and, believe me, she didn't need that rehearsal: she could have done the show there and then – she was fantastic and there was no sign of any drugs. I had dinner with Amy at the hotel and she definitely hadn't taken any drugs, but she did drink a lot, which troubled me. I hoped it wasn't something new to worry about.

Amy's show for the Grammys was due to start at eleven thirty p.m., to coincide with the live show in LA, but I wanted to be there very early to keep an eye on her. I arrived at the venue, Riverside Studios in Hammersmith, west London, at about six thirty. The room had been decorated to resemble a nightclub and looked great. I hung out with the guys from Amy's band, who were looking forward to the gig. When show time came around, Amy looked just great and gave an absolutely brilliant performance for friends and family. It got the night off to a perfect start and we didn't look back.

Via a satellite link, Amy performed 'You Know I'm No Good' and 'Rehab' to us and the Grammy audience, who clapped and cheered her for ages after she'd finished. It was a real high point, and I was reminded of just how magical Amy could be, even in the midst of these very dark times. I had seen her perform on stages in front of thousands of people; I had seen her in small clubs and rooms above pubs; I'd heard her in my sitting room and in the back of my cab – but that night outstripped them all. That show was electrifying. She was vital and alive, at her peak. She knew it and revelled in it.

In all Amy won five Grammys – an unprecedented number for an overseas star – for Record of the Year, Song of the Year (both for 'Rehab'), Best New Artist, Best Pop Vocal Album (for *Back to Black*) and Best Female Pop Vocal.

When Tony Bennett announced she'd won Record of the Year we all rushed on to the stage and hugged – Janis, Alex, Amy and me. 'I can't believe it, Dad,' Amy said, 'Tony Bennett knows my name.'

In her acceptance speeches, Amy kept things sweet and simple, saying very graciously, 'Thank you very much. It's an honour to be here. Thank you very, very much.' And as the crowd chanted, 'Amy, Amy, Amy,' she put her arms around Janis and me, and said, 'To my mum and dad.'

When I heard those words, I started crying uncontrollably. My tears of joy were not only for her success but also for the fact that my little girl was back from the misery she had been suffering for the last six months.

The whole family partied until the early hours and we arrived back at the hotel at five thirty a.m. The room was crowded; I beckoned Amy over and told her I had something to say to her privately. We walked out onto the terrace, where we stood and shivered in the cold. I put my arm round her and said, 'Do you know, darling? Tonight wasn't about the tabloids. It wasn't about Blake. It wasn't even about the drugs. It was about you and your music. Keep it that way and, believe you me, you'll be all right.'

13

PRESS, LIES, AND
A VIDEOTAPE

The following day the newspapers were full of Amy's triumph at the Grammys. Some even reported that her visa had come through too late for her to travel to the US, rather than the truth that it had been declined. In every way it seemed this was a chance for a fresh start.

It didn't last long. Before any of us had any time to relish things, we were confronted once again with the difficult reality that drugs remained a constant problem for Amy. Despite my instructions to the hotel's security guards, Amy managed to have drugs delivered to her suite and my hopes for her recovery were dashed. American Blake had been there, but couldn't stop her. The only consolation, if you could call it that, was that she hadn't taken much, and American Blake had managed to flush away most of what she'd bought. But what difference did it make how much she had taken? The fact was, she was still addicted. We had gone from the incredible high of the Grammys night to another low. I said to Jane, 'Is this what our lives are going to be like from now on? Up, down, up, down?' It wasn't enough to say I was disappointed, the truth was I was simply exhausted.

Around that time I had a call from Roger Daltrey – he wanted to congratulate Amy on her Grammy wins. He and I ended up having a long chat about addiction. I got off the phone feeling slightly better because Roger had convinced me that it was possible for Amy to get clean – but part of me still worried about what was coming next.

I spoke to Amy later that day and, understandably, she didn't want to discuss drugs. Instead she said she wanted to visit Alex Foden, who'd gone into rehab while she was in treatment. When he came out, she said, she wanted him to become her personal assistant. The minute I heard those words, I knew it was a load of rubbish. Personal assistant? Drug buddy, more like.

The next day Amy went to see him, Foden checked out of rehab and Amy installed him in her suite at the Plaza on the River Hotel. Unable to deal with what he knew was to come, American Blake left, and I didn't blame him. With Foden staying, I knew it wouldn't be long before there was trouble. Sure enough, a couple of days later, Amy took drugs again and, as a result, she missed her visit to Blake in prison. I went to the hotel and told Foden he had to leave. I agreed that we would pay his rehab bill if he went back in. Amy wasn't too pleased but in the end he went.

American Blake moved back into the suite and, once again, Amy promised not to take drugs. I told her that her promises were worthless to me, and I would only be convinced that she meant what she'd said if she had a urine test every day. She didn't like that but agreed to it. While I was encouraged that she'd said yes, I doubted she would stick to the regime. I pointed out that the BRIT Awards were looming, and even though she wasn't nominated for anything, they wanted her to perform and receive a special achievement award. I explained to her, though, that unless I knew she wasn't taking drugs, I would make sure she didn't perform.

'I'm gonna do it, Dad,' she insisted. 'Look, I've even emailed Ronson about it.'

She showed me what she'd sent him.

SUBJECT: My God you're ugly.

TEXT: Are you coming to the BRITS, you savage, savage man. I would prefer Maud, but Madonna couldn't even fast-track the quarantine laws. I did everything, trust me. I go bananas over you.

Levi Levine

p.s. Frank Sinatra is and always will be God.

I laughed. 'I suppose Maud's his dog? And why'd you call yourself Levi Levine?' But Amy had drifted off to sleep.

Despite my lectures and threats, Amy's first urine test confirmed that she was back on drugs. I warned her again about the BRIT Awards and told her that this was her last chance. American Blake told me he was leaving again because, despite his best efforts, Amy wasn't going to stop taking drugs. I thanked him for his support and a black cloud of despair fell over me. At least while he had been with Amy I'd had eyes and ears in the suite. Now anything could happen without me knowing about it. Later that night I had a rambling call from Amy. She told me that the prison had called her to say that Blake been cut.

'Bloody good job. I hope it was his throat,' I said, and hung up on her. Never mind my daughter swanning around on a beach in the Caribbean: I needed a holiday – from her.

All at once, everything began to unravel. American Blake had left, and Amy moved back into Jeffrey's Place in Camden Town and started getting high, refusing to go to hospital. She was upset because Blake had told her that Georgette had a tape of me saying I hated Blake. A couple of days later Alex Foden's rehab clinic told me Amy had sent a car for Foden and he was leaving. I berated Amy, but my reproaches fell on deaf ears. Her progress in getting clean had been halted and she was right back where she had been before she'd gone into Capio Nightingale. Just like that, almost two months of hard work were gone.

The BRIT Awards were the next day and I had serious doubts about Amy being there. I arrived at around six thirty and waited on tenterhooks for her appearance. She performed 'Valerie' with Mark Ronson and 'Tears Dry' with her own band. I didn't know whether she was on drugs or not but she was a bit shaky on her feet. She got through it without a disaster, but it certainly wasn't the best performance I'd seen her give.

Phil Taylor, a journalist at the *News of the World*, told me they were going to publish pictures of Amy with bruising and swelling on her face in the next edition. 'Would you like to comment on this?' I declined, and had a little laugh to myself: Amy had recently been diagnosed with impetigo, a highly contagious but fairly minor bacterial skin infection. She hadn't been in a fight, as Taylor had implied. However, when I saw the picture in the *News of the World*, there was indeed a big swelling on her cheek so perhaps she had been in a brawl. I never found out the truth.

As always, another tabloid was there with a theory. A few days later the *Sun* printed a story saying that Amy had caused the swelling on her face. I didn't dismiss this because I knew that, since she'd been with Blake, Amy had self-harmed at least once, that night at the

Sanderson Hotel, although she hadn't done so for a while. It seemed that it was usually a reaction to intense and self-inflicted pressure. According to the *Sun*, Amy had been smoking in a restaurant and when she was asked not to she had stubbed out the cigarette on her cheek. I couldn't bring myself to talk to her about it. I was running out of strength.

In one of our more desperate ideas, Raye and I went to see Blake in prison to ask him to join us in a united front to get Amy clean. It was dancing with the devil, but we were reaching the end of our options. Amy had to want to get better, and Blake was one of the few people whose opinion mattered to her. However, all Blake wanted to talk about were his own problems. We left not knowing whether he would support us.

Blake started talking to Amy a lot more, but it rarely did her much good and it certainly wasn't about getting her clean. In fact it seemed to make everything worse. In mid-March, Amy was scheduled to do a private gig at a party for Universal executives that Lucian had brought in from all over the world. That day, I went round to Jeffrey's Place to wish her luck, but when I got there she was in a bad way. She'd been talking to Blake, who had upset her so much that she no longer wanted to do the gig.

While I was there, Amy was talking to him on and off for at least two hours. I could never understand how a prisoner was allowed to make so many calls; it seemed he was able to use the phone whenever he wanted to. In the end, thanks to Blake, Amy cancelled the gig and ruined the party for all the people who had travelled across the world to see her. She should have done the show no matter how much Blake had upset her – it was her responsibility to fulfil her obligations – and I angrily told her this.

During one visit, Blake told Raye he wanted a divorce from Amy. If only we were that lucky! He was all talk, though – he didn't want a divorce, he just wanted to create drama. It was his way of getting attention. I always knew when Amy had been speaking to Blake, because almost every time she mentioned money, he was behind it. It seemed to me that Blake's ideas had one thing in common: they benefited Blake.

* * *

At the end of March 2008, Amy moved out of Jeffrey's Place to a house just around the corner in Prowse Place. Unprompted, she announced that she wanted to get clean and that she wanted to find a way of doing so quickly. I couldn't believe my ears. I'd waited so long for this moment.

'Right, right, listen,' I said. 'I've got some brochures in the boot of the cab outside. I'll go down and get 'em. You can go anywhere in the world, anywhere you want.'

'Dad, hang on a minute,' she said. 'I'm not getting on a plane or a boat to go to rehab … Well, I might go to Osea Island.'

I roared with laughter. Until she said, 'I want do the detox and withdrawal here.'

I was astonished. 'Here? Are you mad? In the house?'

I knew that would be fraught with problems, but it was her choice. At seven o'clock on 31 March, Dr Ettlinger, his practice partner Dr Christina Romete, Dr Kelleher, Raye and I met with Amy at her house to discuss the detox. It wouldn't be easy, but Amy was confident she could do it.

Amy was to start her drug-replacement programme on 2 April 2008. Two nurses, Sandra and Brenda, were to work shifts to administer the medication. The treatment got off to a terrible start: Brenda called me to say that she was unable to administer the drugs because Amy had taken others; if she took heroin that day she couldn't have the replacements the next day either. The next day the story was the same: Sandra called to say that she couldn't administer the replacements because Amy had smoked heroin the previous evening. Amy told me she wasn't happy with Sandra, probably because Sandra was doing a good job and being strict with her, but Raye and I set about finding a new nurse. Amy had to be drug-free for twelve hours before a programme could begin – which meant waiting another day before we could start again. Amy's big recovery seemed over before it had begun.

Further complicating the drug treatment programme was the fact that Amy was supposed to start work on the new Bond movie theme tune with Mark Ronson. She hadn't been in the studio with him since they'd worked together in New York, in December 2006. Mark was to write the music for the theme to *Quantum of Solace* and Amy the lyrics, but when the date to begin work rolled around in the second week of April, she was in no fit state to start. After she'd missed studio appointments with Mark, he said that he didn't want to work with Amy while she was high, and that something needed to be done.

The studio where Amy and Mark were to work on the Bond song was in Henley, Oxfordshire, and was owned by Barrie Barlow, the sixties/seventies progressive rock band Jethro Tull's sometime drummer. It was in the grounds of Barrie's home. It was self-contained and comprised two bedrooms, kitchen and bathroom upstairs with the studio downstairs – a perfect environment for Amy and Mark to work in. But we couldn't get Amy there.

When Mark had been waiting for four days for Amy to show up at the studio, he started making noises about going back to the US, which would have meant the end of the Bond film for Amy. He was understanding, but he wouldn't hang around for ever – why should he?

Amy seemed incapable of leaving her house. There was always an excuse not to go to the studio; drugs seemed all-consuming. When she wasn't high, she was as passionate about her music as she'd ever been, but those moments were further and further apart.

On Tuesday, 8 April, Amy finally made it to Henley. I spoke to Raye, who was with her, and he told me that she and Mark had begun work. He also said that Amy hadn't taken any drugs and that a nurse was coming to administer the replacements. She might have been drug-free, but within hours, the withdrawal symptoms were making her restless and unable to work. A nurse and a doctor were with her; the doctor gave her diazepam to help her sleep and changed the replacement drug from methadone to Subutex, which started the following morning.

That combination seemed to help. The next day Amy had a meeting with one of the Bond film's producers, Barbara Broccoli. I wasn't there but, according to Raye, they had an immediate rapport and 'Amy charmed the socks off her'.

On the Friday I went to the Henley studio and met David Arnold, who was writing the music for the film. He told me that everyone involved, including Barbara Broccoli, was very excited that Amy was doing the song and he was looking forward to working with her. I had taken Amy some of her favourite Jewish deli food: smoked salmon, fish balls, bagels, chopped liver, and egg and onions. She was asleep upstairs when I arrived, and when she woke, I was told, the first thing she did was to smoke crack. How did that happen?

Someone said to me, 'She's sneaky with it, Mitch. We didn't even know she had anything with her.'

I went upstairs and tried to talk some sense into her but it was a waste of time. When she was high, she would babble about whatever came into her head. It was painful to watch and even worse to listen to. At one point Amy told me to cancel a proposed deal to license a perfume with her name attached to it.

'I don't want to hurt my credibility,' she told me, as she sat there high on crack.

'Hurt your credibility? What do you think smoking crack cocaine is doing to your credibility?'

It was an impossible conversation. I stormed out, with Amy shouting for me to come back. I felt as low as I'd ever been. I didn't think Amy would die, but I just couldn't see a way out of this. You don't become an expert in anything overnight, and I was still learning how best to deal with an addict. Somehow or other I had to speed up the learning process.

The day-to-day changes in Amy amazed me: the next evening Raye called me from the studio to say that she and Mark had had a really good day working. He also said that she had been able to take her prescribed Subutex, as she had been drug-free for twelve hours. When it came time for her next dose, though, she couldn't have it as, once again, she had taken other drugs. As a result, she went into withdrawal and the whole process started yet again.

That Sunday, I drove down to the Henley studio to find Amy in bed. She was filthy and suffering the effects of withdrawal. I managed to get her into the shower, realizing again how painfully thin she was. If Amy had died at that point, I wouldn't have been at all surprised.

I put her back to bed and stayed with her until she fell asleep. Sitting in a chair next to her bed, I despaired. I was running out of ideas. If she took drugs she couldn't take Subutex for twelve hours. If she didn't take Subutex she went into withdrawal so she took more drugs. A horrible vicious circle.

The next day Amy sounded better when I spoke to her on the phone. She said she was working, and determined to beat heroin without Subutex. I doubted that she could do that but gave her lots of encouragement. She said she was missing me.

'I miss you too, darling. I'm there if you want me, you know that, and I always will be,' I told her. 'Why are you crying?'

'I'm feeling broody, Dad,' she replied.

'What? Where'd that come from?'

'We were in the pub before, me and a few of the guys, and there was a baby and I held it. It was lovely, Dad, and it just made me feel … you know.'

I did know. Amy had always loved kids, and they'd always loved her, but I hadn't expected this. I told her it would be very difficult for her to have a baby while she was still taking drugs – her periods had stopped as her metabolism was all over the place. Not only that, it wouldn't be fair on the baby, who might be born with a heroin addiction.

That conversation encouraged me to believe that she had finally found the reason to get clean. I didn't know it then, but this conversation marked a huge turning-point for Amy: it really was the beginning of the end of the drugs. Amy wanted to have children, and what I said to her hit home. Yes, there were lapses and bad days ahead but, from then on, the tone was different. Amy was on the slow, difficult road to becoming drug-free.

Meanwhile, Mark Ronson had completed the music for the song: all Amy had to do was to write the words. But she couldn't concentrate on the Bond song, so she left Henley and returned to Prowse Place where one of her first visitors was Geoff. Slow road indeed.

*   *   *

Towards the end of April 2008 there was a series of incidents in pubs when Amy got into arguments and ended up hitting someone. I was away in Tenerife with Jane when she called to tell me she had been in a pub in Camden Town playing pool and an argument had broken out between her and a man about who was using the table next. Apparently the man had threatened her and Amy slapped him. He had reported the matter to the police. On another occasion, this time in the Dublin Castle, another Camden pub, a man had pinched Amy's bottom and she'd hit him. Quite bloody right, I thought. But it was the last thing we needed as the police were still interested in Amy over the *Sun*'s crack-cocaine video.

I told her to go back to Henley and get on with her work, but she resisted: there had been problems with Mark Ronson. I'm not blaming Mark for any of this because dealing with Amy on drugs was never easy. She claimed she already had three songs, words and music that she thought would be suitable for the movie but, of course, that wasn't her brief. Her brief was to write the words and Mark the music. Mark had listened to the songs and didn't think they were right.

'So what?' I said. 'You've had an artistic difference. Get back to Henley and sort it out with Mark before it's too late.'

'All right, I'll go,' she told me.

The next day the papers were full of stories about Amy's fight. Apparently there had been more than one violent incident, and Amy had also walked into a lamp-post. From the way she looked in the photographs, she had either walked into a lamp-post or somebody had hit her very hard indeed. Another story said that she had been thrown out of a club for allegedly taking drugs. I got on the first plane I could and flew home, leaving Jane in Tenerife.

When I got back, Amy was driving around with Geoff and being followed by paps. Meanwhile, the newspapers were full of stories about Amy and Blake's supposed split – I'd received a call from a journalist at the *Sun* about it a few days earlier. Blake had had a bail hearing but Amy couldn't go as she'd had to see the police over assault charges. Apparently a girl had been in court and had kept blowing Blake kisses. For all I knew she might have been working for a newspaper and doing that to fuel the story of the split.

When it came time for Amy's interview with police about the assault, she arrived two hours late at Holborn Police Station, which didn't go down well. As if that wasn't bad enough, she was not sober. The police deemed her unfit to answer questions and kept her at the police station overnight. They didn't put her in a cell. In fact they bought her chocolates and soft drinks and were very nice to her. When Amy was finally questioned, with her solicitor present, she was told that if she admitted to the assault she would be released with a caution, which was what she did.

As usual, I got all the news from Raye, and as I was taking it in, my other phone rang. It was Phil Taylor from the *News of the World* asking how I felt about Amy having an affair with Raye's assistant, Alex Haines. I was flabbergasted. I asked him where this had come from and he told me he had got the information from Alex Haines himself, who wanted to sell a story.

For weeks the press had been filling their papers with rubbish stories from people who don't even know Amy – there had been false accounts of her smuggling drugs into Pentonville for Blake, and an incredible story about me going to prison in my youth for seven years. When I told my auntie Rene about that one, she said, 'Someone in your family might have noticed if you weren't around for seven years.'

Then the newspapers got all of their Amy Christmases at once. There were stories about her arrest, Blake's bail hearing and the girl blowing kisses, Amy and Blake splitting up, and Amy's affair with Alex Haines, which, by the way, was true.

I wasn't angry with Alex Haines. After all, I would much rather Amy was with him than with Blake. Raye was understandably upset that one of his employees would do something like that. He came back from LA and sacked Alex Haines. When I spoke to Amy about what had happened, she was a little ashamed, but as she saw that I wasn't annoyed with her, she opened up: it had been more of a fling than an affair and she was no longer seeing Alex.

The end result was that Raye decided to pull the Bond gig and cancel everything booked for the near future. I agreed with this and he left me to tell Amy. She was very upset, but so was I.

'You know who's to blame for this, don't you?' I carried on. 'It's you. And I tell you something else. If you want to work again you're going to have to stop living this druggy life.'

'Dad, can't you talk to Raye? I really want to do this Bond thing.'

'Look,' I sighed, 'if you behave yourself during the next few days, we'll see.' I thought about what was coming up in the week ahead. 'And another thing, don't forget you're going to see the police drugs counsellor at the end of the week and that if you don't go you could end up in jail.'

'The police are just bullying me into going, Dad.'

'Nonsense,' I said. 'They couldn't have been more caring or helpful to you.'

She agreed to try her hardest and I said I'd talk to Raye, try to persuade him to hold off pulling the Bond gig.

Amy did behave herself for the next few days, and on 29 April I went to pick her up from Prowse Place to drive her to Henley to continue with the Bond song. When I arrived the house was full of ne'er-do-wells, hangers-on and drug-dealers. I threw them all out, getting the usual protests from Amy, 'No, Dad, no, Dad, no, Dad,' which I ignored. One of the hangers-on got a bit shirty so I punched him, and the others left as fast as they could. Again, it was my frustration coming out. Despite the presence of the lowlifes, Amy was completely sober but said she was too upset to go to Henley.

The next day there was bad news about the *Sun* crack-cocaine video. The police intended to arrest Amy for supplying drugs. I thought this was their way of getting Amy to name the man who had shot the video. What I didn't know was that the police already knew who he was: Johnny Blagrove, a friend of Blake's. Blagrove and his girlfriend, Cara Burton, had been arrested and bailed pending further enquiries. Of course Amy hadn't supplied the drugs, but when I told her how serious this allegation was, she didn't seem at all concerned and referred to Blagrove and his pals as her friends. I wrote in my diary, 'Brian Spiro told me that if the police are successful, Amy will get a custodial sentence. Is this the rock bottom that we have been waiting for?'

I met with our solicitors Brian Spiro and John Reid, and the two police officers who were in charge of the crack-cocaine video case. Fortunately the press didn't know about the meeting and there wasn't a pap in sight. The policemen were very nice, but annoyed with Amy because they felt she was making idiots of them. They told us that the following Wednesday she would be charged with 'allowing her premises to be used for taking drugs and the intent to supply drugs'. To make matters worse, there was another assault complaint against her.

The next day I explained to Amy what the police had told me, and she agreed to go back to Henley to finish recording. After she had been to see Blake in Pentonville Prison, I drove her back to Prowse Place to pick up a few things. I talked to her about her options – there weren't many. I tried to put a positive spin on it but deep down I couldn't see how she would avoid prison. On the way Amy received a 'helpful' call from Blake, telling her not to be bullied into doing anything I told her to do.

When we got back to Prowse Place Amy started messing about, and after an hour or so, I could see that she had no intention of going to Henley, so I left, feeling very down. I called Raye and told him to cancel the Bond gig.

In many ways I was resigned to whatever was going to happen. Her attitude disgusted me. It was one thing for her to be disrespectful to any number of people, including herself, but now it was clear to me that she thought she was above the law. I couldn't see her recovering personally or professionally from this. I wrote in my diary: 'If she carries on taking drugs like this she will die and Blake will be responsible.'

Early on Thursday, 1 May 2008, I found out that Amy had gone to Henley at three a.m. Hurriedly I called Raye but he already knew. Fortunately he hadn't made the call to cancel the Bond song. However, the next day Mark Ronson was on *Sky News* saying that Amy wasn't fit to work and he doubted the Bond song would go ahead. I knew how upset he had been but I didn't see why he'd needed to go on television news to talk about it.

Amy was working at Henley, but it didn't last long. A few days after she arrived, the *News of the World* ran the crack-cocaine video story, explaining that their sister paper, the *Sun*, had passed footage of Amy allegedly smoking class-A drugs to the Metropolitan Police Service (MPS) in January and that the police had later arrested Johnny Blagrove and Cara Burton on suspicion of supplying a controlled drug.

The next day Raye rang: Amy was flipping out at Henley. She had hit someone and cut herself. I shot down to Henley. I had never seen Amy so bad. She had cuts on her arms and face; she had stubbed out a cigarette on her cheek and had a bad cut on her hand where she had punched a mirror. She had been on a two-day bender and, during the course of it, had told Blake she had slept with Alex Haines. What had happened at the Sanderson Hotel was happening all over again: out of shame and guilt she had cut herself.

All this was still going on when I got there and I had to force her on to her bed to stop her harming herself even more. I held her in my arms until she finally calmed down, then got a nurse to patch her up and to stay with her. I wrote in my diary, 'This has been one of the worst days of my life. I don't know what to do next. Please God, give me the strength and wisdom to help Amy.'

Every day brought a new set of horrors.

The following week Amy presented herself, on schedule, at Limehouse Police Station, accompanied by Raye and Brian Spiro, to talk to them about the crack-cocaine video. Of course, she was high on drugs and drink. Amy was charged and bailed to return there later that month. When I mentioned rehab, all Amy could say, in her drink- and drug-fuelled state, was, 'I'm not going to any facility, I want to go to Holloway,' meaning the women's prison in north London.

Although the Bond song had now been cancelled, a couple of days later Amy wanted to go back to Henley to work on other stuff, so I arranged for her to go while I stayed in London. Over the week, I checked in regularly with Dale Davis, her bassist and musical director. Some days they were getting work done, on others Amy was being yelled at on the phone by Blake so she'd get high to console herself.

I drove to Henley to see for myself how she was getting on. When I got there, Amy greeted me with news that I'd heard all too often before: she wanted to quit drugs. I had little faith in this but went through the motions and talked to her about the best way for her to do it. While I was there Raye rang: Salaam Remi wanted to come to Henley the following week to work with Amy. She was delighted, and I was pleased when she told me that she had been drug-free for three days! The nurse confirmed this.

Salaam Remi's presence enhanced Amy's good streak. They worked at Henley during the weekend and laid down a track, which Amy told me I would like. She hoped it would be on her next album, which would come out who knew when – not that there was any pressure on her from the record company to complete it. Much to my surprise, she sounded fine when I spoke to her and still hadn't taken any drugs. I supposed only time would tell me if this was the truth.

14

DRUGS – THE ROCKY ROAD TO RECOVERY

The few days that Amy worked with Salaam Remi did her a lot of good and Raye came back making lots of positive noises about what he'd heard. But when Salaam had returned to the US, there was no reason for Amy to remain at Henley and, once more, she was back in London. She came with a more determined attitude and I felt that things were gradually changing for the better.

Later that week she told me she had made an appointment to see Dr Mike McPhillips, a consultant psychiatrist and an expert in the treatment of addicts, from Capio Nightingale. For me this showed major progress: first, Amy had chosen to see a doctor; second, she'd made the appointment herself; and third, she turned up. Dr McPhillips was very encouraging and started her on a new Subutex programme almost immediately. I'd been nagging her for months, but at long last it seemed that she was trying to take control of her recovery. She had started thinking for herself again, and later that week she refused to visit Blake as Georgette was going to be there.

The second week in May brought the great news that the CPS had dropped all charges against Amy relating to the crack-cocaine video. I breathed a huge sigh of relief. But while I was obviously glad that the police had dropped the case, doubt niggled at the back of my mind. Part of me felt that that the prospect of prison had helped to keep her in check for the past couple of weeks. I hoped that she wouldn't see this as a licence to be bad again.

I knew that Amy wanted to celebrate her good news but my anxiety went through the roof when she told me she was going to Pete Doherty's concert at the Forum in Kentish Town. He had just been released from prison for drug offences and was the last person I wanted Amy hanging around with. Maybe I had to bite the bullet and trust her judgement on this one. After all, it wasn't too early to put her resolve to the test.

The next day there were photos of Amy and Doherty all over the papers. They had partied until the early hours at Prowse Place and the paps had lots of shots of them together, clearly the worse for drink. I heard later that Amy and Doherty had been seen kissing earlier in the evening. What was she thinking? I hoped and prayed that she would think twice before getting romantically involved with another loser. Just a few days before she had seemed to be in control of her life. I didn't understand how everything could change so quickly.

The next day I confronted Amy, making my feelings very clear. 'What are you thinking about, messing around with Doherty? Just because you're getting divorced from one idiot doesn't mean you should start up with another.'

She laughed dismissively. 'Me and Blake aren't getting divorced, Dad. I love him.'

There had been lots of stories about Blake in the press over the past couple of months. In February he'd written Amy a letter distancing himself from Georgette after she'd made some comments in the *News of the World*. I'd shown the letter to the press and told them what I thought of Blake and his family. In response, I got a vile, abusive and threatening text from Georgette. Since then the retaliation had continued in the media. The latest piece from Georgette, in the *News of the World* on 11 May, was a claim that 'Blake must leave Amy or *she* will destroy him'. Georgette added that Blake wanted a divorce from Amy and a mere £3 million as a settlement.

But Amy clearly hadn't taken this to heart: despite her actions with Doherty, she was adamant that she loved Blake. Confusingly, she also said she was still seeing Alex Haines. I asked her how she could do that if she loved Blake. She told me that I wouldn't understand. She was right. And perhaps this was just Amy putting her head in the sand because the next week I heard that Blake was filing for divorce. He said he didn't want any of Amy's money.

But I was really worried about Amy. Her nurse had told me she was doing well with the Subutex, but she wasn't eating properly. She was still painfully thin and, more than ever, she needed her strength to get through her recovery. I'd been regularly delivering the deli food Amy liked to the house, with the hope she might at least be inclined to pick at it, but now she was in Wiltshire with Doherty and I couldn't get hold of her. The news of the divorce might send her into a downward spiral, pushing her back towards drugs.

I hadn't spoken to her for forty-eight hours. Frantically I called around and eventually discovered that she was okay and due back in London later that night. When I spoke to her the next day she was fine, although she was clearly very upset about the divorce, and

I spent a long time on the phone bucking her up. She hadn't slept for thirty-six hours and had spent the whole time drinking, but she assured me she hadn't taken any drugs. When I heard her utter those words I felt like we'd got over another huge hurdle. Until she added, 'Tomorrow's mine and Blake's anniversary. Wish me happy anniversary, Dad.'

The words stuck in my throat.

Delighted though I was at the prospect of Blake leaving our lives, I worried about the impact it would have on Amy. She'd been obsessed with him since they'd first met, God only knew why, and – like a drug – she couldn't get him out of her system. Much as I wanted him and his family gone, I was more than aware of how hard this would be on Amy. The next day I went to see Blake in Pentonville to talk about the divorce. He seemed clear of drugs and insisted that he wanted to help Amy get clean as well – I didn't believe a word of it. Shortly afterwards I learned that Amy had been seeing Christian, another of her friends, and that she had told Blake. Although she was sticking rigidly to the drug-replacement programme, other parts of her life, her marriage in particular, were unravelling and there was no telling how this would affect her current attempt at recovery.

*　　*　　*

On 22 May Amy became the first artist to receive two nominations for what is widely regarded as the top Ivor Novello award, Best Song, Musically and Lyrically. She won the award for 'Love Is A Losing Game', which I thought was a better choice than 'You Know I'm No Good', but the whole ceremony was a bit of disaster.

When I arrived at her house, Amy was feeling fine, on good form, but as usual she wasn't ready. She told me to leave her to it and that she would meet us at the hotel where the ceremony was taking place. By the time Amy's category was called, she still wasn't there. In the end, I went up to accept the award on her behalf. I followed Phil Collins – it was a surreal experience, but my speech was well received, and when I got back to the table Amy was there. She looked fabulous, in a gorgeous yellow dress and red shoes. It was a stark contrast to how she had looked at Henley just a few weeks earlier and I was delighted to see her looking like this. The only thing I didn't like was the heart-shaped hairpin with Blake's name on it.

Much like the Grammys had been, this was another wonderful celebration – the Ivors always meant so much to Amy – and that night she told me she was going to a studio in Bath the next day to work with Salaam Remi. Sadly this didn't happen – pick your own reason why. I was fed up with making excuses for her. Despite this no-show, though, she seemed to be focusing on her music again. After months of sinking deeper and deeper into the mire, she was writing properly again. I felt liberated.

The following week she had a gig in Portugal. The day before she was due to fly, I went around to her house to wish her good luck. To my horror, Geoff was there. Amy said he had called around uninvited and that she was still clean, and Geoff claimed he wasn't there to sell Amy drugs, but I was furious. I kicked him out and had a huge row with Amy. I didn't understand how she could be so stupid, but she insisted she hadn't taken anything. I wished her good luck for Portugal and she hugged me, but I left feeling incredibly anxious. Once again, we were teetering on the edge of the mire. Deep down I was waiting for something to push Amy in.

Amy made her flight to Portugal, even cutting short a visit to Blake to be sure she didn't miss her plane. According to Raye, she gave a fantastic show to the 90,000-strong crowd. Apparently the audience couldn't get enough of her. When I spoke to her later that day, she had a sore throat from singing, but she'd loved it and told me she wanted to do more live gigs, which confirmed to me that she was on the road to recovery. This cheered me up, and I rang my son Alex to tell him, then Jane: 'I'm finishing work early. I'm on my way home. Let's go out for dinner.'

A couple of days later Blake's trial started at Snaresbrook County Court; Amy turned up late and left early, but she'd bought an outfit especially for the occasion and looked very smart. She called me late that night and told me how much she still loved Blake. At that stage, she was unaware that our solicitors had received a letter from his, confirming his intention to divorce her. Being the coward that he is, he hadn't mentioned it to Amy when she saw him before she went to Portugal.

On 6 June we were told that if Blake pleaded guilty he might only serve another eight weeks in prison. He stood in the dock and giggled as he pleaded guilty to inflicting grievous bodily harm and perverting the course of justice. His co-defendant, Michael Brown, pleaded guilty to the same charges. They were both remanded in custody for sentencing at a later date. James King was aquitted of his charge. My heart sank as I left court. I had visions of Amy and Blake tumbling back into the black hole of drug abuse if he was freed. The only solution I could see was to get Amy completely clean over the next two months, but with the constant setbacks, and the drug-dealers, who were always hanging around, that seemed impossible. The following Sunday I had to throw four people I didn't like the look of out of Amy's house.

It turned out that I'd been fooling myself in thinking we had two months to go before a problem arose. On Monday, 16 June, Amy had another seizure. By the time I got to Prowse Place Dr Romete was with her. I asked her if the seizure had been brought on by drugs; she didn't know but wouldn't rule it out. Amy was in no fit state to ask. She was taken to the London Clinic, where she had lots of tests, but nobody could tell me if she had been taking drugs. I suspected she had, although I decided not to question her. I couldn't face either of the alternatives: the lie or the truth.

Amy had a comfortable night and the following day she was given Subutex. But Dr Paul Glynne, in charge of Amy's medical team, told me he was unhappy with the results of Amy's CT and ECG scans. She had gunk in her lungs and possibly nodules too. The bottom line was, she could die if she didn't change her lifestyle. It was a stark and shocking diagnosis, but I wasn't surprised. I wondered how Amy would react to the news.

For at least a year, I'd known that Amy's recovery wouldn't be easy, but before the seizure, she'd been on such a good stretch that I had lulled myself into a false sense of security. This diagnosis brought me crashing down to earth. I feared, I suppose, that one day I might have to face the worst outcome of Amy's addiction; I'd tried to pretend it wasn't going to happen, that I wouldn't need to consider it, but here it was. Amy could die from the misuse of drugs, and everything a father could want for their daughter might end with me in tears beside a hospital bed.

To make matters worse, Blake wouldn't leave me alone: he was calling and texting non-stop. 'I feel I'm out of the loop,' one message said. 'Tough!' I replied. I was at the end of my tether.

Amy slept through that night, and I was back at the hospital at seven thirty the following morning. At three o'clock she and I saw Dr Romete and Dr Glynne. They were both very blunt: if she continued for one more month in her current lifestyle, she would be dead. Perhaps the seizure had been a blessing in disguise, the doctors said, and I agreed. Maybe it had been the wake-up call Amy needed. She could hear it in no more certain terms than that.

Amy was very frightened. Her hand was shaking when she clasped mine – I'd never seen her so scared before. She assured us that she was off drugs for good. But it wasn't as simple as that.

The next day Amy felt and looked a lot better. We had a good long chat and covered a lot of ground. We talked about my mum and dad, our favourite Sinatra songs, what colour she should paint the living room in Prowse Place, who in our family made the best cup of tea – that sort of thing. I kept steering the conversation back to her getting clean, but she was smart and kept spotting it. Eventually we were both just laughing. There was further good news when Dr Glynne showed us Amy's CAT scan results and confirmed there was no need for a biopsy.

Every day after that Amy improved, and on 22 June, six days after her seizure, the doctors allowed her out to rehearse for the forth-coming concert in honour of Nelson Mandela's ninetieth birthday.

A couple of days later Dr Glynne told us how pleased he was with Amy's progress. I was thrilled to hear Amy was doing well, but she wasn't really taking her illness seriously any more. Dr Glynne had emphasized how careful she needed to be with her lungs, but as soon as he left she went out for a cigarette. The next day, she rehearsed again for the Mandela concert, and had too much to drink. There was no talking to her. All she wanted to talk about was Blake and getting him to do rehab at the London Clinic. I told her she must be crazy.

But 27 June was the sort of day that made all of the aggrava-tion and bad times worthwhile ... well, almost worthwhile. Amy's performance at Mandela's birthday tribute was stunningly brilliant: she looked great, she sounded fantastic and the audience loved her. Most important of all, she enjoyed herself. She didn't drink or smoke on stage and sang two songs, 'Rehab' and 'Valerie', then took the lead vocal in the final song, 'Free Nelson Mandela'. I don't know how many people noticed that in 'Free Nelson Mandela', Amy was singing 'Free Blakey my fella'. She hadn't planned it, she said. It had just come to her while she was singing.

But after a fantastic high there's always a fall, and the very next day I found out Amy had had drugs delivered to the hospital. Before they were taken away from her she had smoked a small amount of heroin. After all of the promises she had made, all of the warnings she had heard, here we were again. I didn't know how much more I could take – I was devastated.

Perhaps the most difficult thing about loving and helping an addict, which most people who haven't been through it don't understand, is this: every day the cycle continues is your new worst day. When looked at from the outside it seems endless, the same thing over and over again; but when you're living it, it's like being a hamster on a wheel. Every day there's the chronic anxiety of waiting for news, the horrible rush when it turns out to be bad, the overwhelming sense of *déjà vu* – and the knowledge that, despite your best efforts, you'll probably be here again. Even so-called good days are not without their drawbacks. You enjoy them as much as you can, but in the back of your mind there's the lurking fear that tomorrow you could be back to square one again, or worse.

For me, this was life with Amy. If I was stopped by someone in the street and they asked how Amy was doing, I knew they wouldn't understand if I told them what was going on. I'd learned that it's nearly impossible to explain how this could keep happening. I'd imagined that, as they offered sympathy, they'd be wondering, How can her family let this carry on? Or, Why didn't they lock her up until she was clean? But unless an addict wants to quit, they'll find a way to get drugs, and as soon as they leave the rehab facility they'll pick up where they left off.

Long before Amy was an addict, no one could tell her what to do. Once she became an addict, that stubbornness just got worse. There were times when she wanted to be clean, but the times when she didn't outnumbered them.

Amy was meant to be playing at the Glastonbury Festival that day and I was surprised when I learned that she had turned up. I watched her performance on television. She started off okay but her voice quickly became very weak and she was drinking on stage. She wasn't teetering about, as she usually did when she drank, but she was definitely drinking. Just before she finished her set, she went down into the crowd. They loved it and she was beaming.

Straight afterwards she was driven back to the London Clinic. We had security guys working shifts to look after her by this time and the next day I took a call from Andrew, on duty at the time: a package was on its way to Amy. I jumped in my cab, headed to the hospital and got there just in time to see a known drug-dealer with a bunch of flowers for Amy. He swore that there were no drugs in the flowers, but Andrew searched the bouquet and found a rock of crack cocaine. The dealer was immediately escorted off the premises. Amy went mad when she found out we'd intercepted the drug. But I no longer trusted her, and I told her as much. 'You can shout and scream all you want. When you're at home there's nothing I can do to stop them coming round, much as I'd like to, but here in the hospital there are doors that can be locked, and security, and I'll do anything I like to make sure that shit doesn't get in here.'

Amy was sullen when I'd finished, but she didn't argue back.

She left the hospital a couple of days later and went back to her home in Prowse Place. I was relieved that she agreed to my idea that she should have live-in security, and the boys took it in turns to be on call, meaning I could relax a little, knowing that someone was with Amy 24/7. I also arranged for a nurse to visit daily to administer the Subutex. 'No more drugs, Dad,' Amy promised, yet again, and we were back on the road to recovery. How long for, I had no idea, but I was determined that, no matter how many times Amy came off the rails, I would be there to put her back on. I know how this must look to an outsider: either I was fooling myself, willing to believe Amy time and again, seeking a little false comfort for me and the rest of her family, or I truly thought, each time she declared, 'No more drugs, Dad', that she was one small step closer to achieving her drug-free goal. I'll leave you to decide which.

Andrew and Amy quickly became friends and I trusted him implicitly to care for her, which he did for the rest of her life.

But it wasn't very long after the security guards had been employed that Amy told me she wanted them removed. That made me realize what a good job they must have been doing in keeping drugs out of the house, but I also had to face the fact that Amy still needed drugs, despite the Subutex.

'The security is for your own good,' I told her.

'Well, I'm fed up with having them hanging about all the time,' she snapped.

'Yeah? You better get used to the idea because they're here to stay.'

The next day Amy called me in a state of excitement to say she was having period pains, which she hadn't had for ages. This meant her body was starting to recover and one day she might be able to have the babies she desperately wanted. I'd rather she'd discussed it with one of her girlfriends, but it shows how close we were and how much she was confiding in me.

A few days later Amy was due to fly to Madrid for a gig, but she was in a bad way when Raye arrived to pick her up. She was clearly craving drugs and wanted to cancel the gig. After much cajoling from Raye, and some members of the band, Amy changed her mind – and the performance went very well – but Raye was convinced someone who travelled with them to Spain gave Amy drugs. Naturally she denied it.

One of the nurses at home was also concerned that Amy was still taking drugs. I had no idea how she could get them past her security team, but I'd learned that if you're desperate you'll find a way. Amy denied it when I confronted her, but Andrew and the nurse, Michelle, raised their eyebrows. Dr Ettlinger examined her that day and he said he doubted she had taken heroin, but he couldn't rule out cocaine.

I didn't know what to believe. It felt like it was just one instance after another. I asked Andrew if he knew where Amy could have got drugs. He thought for a moment, then said that someone might have catapulted them over the garden wall, where Amy had picked them up, without anyone knowing. It was shocking the lengths to which people would go to squeeze money out of my daughter.

A few days later Andrew called me mid-morning to say Amy had exploded: she was screaming and shouting and throwing things around the house. He couldn't quieten her. I arrived ten minutes later and calmed her down. She'd had a terrible row on the phone with Blake and had taken some cocaine. It was clear to me, whatever progress she had made, she still had a very long way to go. When

Blake was released from prison the situation seemed likely to get even worse.

Later that month there was a meeting at Dr Ettlinger's office, with Dr Ettlinger, Dr Tovey, a new member of Amy's medical team, Raye, Lucian Grainge and myself, to discuss Amy's progress. When you're talking about addiction, 'progress' is a funny word. Sometimes you measure it day to day, sometimes it's month to month. Despite the recent setbacks, everyone agreed that Amy had generally been doing well. But Lucian didn't want Amy to do any more live gigs: he thought it was best for her to concentrate on recording her new album, mostly to get her out of the limelight. The conversation became slightly heated, and Raye nudged me. He asked Lucian for a five-minute break.

The two of us stepped outside. 'Do you think Lucian's right?' I asked Raye

'Yes, Mitch,' Raye said, 'I do think he's right. She needs the pressure of live gigs taken off her for now. You know how bad she can get – remember Birmingham?'

That did it for me. 'You're right. He's right. Let's go back in and tell him.'

Amy had a couple of gigs booked and it was decided those would be her last for a bit. They were in Dublin and Glasgow, and she performed brilliantly. I spoke to her after the shows and she sounded fine – she assured me she hadn't taken any drugs, but admitted she'd had a couple of drinks before going on stage. A couple?

*   *   *

Then came the day I had been dreading for months: Blake was back in court for sentencing and everyone was convinced it was only a matter of time before he'd be released. Amy didn't want to go to court: the previous day Georgette had told the *News of the World* that she feared Amy would reintroduce Blake to drugs. Amy was hurt and didn't want to see Georgette and Giles.

On 21 July 2008, Judge David Radford sentenced Blake to twenty-seven months in prison for 'wounding with intent to do grievous bodily harm and perverting the course of justice'. The sentence notes read: 'The victim, James King, was bullied and offered a £200,000 bribe to drop the assault complaint.' But after the trial there was some confusion over how much longer Blake would remain in prison. At first we were told he'd be released straight away, as he'd already served 276 days in Pentonville. Then we heard he'd be released around Christmas. Then we were given a release date of 6 September 2009. None of it made much sense and I left the court unsure of where we stood. It was all very confusing, but I was glad to have it confirmed that Blake wasn't being released yet. I knew it was in Amy's interest that he should stay behind bars, but I was worried as to how she would take the news.

I drove straight to Prowse Place and discovered that Amy had already heard that Blake wasn't being released. She wasn't too bad at first, but after I had been there for five or ten minutes she stood up and said, 'I don't want to do today,' went upstairs to her bedroom and wouldn't come down. After a while I crept up and peeped round the door. She was curled up on her bed. I inched closer and saw she was asleep with her headphones on. I closed the curtains and left her to rest.

She had a tough couple of days after that, breaking down in tears over 'poor Blake'. She missed doctors' appointments and was drinking heavily. I was worried about what lay around the next corner.

Five days after Blake's date in court, I received an anonymous letter with a Derby postmark:

Dear Mitch,

Can you please get yourself and your drug-addled and disease-ridden daughter out of the media? We are all sick to death of reading about this disgusting woman's life. Even worse, my children have to look at this scum all the time in the media. You must be a right c**t to have brought her up to turn out like this. Do us all a favour and get Auschwitz reopened and then hold a charity concert for as many Jews as you can get in there. If you need any help turning on the showers, please let me know.

Yours Faithfully

A disgusted Englishman

It was repulsive to read and the last thing I needed. I showed it to my solicitor, Brian Spiro, who was shocked. He passed it on to his colleague Angus McBride, who handed the letter to the police. The advice was to wait and let the police take action.

*   *   *

Amy was asleep when I called her that afternoon, but I spoke to her new PA, Jevan Levy. After the news about Blake, I was still worried about her. I asked him to keep an eye on her and said I'd be over later. Jevan had been checking on Amy every hour and said he would continue to do so until she got up.

It was a hot and sticky night, one of those when one minute it's dry and the next there's a storm. I was on my way to Prowse Place. I'd spoken to Jevan again and learned that Amy had got up but gone back to bed. To make matters worse, Alex Foden was in the house. The cab was hot; I switched on the air-con. I arrived at Prowse Place just after seven thirty, fought my way through the paps camped outside – nodding to a few I'd got to know – and found Foden on his way out. Jevan had probably warned him that I was on my way over. I'm always – well, nearly always – polite, so I said hello to Foden, who decided to give me his opinion on Amy's problems. I told him what he could do with it, and let's just say he left in a hurry. I was furious. How dare he, one of Amy's drug buddies, tell me what was best for my daughter?

Jevan calmed me down. He'd been to check on Amy five minutes before I arrived and she was asleep but fine. I asked him to make me a cup of tea while I went upstairs to see her.

I walked into Amy's room and my heart stopped. She wasn't asleep. She was sitting on the edge of the bed, her face ashen, fighting for breath. I shouted down to Jevan as I fumbled with my phone, desperate to find Dr Ettlinger's number. When I got hold of him he said he'd be there in five minutes but, in the meantime, we should call an ambulance. Jevan dialled 999 while I struggled to get Amy to breathe. She was in a terrible state, wheezing and croaking. It was terrifying – I had been dreading this moment, hoping and praying it would never come, yet here it was. I started acting instinctively. I lifted Amy off the bed and put her into the recovery position on the floor. It was weird – all the time I was helping her, I felt as I was watching someone else. Then Dr Ettlinger arrived and took over.

Amy's breathing was getting worse. Normally I'm very calm in emergencies – but this time I was panicking. Dr Ettlinger wanted to put something down her throat to help her breathe, but warned it might damage her vocal cords.

'Just do it,' I shouted at him. 'Do what you've got to do.'

But before he could do anything the paramedics arrived, charging up the stairs like a small commando unit. They pushed me out of the way and began to work on Amy. With Dr Ettlinger, they stabilized her breathing but said she needed to go to hospital straight away. They asked me if she'd taken any drugs. I didn't know, but I couldn't rule it out.

Taking Amy to hospital meant carrying her out in front of the paps, many of whom had made 'Outside Amy's House' their second home. I told the paramedics I'd fend them off while they got Amy into the ambulance. And we did this with a lot less trouble than I'd expected – some of the paps looked genuinely concerned. The ambulance drove off, sirens blaring and blue lights flashing, and I followed in my taxi. We arrived at University College Hospital at about eight fifteen.

Amy was whisked away and I was left to sit and think about what had just happened. Jevan had checked on her at seven thirty and I'd arrived just after that, which meant that Jevan probably wouldn't have checked on her again for another fifty-five minutes. Thank God I'd arrived when I had. If I hadn't, I think Amy would have died.

I paced up and down. Nobody was telling me anything. I kept asking what was going on. They told me that the doctor would come and see me as soon as he could.

I was driving myself mad. There was a sign saying no mobile phones but I needed to talk to Jane, so I phoned her. She calmed me down a bit and asked me if I wanted her to call Janis. I said that I would call her when we had more information, but I phoned Raye and told him to manage the press. He called Chris Goodman at the Outside Organization straight away.

Still nothing was happening. I kicked up so much fuss that eventually security threatened to throw me out. After a while a nurse came and told me I could see Amy.

'How is she?' I asked, desperate for anything.

The nurse mumbled something and scuttled off. In my fertile imagination I convinced myself that she felt uncomfortable telling me just how bad Amy was.

I didn't know what to expect and was shaking when I walked into the room. Amy was in bed, asleep, with an oxygen mask over her face. She was hooked up to about a hundred tubes and there was a machine monitoring her heart. The doctor was there; he told me he'd have a better idea of her condition when they got the blood-test results. I couldn't get anything else out of him. His bleeper went and he was gone and I was left alone with Amy.

So what had happened? Another seizure? Had she overdosed? I had no idea, but she was alive and I prayed that she was going to be okay.

I picked up her hand. What had happened to my little girl? She'd been doing so well and now this. I felt faint. I let go of her hand and poured myself a cup of water from the jug next to her bed. My hands were shaking so much that, by the time the cup reached my lips, most of the water had spilled down my shirt.

I sat down hard on a chair next to the bed and put my head in my hands, not knowing what more I could do to help Amy if she survived; and what I would do, God forbid, if she didn't.

My head was pounding and I stood on wobbly legs, took deep breaths and gave myself a good talking-to. I poured another cup of water and sat down. It was now ten forty-five and I was preparing for a long vigil.

I was dog-tired and, as hard as I tried to stay awake, I dozed off. A clap of thunder woke me just before midnight. The lightning lit up the whole room as rain pounded the windows, but Amy slept on. What with the thunder and lightning, and the shadows bouncing off the walls, I felt like I was in a Hammer Horror film.

Eventually the rain stopped and I pulled myself together. I needed to go to the lavatory but I didn't want to leave Amy, so I crossed my legs and slumped back in the chair.

At about half past midnight Amy woke up. She lifted her head from the pillow, looked around her, pulled off the oxygen mask and simply said, 'I'm starving, Dad. Fancy a KFC?' She looked at me a bit strangely and said, 'Dad? Why are you crying?'

I was in floods of tears.

When I'd gathered myself back together I told her what had happened. She had no recollection of any of it. I asked her if she had taken any drugs, but she didn't want to talk about it and I couldn't press the issue. Then she thought for a moment, and said she remembered asking someone for headache pills; she couldn't remember if she'd taken them or not.

Apparently there had been people in and out of the house all day. 'Perhaps somebody slipped me something, Dad,' she suggested. Either on purpose or by mistake, I thought. The last thing she remembered was listening to music in her room.

I thought about asking the doctor if Amy could have something to eat but as the answer would probably be no I decided not to bother.

There was a twenty-four-hour KFC just up the road from University College Hospital and that was where I went. There were loads of paps outside the hospital, and on my way back in one asked how serious Amy's condition was. I held up a bag of KFC and said, 'That's how serious it is.'

We both loved KFC, so I'd bought buckets of it, and by one fifteen Amy and I were tucking in. She seemed fine and was remembering more of what had happened. Someone had given her some temazepam, a sedative used to relieve anxiety. We found out later that Amy had had an adverse reaction to it, which had caused a fit. After we'd eaten, Amy said she felt fine and wanted to go home. I told her I'd ask, and I did, although I knew what the answer would be: the hospital wanted to keep her in for observation.

15

CLASS-A MUG STILL TAKING DRUGS

The next day the news was out that Amy had been taken to hospital, and I got a lot of calls and messages from well-wishers. Amy was in good spirits and Andrew took her home around lunchtime, where Jevan looked after her until I arrived to take her for a five o'clock appointment with Dr Tovey. She kept messing around and wouldn't get ready, and I was getting annoyed. I didn't want to shout at her after what she had been through the night before, but I was already having problems with Amy's doctors, so I didn't want her to miss the appointment. The doctors kept contradicting each other. One would say that Amy must be treated in a clinic, and another would say it was best for her to be treated at home. I didn't know who to believe. To add to the problems, Amy didn't like most of her doctors so I was contemplating starting again with a new set. I had faith in them, but it was imperative Amy did too. As Dr Tovey was prescribing the Subutex, I decided that, for now, I would go with his advice. In the end he agreed to come to the house, where he examined Amy and prescribed her more Subutex.

A couple of days later Amy was meant to see Dr Tovey again, but she couldn't bring herself to leave the house. She knew she only had three more days' supply of Subutex so at some point she would have to go and see him. Of course, I could have asked him to come to the house again, but I didn't want to make it too easy for Amy. I thought it was important for her to be proactive in her recovery. I'd observed that she felt vulnerable on the street, where paps and temptations lurked, but I didn't think she should hide away at home.

During the first week of August Janis had a minor car accident and was hospitalized at Barnet General Hospital, north London. Thankfully, it wasn't too serious, but Amy, Alex and I all went to visit her – I was encouraged that Amy was able to leave the house for this. It seemed that almost every day something bad was happening to my family, and it was taking its toll on my health. I was anxious, I was short with people, and poor Jane bore the brunt of everything. I needed a break but I was scared to go away, fearing that something terrible would happen if I wasn't there. That feeling stayed with me for the next three years and in the end, sure enough, I was right.

Later that week Amy missed her appointment to visit Blake in prison because she couldn't get up. She was very agitated and angry with herself, until Jevan administered the last of the Subutex. Then she calmed down quickly and we ended up having a nice afternoon together, looking online at potential properties for her to rent in the country. Leaving the house was a real problem. She had wanted to play at the upcoming V Festival gigs in Leeds, and at Chelmsford the following week, and I knew she needed to prepare herself, but she couldn't even face the idea of a walk. I made a mental note to put Raye on standby to cancel her appearances, and started to wonder if Amy's staying in was a sign of something deeper.

A couple of days later Amy was due to visit Blake again – he'd been moved now to Edmunds Hill Prison in Suffolk, about sixty-five miles and an hour and a half's drive from London – but she had been up the previous night until two and again couldn't get up in the morning. She and Andrew were late leaving, and about halfway there they realized they weren't going to arrive in time, so they turned around and drove home.

Jevan called later that day: a drug-dealer was hanging about outside the house. I called the security guy and told him not to let the man in. By the time I arrived the drug-dealer was nowhere to be seen and Jevan had gone home for the day. Amy was alone, deserted by her 'friends' now that she wasn't doing drugs. She was lonely and wanted to go out, but couldn't persuade herself to leave the house. It was heartbreaking to see her like that. She'd always been such a strong character, always at the centre of every gathering, and now she was quiet and on her own. I felt so sorry for her. I managed to cheer her up a bit with some of my boyhood stories and 'Mitchellisms' though, and it wasn't long before I had her laughing.

I told her that after my father passed away, a friend of his, Sammy Soroff, had come to see me. 'He said to me, "I've come for the money your father Alec owes me." Now, I didn't know what he was on about, and I was only young so I didn't know what to do. Sammy said, "Your dad and I went up north to do a bit of business, and I paid the whole bill. Your dad never paid me back. I want my money." Now I was really worried – how could I afford to pay him back? I said I'd find a way one day to pay the debt. And to this day I still owe it to him.'

Amy was entranced, and I knew I had her when she asked, 'How much do you owe Uncle Sammy, Dad? I'll give it to you.'

'Oh, about forty pounds,' I replied, laughing, and she got it, and laughed too.

I believed that getting Amy out of Camden Town might help her get her confidence back; I also knew her whole family would be happier if she was away from that environment, so a few days later I started house-hunting. I looked at some very decent places, all just outside London, in Rickmansworth, Hemel Hempstead and Hadley Wood. I thought any of them would be great, but Amy was more concerned about how she would get her next dose of Subutex.

I talked to Raye about the possibility of Amy not being able to sing at the V Festival, but we decided to leave it until the last minute to make a decision. Raye had also had an offer for Amy to do a big concert in Rio on New Year's Eve.

'Right now, she won't leave Camden,' I said. 'How the hell are we going to get her to Rio?'

In the end Raye managed to persuade her onto the tour bus for the V Festival. She came onstage about half an hour late, but performed pretty well. The next day she was late onstage again, but Raye said she was very well received by the huge audience. He thought she was stupendous that night and had nailed it. When I watched it on TV, I'd have called her performance average.

Once Amy was back in Prowse Place the same problems returned. She was still anxious about going out and Dr Tovey had to visit her at home to prescribe more Subutex. One day she was planning to go to the gym for some much-needed exercise, but she got to the front door and couldn't leave the house. Her mental state was getting worse day by day. Most of her doctors had washed their hands of her as she wouldn't listen to them. I was rapidly losing confidence in her current treatment regime, and needed to come up with new ideas and methods. I rang round my pals and got the jungle drums beating.

Amy was also having rows with lots of her friends. I heard from Jevan that Geoff had been around again, although he hadn't given her any drugs, and Lauren was giving her a hard time about how she was handling her recovery. Some of Amy's clean friends weren't supporting her. She was always on her own and they'd given her no credit for embarking on the drug-replacement programme that appeared to be helping her recover. In the end, they had their view of how she should handle it, and I had mine. We agreed to differ.

To add to our troubles, I discovered that, over the last couple of months, Amy had used her debit card to draw seven thousand pounds from her account. I felt sure that this was a payment for drugs – what else could it be? I was trying to convince myself that it was for an old drug debt, but later that day Andrew called to say a new drug-dealer had managed to get into the house. Apparently Amy had called him, and welcomed him at the front door as an old friend. 'I fear that Amy is back on drugs.' I wrote in my diary that night. 'Here we go again.'

We could find a way to stop Amy withdrawing cash, but if she was still determined to get hold of drugs she'd find a way. In the end I confronted her about it and told her I knew that huge sum had been spent on drugs. She went mad, and we had a bit of a row, but eventually she admitted she had paid other people's drugs bills, and assured me it would never happen again.

We still had the problem of Amy's remaining gigs. She had three more booked and she was supposed to be focusing on her new album. The first was in France. Raye had managed to get Amy out of the house, and they were on the Eurostar together, when Blake phoned her from prison and told her not to do the gig. It seemed Amy would do anything that Blake said. He told her she was being bullied into it and she shouldn't go. As the train was about to pull out of the station, Amy got off, jumped over the barrier and into a cab to Prowse Place. The no-show ended up costing 150,000 euros.

After that, Raye cancelled her performance at the GQ Awards. Amy wasn't in a good state, but she was livid, protesting that she was well enough to go. She wasn't. And she was blaming everyone but herself for her inability to perform. She told me that she was totally bored with her life and wanted to move away from Camden Town. But when I said I had properties for her to view, she said she wasn't up to it. I went outside and kicked the wall. My plan had been to find a place where she had enough space and privacy to write and record at home, so that when she didn't go out at least she could be working. I wanted her to get over her boredom by finding new inspiration, away from Camden. That she chose not even to consider the options was infinitely frustrating.

I was also worrying about Blake being able to stake a claim on Amy's money. He had told me again that he definitely wanted a divorce and was going to send me a visiting order so we could discuss it. If Blake went through the courts he might be awarded a cash sum from Amy on their divorce. I wanted to avoid this, but Amy's accountant, Margaret Cody, said it would be very difficult to obtain a protection order to stop Blake getting his hands on Amy's money. And if we did that we might alienate Amy. We had to find an alternative.

The next day when I saw Amy she looked and sounded a lot better. One day she was at death's door and the next she was fine. She was sticking to the Subutex regime, but I suspected she was also taking other stuff.

The last of Amy's scheduled gigs was on the Isle of Wight. Amy was responsible for the costs of production, staff, her band, travelling and other expenses, which amounted to some £96,000. She was being paid £150,000 for the gig. But if there was another no-show, the £96,000 would still have to be paid. I was concerned that Blake would phone her at the last minute and tell her not to go. Thankfully, she made it onstage, albeit half an hour late, and the show went very well.

That was the last of her live shows for the foreseeable future and I was glad, but I couldn't read how Amy felt about it and had no idea how she'd fill the gap. At least they had kept her active, when she was becoming so depressed and lonely. Now she was meant to be spending all her time on the new album, but I felt we might be entering a dangerous period. It seemed that Amy's drug habit was diminishing, and I felt incredibly positive about that – she always took her Subutex – but I found it hard to understand why she was still doing drugs if the Subutex was working. I asked Amy about it repeatedly, but she had no answer for me. I found out later, from talking to other recovering addicts, that this is often the way.

*　　*　　*

With things looking up with Amy, Jane and I took a much-needed break in Tenerife. When we got back there were new problems: Blake was rearing his head once again.

He was being released with a tag. I was devastated, but Amy was very pleased, saying she'd put him on Subutex and was going to help him get clean. I knew that if he and Amy ever got back together, Subutex would become the poor relation and they would be back on drugs in no time at all. Meanwhile, Amy still didn't know that

Blake intended to divorce her; if she did, she kept very quiet about it. I wanted Blake out of the picture, but if he went ahead with the divorce before Amy was clean, there was every chance that she would flip out and we'd be back where we'd started – or worse. It was a lose-lose situation, really.

Blake wasn't released when he was supposed to be because the police were concerned about the drugs goings-on in Prowse Place, his named address. He was told he could be released to Georgette's address, but he said he'd rather stay in prison. When she heard that, Amy was beside herself and told me she wanted to find a new house immediately. Then she had a really bright idea: she wanted Blake to be released to my house. I was totally gobsmacked. She couldn't understand why I said no.

A few days later we had a bit of good news. Raye spoke to Blake's solicitor and discovered Blake wouldn't be released until the end of his sentence on 6 September 2009, a whole year away. That *must* be enough time for Amy to get clean, I thought. I had to contend with her disappointment, but I could handle that if it meant we had twelve more months without Blake. Her disappointment was short-lived. By the beginning of October she seemed okay and hardly spoke about Blake at all. She was still very thin, but she looked a lot healthier, and Jevan confirmed that visits from drug-dealers were non-existent.

I had arranged to talk to Russell Brand about Amy and met him at his house in Hampstead, north London. He is a recovering addict and gave me some very helpful advice about her situation. He was impressed that she was sticking to the Subutex, and introduced me to his drug counsellor, Chip Somers. I set up an appointment to meet him right away. My conversation with Russell left me feeling optimistic that the end of the road could be in sight. A lot would depend on whether or not Amy got back with Blake, but time was on our side now, and she seemed to be coping well.

I met Chip Somers at Focus 12, the drug and alcohol rehabilitation clinic, in Bury St Edmunds, Suffolk, and was very impressed with the work he was doing. If only we could get Amy there, I thought, this would be a good place for her to be now that she appeared to be nearing the home straight.

But the daily frustrations continued, with Amy missing appointments and Blake persuading her not to do things. Eventually I'd had enough, and I tore into her. She screamed and shouted and we both got very worked up. I can't remember what we said in the heat of the moment, but in the end Amy promised, 'I'll keep my next appointment, Dad, but it's really hard without Blake. Can you stop going on about him all the time?'

'I would, darling,' I said, 'but I don't like this hold he has over you.' I thought about my recent conversation with Chip Somers and his advice on how to handle an addict in recovery. 'You've got to learn to say to yourself, "No, I'm responsible, I'm going to take control of what happens in my life."'

Amy put a hand to her forehead. 'I know, Dad,' she said. 'I know Blake manipulates me, but I kind of like it, and I know I've got to stop.'

She kept talking about the good times they'd had and how much they loved each other. I pointed out to her that all of the so-called good times had involved drugs. At first she said this wasn't true but then, after she'd thought about it, she agreed. I asked her what she was going to do about Blake. She said she loved him and she really couldn't see beyond that. I felt very sorry for her.

Despite her promise, Amy didn't keep her next appointment with Dr Tovey. The Subutex was rapidly running out, and once she stopped taking it, it wouldn't be long before she went into withdrawal. I tried calling her, but she wouldn't answer the phone. That was unusual. I wondered if she had repeated our conversation to Blake and he had banned her from talking to me. I went over to see her. She had run out of Subutex and was having a really tough time. I finally persuaded her to let me take her to Dr Tovey, who prescribed more Subutex.

*   *   *

As all of this was unfolding, there was the constant pressure of the press. When Jane and I were in Tenerife, I'd received a call from Phil Taylor of the *News of the World*. They were publishing two stories about Amy and he wanted my comments. The first was from Georgette, saying it was disgraceful that Amy had missed so many visits to see Blake, and the second was that Amy was being kept under house arrest as she was in a terrible state, talking to herself and incontinent. It was unbelievable. I, of course, denied it all. Now Phil Taylor was in touch again. The *News of the World* was publishing a story that damned Blake and his family and they wanted my reaction. At the time I believed the best way to fight Blake and his family, and protect Amy, was publicly in the press, so I talked to him. I wanted the world to know there was always someone in Amy's corner. In retrospect, that was a mistake. It didn't do any of us any good and I regret the way I handled it, but at the time I was angry.

I'd also been receiving lots of anonymous calls. They were from a withheld number and the woman, whose voice sounded familiar, swore and ranted down the phone at me. I alerted my solicitor, Brian Spiro, and he chased the police about the anonymous letter and texts.

A few days later I was called by Kent Police to discuss the anonymous anti-Semitic letter, anonymous calls and abusive texts in more detail. I was told this was more than just harassment and the police were treating it as a very serious case. The letter had been sent for forensic analysis.

On 18 October Amy called to say, 'I love you, Dad.' That cheered me up immensely. When I spoke to her again later, she said she wanted me to help her with some designs she was doing for a collection of clothes that Fred Perry were interested in producing. I had known about this for a while and was pleased that she was starting to work on it. The idea was that Amy would design and draw the clothes and Fred Perry would produce the Amy Winehouse Collection. Amy was a very good artist and loved designing and drawing clothes. Fred Perry could see that she was stylish in the purest and most original sense, and believed that the collection would sell. It was eventually launched on 10 October 2010 and did extremely well. Amy's collaboration with Fred Perry went from strength to strength and I treasure the original drawings.

I don't know where she got her ideas from. She might have spent hours flicking through fashion magazines, both new and vintage, but I think her real source of inspiration was the street. Whenever she went out, Amy was always looking about, her keen eye picking out individuals who'd created their own look. If she saw someone wearing something that interested her, she'd go up to them and ask where they'd bought it. She'd do this wherever she was in the world, not just in Camden: I'd been with her in Spain when she'd go up to strangers and ask them.

The Fred Perry project was a good distraction, but things were getting on top of Amy again. She was trying hard to beat the drugs, but she certainly wasn't clear yet. At one point she suggested she came to live with me and Jane for a while, but at the last minute she changed her mind.

Once again, she was struggling to leave the house and it wasn't long before the Subutex ran out and she went into withdrawal. This time, though, instead of doing as she had previously done and taking drugs, she wanted to be admitted to the London Clinic. It was a big step forward: she really was taking control. I took her in, and she was examined immediately: apart from the withdrawal symptoms and a chest infection, there was nothing wrong with her and they confirmed that she hadn't recently taken drugs. Her security guys were posted at the hospital and told that there were to be no visitors or calls without my permission, unless the visitor knew the password, which only I would give to permitted visitors. The password this time was my mother's name, Cynthia.

Over the next couple of days, Blake called me repeatedly asking for the password. Obviously I wouldn't give it to him, so he made a nuisance of himself, calling the hospital and being abusive to the nurses because they wouldn't put him through to Amy. I felt awful about what we were putting the nurses through, but I was very glad they were standing up to him: I certainly didn't want him talking to Amy because I was worried he might persuade her to leave the hospital.

After a few days Amy was doing very well, and all of her test results were much better than the doctors had expected. She had brightened up and was having a good time with her permitted visitors, who seemed to be there day and night.

I took some deli food into her one lunchtime. She picked away and actually cleared her plate, then said, 'Dad, I was talking to someone in here about eating and that, and I realize I've had some trouble with this over the last couple of years. Was it the drugs? I ain't certain, but it could've been, couldn't it?'

I was pleased she'd brought it up because, as I've said, we'd all noticed how thin she'd got. I'd put it down to drugs, but suggested she ask a doctor.

After a week she left the London Clinic, and she looked as if she'd put on some weight. Dr Tovey was pleased with her progress, so I took her back to Prowse Place. Later that day she called saying she was worried about a rash that had suddenly appeared on her body. I arranged for Dr Ettlinger to visit and straight away Amy asked if she could be readmitted to the London Clinic. I later learned that she had told Jevan she wanted to go back even before she had noticed the rash. She had been home just a few hours, but it was clear she felt safe at the London Clinic, away from the temptation of drugs. I doubt it had anything to do with the rash.

Despite Amy's wish to go back to the London Clinic, I got a call two days later to say that she had left the hospital at nine thirty the previous night and hadn't returned. She had gone back to Prowse Place to get high. Twenty-four hours later she returned to the London Clinic. She seemed to be treating it as a hotel. By this time, though, I'd spoken to a number of recovering addicts and drug counsellors, who had all told me that it was fairly common for addicts, even those close to quitting, to lapse, so I didn't take the news too badly. I suppose I was becoming more informed about the whole process so I no longer overreacted to every last little thing. The bottom line was that Amy wanted to be helped.

*　　*　　*

On 5 November 2008 Blake was released from prison, some months early. His release was conditional upon his admission to Life Works, a rehab treatment centre in Woking. Of course he asked Amy to pay the fees, and sent her a form to sign while she was at the London Clinic. Surprisingly, she refused. 'I'm not paying, Dad,' she told me. 'I'm totally pissed off with him. He can go where he likes, but I ain't paying.'

I was over the moon. This was the big breakthrough I'd been waiting for. I'd worried constantly about how Amy would react when Blake was released and I couldn't have hoped for anything better.

A few days later Blake was quoted in the newspapers as saying, 'When I see Amy, I'm going to take her knickers down.' I wanted to kill him when I read that.

When Amy left the London Clinic she still hadn't agreed to pay Blake's fees, so he was pestering me instead. He texted, 'Can we be pals?' I replied, 'No.' He'd been trying to speak to Amy as well, but she wouldn't take his calls, which I was very pleased about. If Blake didn't find some way of paying his fees in the next couple of days he'd return to prison. Sadly, the day before he was due to be sent back, Amy paid the fees, saying she owed him that and calling his rehab a 'hotel stay'. At least she wasn't deluded.

She seemed to be staying off the drugs still, but I was getting lots of calls from Amy's friends about her drinking. She'd been dancing in the streets of Camden in the early morning, and American Blake said it was the worst he'd seen her in months. I called Amy to talk about it, but she shouted at me, so I hung up on her.

A few days later Amy had another lapse. She had locked herself out of Prowse Place and gone to stay at Jeffrey's Place instead. My heart sank: every drug-user in Camden seemed to know where that place was. Later Amy admitted that she had taken drugs when she was there, but she assured me it had been a one-off. I wasn't so certain.

The rollercoaster continued a few days later when Amy was on top form and making me laugh a lot. I'd been foolish enough to allow someone to persuade me to have a Botox injection in my forehead – I couldn't move my eyebrows for three days afterwards. Amy sighed, looked at me and said, 'I don't want you wasting your money on drugs, Dad.' She had a great sense of humour, and when she was in that sort of mood she enjoyed my old stories of growing up in the East End. For those few hours, drugs, Blake and all of the other problems we were dealing with were a million miles away. It was just like it used to be. That night I wrote in my diary, 'I really, really think this time we are near journey's end with the drugs. I pray that I'm right.'

The next day Amy spoke to Blake on the phone and went on a bender, drinking in several Camden pubs with whoever was in there; she was in such a bad way she ended up spending the night at the London Clinic as she couldn't stop throwing up. Blake was calling everyone to find out where Amy was. He called me, but of course I wouldn't tell him. The last thing we needed was Blake pestering Amy at this crucial stage in her recovery.

The following day Blake was in court for his sentencing appeal hearing. His appeal was rejected and I have to say I was thrilled, but I knew this wasn't the end. That night I wrote in my diary, '*He* called me and said that he would leave Amy if it would save her – normal shit from him, but I do believe that things are coming to a head with him. Although at the hospital Amy showed me a letter he sent her. No mention of divorce, he said that they were like Bonnie and

Clyde and destined to be together for ever.' Blake was telling Amy one thing, and me another. This was far from over.

The next day I got a call from him: he asked if we would help him out financially to rent a property. I told him I would only do that if he started divorce proceedings. He assured me he would and said his solicitor would contact us to confirm.

I was still looking at properties for Amy as part of the effort to get her out of Camden Town. That day I'd been with Amy's friend, and fellow singer, Remi Nicole and Jevan to see a beautiful house in Hadley Wood, Hertfordshire, and I showed her the brochure with all the pictures. At last Amy became animated, and my reward for weeks of house-hunting was a lovely cuddle. 'It looks perfect, Dad.'

Shortly after this Blake was interviewed in the *News of the World*. I thought he would finally admit that he was divorcing Amy, but in many ways he went further than I could have hoped. He was quoted saying:

'I dragged Amy into drugs and without me there is no doubt that she would never have gone down that road. I ruined something beautiful. I made the biggest mistake of my life by taking heroin in front of her. I introduced her to heroin, crack cocaine and self-harming. I feel more than guilty.'

He had admitted he had turned Amy into a junkie, but there was no mention of him divorcing her. Instead, he put the ball in her court:

'I will do anything for her – and that includes walking away. If Amy wants a divorce I'm not going to fight her for anything. It's going to be the saddest day of my life.'

Blake was trying to portray himself as a martyr and there was no mention of how well Amy was doing in her battle to get clean.

The same day I received the following text from him:

You are trying to buy your daughter's divorce. Stop hiding Amy's money. I want a contract.

He was after something in writing – I assume about the property he wanted my financial help with – before he'd agree to a divorce. I texted him back telling him not to contact me again.

Amy was in a terrible way after she saw that article, stomping around and banging doors. Andrew told me she had arranged for a drug-dealer to visit her later, but I managed to put a stop to it. She was in complete and utter denial, insisting Blake hadn't actually said the words printed in the *News of the World*, that he'd been misquoted and they were the words of the journalist. When I asked her how she knew that, she said Blake had told her.

I had no choice but to show Amy the text I had received from Blake. 'I don't want to hurt you, darling, but you've got to know the truth.'

She was stunned and just stared at the words on my phone, trying to make sense of what was going on. I think it was then that it finally sank in. It was then that she realized Blake had been lying to her and that all he was interested in was her money. It was a hard blow and I feared she might resort to drugs in an attempt to ease the pain.

Eventually she spoke: 'I love him, Dad. I'll love him no matter what.' This worried me, but she went on, 'I'm stronger now, and what he says to you only makes me want to get clean and stay clean. Then I can help him get clean as well. It's what I want to do.'

I never understood why Amy was so in love with Blake. It wasn't as if he'd brought much good into her life, or so it seemed to me. Just drugs and misery. Maybe she'd wanted to experiment with things, as a lot of people do in their early twenties, but she chose the wrong man to do it with: he took her down a path she couldn't come back from easily. It's the one thing I never got clear in my head about my daughter. I like to think I knew Amy as well as anyone in the world; I could relate to so much of her because she always reminded me of myself. But this was the one part of her that didn't make sense to me, ever.

Sure enough, as soon I left, Amy and Blake made up and she told him to come home when he got out of rehab.

*   *   *

By the beginning of December Amy was back at the London Clinic and I learned that Blake had failed a drugs test at rehab. We were told he would be sent back to prison, but the next I heard was from our security guys at the London Clinic: Blake had absconded from rehab and turned up at the hospital, demanding to see Amy. 'Turn yourself in to the police,' I said to him, when security passed me the phone.

He said he would, but he pleaded to see Amy before he did that. Against my better judgement, I agreed he could spend some time with her. What a mistake that was. To my amazement, I got a call less than an hour later from Amy's security to say that they thought Blake had given her drugs.

You couldn't make it up if you tried. There he was one day, saying he wanted to save her, and the next he was giving her drugs. I had learned that addicts lapse, but this man had told me he liked being a drug addict. What I thought of him at that moment is unprintable.

I headed straight for the hospital, but by the time I arrived Blake had left. I asked Amy about the drugs he had given her and was very relieved when she produced them from under her pillow. 'Dad, I'm not that stupid,' she said, handing them over to me to flush away. I was thrilled she was keeping control of her recovery, but I couldn't help wondering if she had taken some. I wanted to believe her denials but my cynicism was born of long experience.

When Amy learned that Blake had turned himself in at Shoreditch Police Station, she was pleased and, frustratingly, became even more devoted to him. It was as if he was some kind of hero. She told me that from then on they would have a completely drug-free relationship.

On 4 December 2008 it was my fifty-eighth birthday. I spent most of it with Amy at the London Clinic. She talked a lot about going back into the studio to work, which I took as a very good sign. But Amy knew me only too well: 'You think I took some of those drugs Blake brought in, don't you, Dad?'

'Well, did you?' I was blunt because I was tired of this game.

'I'm not stupid, Dad,' she replied. 'Course not.' I obviously didn't look convinced because she carried on, 'I promise. Look, I'll swear if you like – I swear on a hundred Bibles I didn't.'

I smiled. 'All right, darling, I believe you.'

I did too. She really was getting better. All I had to do was make sure that there were no more lapses. That was easier said than done, but my little girl was stronger now and I knew we could do it if we all worked together.

Three days later Amy was involved in an altercation with another patient at the hospital. Dr Glynne was very unhappy about her behaviour and warned me that if it happened again he would have to ask her to leave.

Meanwhile I had made a lot of progress on the Hadley Wood house. Amy would be able to move in by the third week of January, but I'd only let her do that if she agreed to my terms (something I'd learned from my meetings with drug counsellors to do: the stick-and-carrot approach): no drugs in the house; a weekly urine test to confirm that she hadn't taken any drugs; and 24/7 security.

'Thanks, Dad. I won't let you down,' Amy said, giving me a big hug and agreeing to all the rules.

I told her that if she didn't obey the rules it would be herself she was letting down, not me, but as I was doing so well with my rules I added a few more: no misbehaving in the hospital and no dramas. I was on a roll. She said okay.

By this point Amy was quite happy to call the London Clinic home but she was bored, so every couple of days I took her to a gym in the Strand, which seemed to help. It was good to see her strength and health improving. Afterwards we'd sometimes go to Joe Allen's restaurant in Covent Garden for something to eat, which Amy loved. We'd been there many times in the past after her early gigs and just being there brought back lots of good memories.

In the middle of December things came crashing back to earth again when the *News of the World* published a story they'd received from Georgette. She was claiming that a man close to Amy had offered Blake five thousand pounds to hire a hitman to kill her drug-dealer. The story was so ridiculous it was almost laughable, but it was an absolute disgrace that people would keep making up stories about Amy, and that the *News of the World* would keep printing them.

I later heard that Georgette had told the paper that the man close to Amy was me. I didn't know whether to believe this or not; we'd heard it from the editor, but the *News of the World* had such a history of lying to me and manipulating stories that it wasn't impossible they'd make this up too, just to provoke a response from me. I really didn't know what to believe. But if it was true, I had to find a way to prevent this woman using the press in that way. The paper was paying Georgette each time she came up with another 'exclusive' story concerning Amy and I was worried about what else the paper would write. My solicitor added Georgette's allegation to the growing list of complaints that he had already given to Kent Police.

I kept all of this from Amy, of course. She was very bored and desperate for something new to do but she was still coping well with her recovery. And by now she had taken under her wing a thirteen-year-old singer called Dionne Bromfield. The press often referred to Dionne as Amy's goddaughter. That wasn't true: Amy had met Dionne on her eleventh birthday, but she had recognized her talent instantly and wanted to help her. I was less than pleased, though, when I was asked to sign a cheque for thirteen thousand pounds in payment of studio time for Dionne. The bills for the hospital and the security boys were already astronomical and I thought this was preposterous. But Amy was determined to help Dionne. She thought Dionne had an incredible natural talent, and eventually persuaded me to change my mind. It was money well spent: in September 2009 Dionne became the first artist to be signed to Amy's own label, Lioness Records. Amy set up the company just to sign Dionne. The name came from a lioness pendant my mother had given her. 'When I was thinking of what to call the label I picked up the necklace and knew straight away that I'd call it Lioness,' Amy told me, 'in honour of Nan.'

On 19 December Amy left the London Clinic and flew to St Lucia for a holiday. She took with her Andrew, Jevan and, of course, her good friend Subutex. I had been a bit nervous about Amy going away, but I believed she was strong enough by now to resist temptation, and I was reassured because she had the boys with her. I spoke to her nearly every day while she was on the island, and it quickly became evident that she loved it. I also got lots of texts from Andrew and Jevan confirming that she was fine, although she had too much to drink on one or two occasions.

Driving past King's Cross station one afternoon, I saw a small group of addicts huddled together – I recognized the signs now, sadly. I felt very sorry for them and wondered how those young people had got into drugs. I knew what had started Amy off: Blake. To quit for good, she would have to accept that uncomfortable fact.

On New Year's Eve Raye and I met for lunch to discuss Amy's plans for 2009. There was a lot of interest from all over the world in booking Amy for live gigs, but we resolved to see how she was when she returned from St Lucia before we made any arrangements. We'd moved a million miles from where we'd been the year before, not just Amy but me as well: I had learned so much more than I'd ever expected I'd have to about addiction and recovery and had gained a new respect for those people who devoted their lives to working in the field. I also began to realize that, for most people, addiction is an illness, an illness that needs treatment, just like any other.

Thankfully, as 2008 came to a close, it finally looked as if we were near to getting Amy off drugs for ever. It was undeniable that she was doing better than she had been even just a few months ago. I had no illusions that she was cured, but St Lucia seemed to be doing her no end of good. She wanted to stay on for as long as possible, which we all thought was a great idea.

'Let's hope that 2009 will be a better year than 2008,' my final diary entry for 2008 reads. 'Things are already looking a lot more hopeful. Amy has worked so hard to become drug free. I'm a very lucky man to have such a wonderful family.'

16

'IT AIN'T BLOODY FUNNY'

Though it was clear in my mind as 2009 began that Amy was continuing to recover, I expected the drama around her to carry on. The tabloids hadn't presented to their readers the complex picture of Amy's recovery. Instead they'd dwelled on her lapses. It was hard for the general public to understand that overall she was getting better. If I had a wish for 2009 that was anything other than health and happiness for Amy and the rest of my family, it was that the papers would treat her more fairly. She had her own part to play in that as well, and I was determined to help her find the strength to do so.

That Amy was enjoying St Lucia so much was music to my ears and I wanted to encourage her there as much as I could. The only problem was that she was running out of Subutex. She spoke to Dr Tovey, who gave me a prescription. Jevan, who was now in London, flew back to St Lucia with the Subutex. I was going to join Amy a fortnight later, so she spoke to Dr Tovey again and he gave me another prescription so that I could take the medication with me.

My mum and dad, Cynthia and Alec, in their flat in Rectory Road, Stoke Newington, 1953. Amy never met Pop Alec as he died long before she was born. She felt she knew him from my stories, though, and his style certainly played a part in her love of retro.

Above: Me aged six with my mum. Amy loved my mum as much as I did. We spent many hours listening to jazz together — a habit she later repeated with Amy.

Below: A proud dad and his darling daughter. I'd probably just woken her up on coming home from work, much to Janis's irritation.

Above: Janis and I were engaged in 1975. Who does she remind you of?

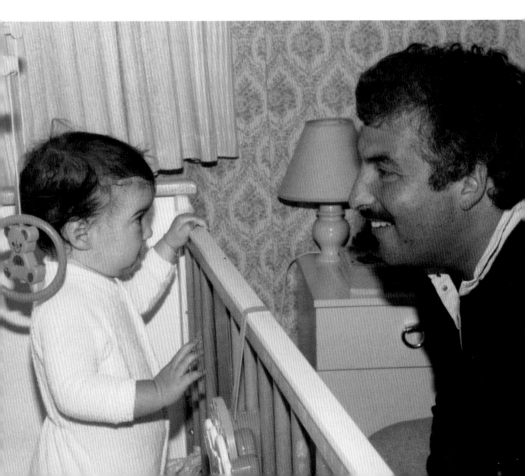

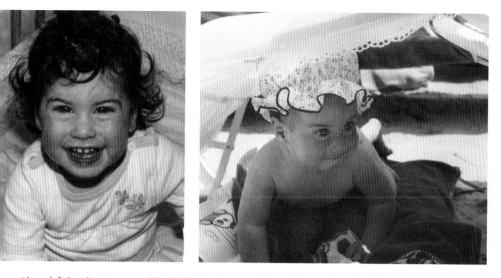

Above left & right: Amy was a delightful baby, always smiling and happy, but when she wasn't we all knew about it. We took her abroad from an early age where she immediately loved the beach.

Amy with her most adoring fan, my mum.

Amy in Spain, aged three. Everything she wore had to be pink.

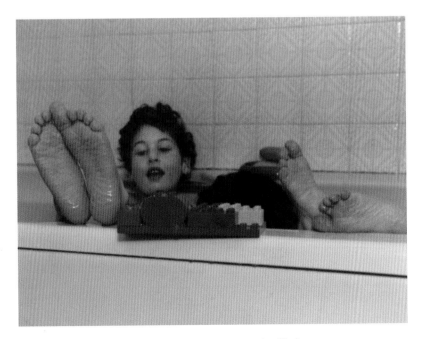

Bath time for the kids was a tangle of limbs
and always a soaking wet floor.

Above left & below: Some of Amy's drawings from school: Amy with her friends Juliette and Gemma. Why she didn't use the correct colour for her own hair, I don't know. I've always liked her schoolgirl habit of using hearts to dot her i's.

Above: My lovely two: Alex and Amy, in their Osidge Primary school uniforms. Alex always looked after his baby sister.

On my first day at School I was hanging around with Juliette because She was the only one I also knew gemma. When I Started school I was with Juliette and gemma! mrs. Strachan was our teacher

on my second year at School I was in miss mehmet's class! I kept getting told off I was still hanging around with gemma and Juliette!

Above: The precocious talent that was my daughter. Never happier than when she was performing. 1988 at our home in Osidge Lane, Southgate.

Opposite: A thoughtful Amy, still in pink and with her heart symbol of course, at her school Summer Fête.

Above: Amy at Camber Sands 1988 — a rare moment
when she was still long enough for me to take a picture.

Above: Amy proud of her brother Alex at
his Bar Mitzvah, 1992.

Amy's class photo, 1994. I know as her dad you'd expect me to say this, but she stands out so much in this picture. Perhaps because she is in the middle and gazing intently into the camera.

At my mother's house with Alex and Amy, 1995. A quiet moment just before a Friday night dinner.

Amy dressed up for an early performance. Her makeup skills certainly got better.

Amy on the set of the 'Back to Black' video, 2007. It was freezing that day and I had to rush over in between takes with a thick coat for her. This is the look that most of Amy's fans around the world fell in love with.

Amy shortly after the release of *Frank*, still playing a guitar as she performed on stage, 2003.

Amy performing 'Valerie' with Mark Ronson, Brit Awards 2008.

Amy in the spotlight. Performing 'Rehab' at the Brit Awards 2007.

Amy on the Pyramid Stage at Glastonbury, 2008.

Amy collecting her second Ivor Novello
Award for 'Rehab', 2007.

Amy with Janis and me at the Ivor Novello
Awards 2008, picking up her third — well,
technically I picked up this one as she
arrived late.

Amy with all of us — Alex, Janis, Jane, me and my sister Melody — at the live TV link for the Grammy Awards, 2008.

Amy at one of my shows, October 2010. This was the night she joined me on stage and stood beside me while I sang.

Hand in hand with my lovely daughter, snapped by the paps leaving a hotel in Central London.
I was always very proud to be seen with her, especially when she looked as lovely as this.

Amy and I singing together at a family party in 2010 ...

... and then dueting on 'Fly Me to the Moon' at Pizza on the Park, June 2010.

In the studio recording the video for 'Body and Soul' with Tony Bennett, March 2011.

Amy with my friend Paul's daughter Katie at the 100 Club, Oxford Street, June 2011. This is among the last private pictures known to have been taken of Amy.

The worst week of our lives. With Alex, Reg and Janis, visiting Camden Square and reading the beautiful and moving tributes left to Amy, 25 July 2011.

Not even my daughter's glorious voice and fabulous songs made me as happy as the times when she said, 'Give me a cuddle, Dad'.

Her stay on St Lucia was not without its problems. On 9 January Jevan called me to say they were going to have to move hotels, following some complaints about Amy and her drinking. That soon hit the press, and the following Sunday the *News of the World* ran a story saying that Amy was drunk most of the time and upsetting guests in her hotel. They also reported that Amy had slept with the rugby player Josh Bowman, who was holidaying on the island. She had supposedly said, 'Josh is better than Blake in bed.' The only good thing in the story was that Amy was happy and free of drugs.

Coincidentally Blake called me to say that he definitely wanted a divorce, and the following day, our solicitors received the petition from his. I didn't want Amy to find out from someone else, so I rang her. She didn't sound too upset so I scolded her about her drinking and she told me she would cut down. It was hard to believe what she said, but at least when I was there we could have the conversation face to face.

When I arrived in St Lucia, I couldn't believe how well Amy looked – she was tanned and had even put on some weight. She was happier than I'd seen her in ages, and she was as pleased to see me as I was to see her. I was looking forward to us being father and daughter on a nice holiday together – I'd left in London my role as buffer between Amy and her troubles. I liked her 'islander' look of sports bra and shorts, but when we went into dinner that night there were a few tuts from the other diners about the way she was dressed. Amy paid them no attention: she was always friendly and loved fooling around with people, making them laugh. The trouble was, she expected everybody to go along with her, which was fair enough, but some people don't like that kind of thing. Most of our fellow diners were okay with it, but I had to speak to one man who was rude about Amy.

The hotel was far too public. A couple of days later I was awoken by a telephone call from a *Sun* journalist, who wanted my reaction to pictures he had of Amy crawling around on all fours in the hotel bar, supposedly begging people to give her drinks. The truth was, Amy had been fooling around. I know because I was there. Why would she beg for drinks when there was plenty of alcohol on our table? As usual, the press wanted to paint as black a picture of her as they could.

After that we checked out of the hotel. I had rented a superb villa for us all to stay in. Amy preferred it as she had more privacy there. Over the next few days she hardly drank at all and only once did she have too much. It was then that she started to talk about Blake. I said, 'Be quiet, Amy,' the way I had when she was a little girl. We ended up laughing and she didn't mention him again that night.

While we were at the villa, Amy went to another hotel to use their gym. Andrew called to let me know there were a lot of paps around. I rushed over and sent them packing. The press wouldn't leave Amy alone and one tabloid printed a story that when Amy had been at the hotel she had blown ten thousand pounds in one night on drink. Had they bothered to do any research, they would have found out that the resort where Amy was staying was all-inclusive, meaning that no one pays for drinks.

The story might have been wrong, but her drinking was becoming more of a problem. That night, Amy got drunk at the villa. I was pleased there was no sign of any drugs but I went to bed thinking I now had something else to worry about.

The next morning, thanks to her amazing ability to recover, Amy looked marvellous. She apologized and promised not to drink for two days. A few days later I flew home, but Amy stayed in St Lucia, moving to yet another villa. I was nervous about leaving her after I'd seen how much she was drinking, but I needed to be at home to get on with my own life. I couldn't spend all my time on St Lucia, unlike my daughter, who could work anywhere.

On 24 January Raye flew to St Lucia and set my mind at rest by telling me how well Amy was and that she had started working with Salaam Remi. However, the *News of the World* was going to be running a story in which Georgette was saying that Amy was funding Blake's drug habit. After some delving I discovered that Georgette's story might have come from letters Amy had sent Blake, which Georgette had given to the *News of the World*.

Here we go again, I thought. It was hard enough that we had to contend with Amy's struggles, but the continual fight with Georgette in the papers was exhausting. At least I knew Amy was getting better but it was unclear what, if anything, would placate Georgette; the battle in the media was relentless. I no longer heard from her directly as, following the abusive text I'd received in the spring of 2008, the police had given her an official warning to leave me alone.

As I did nearly every time an issue with Georgette came up, I spoke to our solicitors, John Reid and Simon Esplen. They were very bullish about the letters, saying they were Amy's intellectual property and if the *News of the World* published them they would be infringing Amy's copyright; it would also be an invasion of her privacy. If the letters were published we would sue Georgette and the newspaper. Both Simon and John were confident of our success. Their firm, Russells, would deal with Georgette, and another firm of solicitors, Schillings, would deal with the *News of the World*. Russells wrote to Georgette about Amy's letters. They heard nothing from her. Eventually Simon

Esplen told me that time had run out for Georgette to respond so they were starting legal proceedings against her.

In mid-February I flew back to St Lucia, taking another prescription of Subutex with me, as Amy had told me she was again running out. When Andrew met me at the airport he told me Amy had used up her supply of Subutex, gone into withdrawal and was in hospital. I went straight there. Amy was asleep but woke up as soon as she heard my voice. She immediately took two Subutex and half an hour later she was fine. We had dinner that night and she was her usual loud self, talking about Blake a lot and saying she was going to give him her Subutex. I didn't comment, but I noticed she was also talking about young men she had met on the island, so I hoped that said more than her words about Blake.

The next evening we went to a karaoke bar in town. Amy and I sang 'The Girl From Ipanema', and had a lot of fun, but as the evening wore on she had too much to drink. When a drunken punter grabbed her arm, wanting to drag her up to sing with her, Amy roared at her and I had to get her out of there quickly. As bad as her behaviour was, it was more predictable than it had been when she was on drugs. I gave her what for and told her that this had to stop. As always, she promised to behave, but I had no faith in that promise. That night I wrote in my diary, 'Four months ago every day was a bad day, now it's every so often and only when she's had too much to drink, so I suppose there is progress.'

*   *   *

At the end of February, I flew home to pick up the keys for Amy's new home in Hadley Wood, a big house that was a step up from Prowse Place. A few days later Blake was released from prison to go to the

Phoenix Futures Rehab Centre in Sheffield, in the north of England. On hearing the news, Amy said she had to come home immediately. I told her that there were no flights until 6 March, which was a lie, but I wanted to delay her return until I had formulated a way of keeping her and Blake apart. It didn't work: Amy arranged her flight home herself.

A couple of days after her return, Amy was arrested for allegedly hitting a fan in the eye backstage at the Prince's Trust ball six months previously. She had been at the ball to support Dionne Bromfield, who was doing her first high-profile gig. The police charged Amy with common assault but granted her bail. She was due to appear at the City of Westminster Magistrates' Court on 17 March.

I stayed overnight at the Hadley Wood house the night before Amy's court appearance to help her get ready. Thanks to Amy's usual time-keeping, we were late arriving at the court and what seemed like hundreds of paps were waiting outside. Amy pleaded not guilty to the charge but came across as disrespectful and her solicitor was very annoyed with her. The case was adjourned until later in the year. Amy was granted bail with no restrictions, which meant she could go back to St Lucia if she wanted to. This was good, but I was increasingly concerned about her drinking. It really was getting out of control and the press had started calling her 'Amy Wino' or just 'Wino', which I found very upsetting.

I didn't know at that time if Amy was planning to go back to St Lucia or not. I found it difficult talking to her when she'd been drinking, so we hadn't discussed it, although I was delighted that she was avoiding Blake. She seemed intent on maintaining her distance but he called incessantly. Generally, she just didn't want to talk to him. He'd call and she'd simply dodge it and go back to sleep. Of course, when he did get her on the phone it always led to trouble.

In Raye's view Amy drank as often as she did because her conversations with Blake upset her so much. She had to cancel a session with Mark Ronson in the studio because she was too drunk, but she was better the following day and worked with Salaam Remi at the Hadley Wood house.

I rang her to find out how the work with Salaam had gone. She didn't tell me because she wanted to rant about the paps outside the house. She'd arranged with her next-door neighbours that she could climb over their fence and leave through their front door to avoid the photographers, but the whole thing had backfired when the newspapers got the pictures they wanted of Amy stuck on the fence.

'It's not funny, Dad, stop laughing,' she said.

I couldn't help myself. 'Those photos, Amy, you should see 'em. You looked so funny stuck on that fence.'

'Yeah? Well, it ain't bloody funny. I've had enough. I'm going back to St Lucia. And you ain't coming cos you're laughing at me.'

I was happy to hear she was planning to get away again, and happier still that she could joke with me. 'Oh, yeah?' I teased. 'I'll just buy one plane ticket, shall I?'

She ended up going with her friends Tyler and Violetta Thalia. This worried me because I knew Tyler was drinking a lot. I couldn't help wondering if this was part of a familiar pattern: when she'd been taking drugs, she'd surrounded herself with drug buddies and now … I didn't know about Violetta.

She'd picked a good time to get away. On 12 April, the *News of the World* published the story, 'Blake Gets Junkie Pregnant'. The article said that a woman called Gileen Morris had told them Blake had made her pregnant while they were both in the Phoenix Futures Rehab Centre in Sheffield. Blake, she told the paper, was 'going to stand by her'. The paper went on, 'Regarding the *Back to Black* star, she said: "If Amy wants to be a step-mum I wouldn't mind, as long as she steers clear of drugs and self-harming." These sordid revelations will damage Blake's efforts to bank half of Amy's £10-million fortune on the grounds of the singer's infidelity.'

My concern was that, when Amy saw the story, she would flip out.

A couple of days later Amy called me, drunk, from St Lucia. I guessed that she hadn't seen the *News of the World* because she was debating what to get Blake for his birthday, which was two days away. She was drunk the next day too, and for several days after that. But when Andrew called me from St Lucia I knew something was really up. Amy had checked herself into hospital as she wasn't feeling well after days of drinking heavily.

Strangely, this moment marked yet another turning-point for her. She didn't curb her drinking (though I wish she had), but from then on, whenever she felt ill, she would check herself into the hospital. When she'd been a drug addict, it was almost impossible to get her to set foot in a hospital, but suddenly she was going on her own. The next day when she called me she sounded fine. The whole episode made me wonder if perhaps she'd checked into the hospital because she knew she couldn't get a drink there. Maybe that was her way of stopping herself drinking. A few days later she was out of the hospital, but Tyler had been admitted with alcohol poisoning.

Raye went to St Lucia to sort things out. As much as I wanted to go myself I couldn't. A few months previously, I'd been approached by an independent production company, Transparent Television, about a documentary they were producing on families facing problems with addiction, which was to be shown on Channel 4. They'd wanted to know if I would be interested in fronting it. I ended up meeting with Jazz Gowans and Richard Hughes, who explained that the documentary wasn't specifically about Amy, and I would interview families about their experience in dealing with addicted relatives. This was right up my street as I wanted the public to know about the heartaches and dilemmas that such people live with. I'd agreed to do the documentary.

Raye called me and brought me up to speed with how Amy and Tyler were. Since they'd known each other, they'd been like two peas in a pod. I'd always thought that was a good thing but maybe now it wasn't.

I flew out to St Lucia towards the end of April 2009, with Jazz and Richard, who were with me to film there. I bumped into Tyler, who was flying home. He was gaunt and pale, and it was clear the drinking had taken its toll. He was still a good-looking guy but I was worried by his appearance and told him so. When I arrived at the villa, Amy was pleased to see me, but tipsy. As the day wore on she got increasingly drunk. I didn't see her drinking so assumed she had a secret supply.

Every time she drank she seemed to get herself into trouble. At the resort, she was rude to a British couple, who had asked her to pose with them for a photo on the beach. I didn't want to be around her that evening because I was depressed. It was evident to me that she had swapped one addiction for another. Instead I spent the evening with Andrew, Anthony and Neville, the security boys, who were all on St Lucia with Amy, to discuss her drink problem. They told me that there was very little they could do to stop her drinking but assured me they were always watching her back and had pulled her out of several nasty situations.

The following week Amy was due to perform at the St Lucia Festival. When I returned to London, I saw Raye and told him I doubted that Amy would be up to appearing. Raye, who was going to St Lucia, said he would take a view when he got there and pull the gig if he had to.

As it turned out, Amy was sober for the open-air Festival gig, but there were other problems, which, for once, went beyond drugs and alcohol. For one thing, there was torrential rain so there were technical issues. Beyond that, though, Amy sang four songs, then said she'd had enough – she was bored singing the same old songs.

I was a bit surprised to hear that, but as I listened to her, I got the sense that there was slightly more to it. As I've said, Amy wasn't the most confident of performers and if something went wrong, like her forgetting a lyric, her confidence would be blown for the rest of the show. According to Raye, that was exactly what happened. Amy forgot the words to one of her songs, stopped singing and the band started the song again, which threw her. Then the heavens opened and Raye was on the stage mopping up rainwater. He was worried about it – that's how people get electrocuted onstage. He told Amy to come off and she did, as good as gold, no problem at all. In fact, after her stumble with the lyric, I think she was relieved.

She sounded fine when I spoke to her later that day. 'I've haven't had a drink for two days now, Dad. Aren't you proud of me?'

I told her I was. Then she said she was happy that Blake was divorcing her. 'I want to meet someone else, Dad. I want to fall in love again, I want to get married again, and I want to have babies, Dad – lots of 'em.'

'That's lovely, darling. What about your music?'

I liked her fantasy but at that moment that was exactly what it was. I knew she wasn't over Blake, not yet anyway. For now, it was better to get her focused entirely on writing and singing. Everything else would surely follow.

'Yeah, I want to do that as well,' she replied. 'I want to sing some new stuff.'

Raye had proposed a Brazilian tour, but after the Festival in St Lucia, he felt it couldn't go ahead until Amy had some new songs to sing: the *Back to Black* songs, apart from 'Rehab', were still bringing her down. When I told Raye what Amy had said about the divorce, and suggested that at last she was over Blake, he was surprised. His impression was that nothing had changed on that score. As always seemed to be the case, her mental state changed from day to day – it all depended on which day you happened to be talking to her.

While we all had conflicting impressions of what Amy could handle, she continued to do well on St Lucia and the reports from her security team were encouraging. Although she was still drinking, it wasn't every day, and when she did drink, she wasn't getting drunk. The papers were still running pieces about it, but it was useless to tell them she wasn't drinking as much as she had been.

Interestingly, she started spending a lot of time in the gym, and I think all that exercise was incredibly helpful. When we spoke, she'd reiterate that she never wanted to see Blake again and that, of course, was what I wanted to hear. Some friends of hers were due to join her for a short stay. While they were there, Amy told me she'd had a great time with them, had cut down on her drinking and felt a lot better for it. Meanwhile, the Subutex was doing its job: there were no signs of withdrawal.

One night she called me up and said, 'Dad, I want you to know, I'll never take drugs again.'

I'll be honest: when I went up to bed that night, I had a little cry. At last, I thought. And the best part was this time she had been telling the truth.

17

BEACHED

I flew back to St Lucia on 26 June and Amy met me at the airport. As we arrived at the villa, she took my hand and led me to the beach. 'Come with me, Dad,' she said. 'Somebody needs our help. I hope you've brought plenty of money with you.'

As there were various bills to pay on St Lucia, I'd brought eight thousand dollars in cash. Amy walked me down the beach until we came upon an elderly man called Julian Jean-Baptiste, who was sitting under the shade of a small tree. He looked to me like he was dying. 'George needs our help, Dad,' Amy said – she called him George, I don't know why.

Amy had caught me by surprise and I didn't know quite what to say, so I decided to start at the beginning. 'Hi, George, what's the problem?'

'I'm in agony,' he told me. 'My hernia's ruptured.' As a result, he literally couldn't move, but this was only the start of the problems. His family couldn't afford to pay for medical care and it was almost like he had been left to die on the beach. I could see a huge lump in George's stomach and his pain was written on his face. He was a pitiful sight.

'George,' Amy said, helping him to his feet, 'we're going to get you to a hospital straight away.'

George couldn't walk, so our security boys carried him to our car and we drove him to Tapion hospital. All the way there George moaned with pain and Amy stroked his head and told him he was going to be okay.

We got to the hospital, the same one Amy had been in when she'd had a seizure a few weeks earlier. She made sure he got the best possible treatment and instructed the doctor that he was not to be let out of hospital until he was completely better, then explained that we would be footing the bill. I asked the doctor how much it was going to cost and he told me that the operation and aftercare would come to about five thousand dollars. I paid the hospital, said goodbye to George and we drove back to the villa.

There, Amy asked me to go with her to see another guy on the beach. 'If this guy's got a ruptured hernia, he's out of luck,' I told her. 'I've only got three thousand left.'

He wasn't sick: he owned seven horses, which he rented to tourists to ride up and down the beach. Amy told me that she owed him some money. I introduced myself and asked how much Amy owed him. To my disbelief, the answer was fifteen thousand dollars. Amy had discovered that the local St Lucian kids, who regularly played on the beach, couldn't afford to rent horses from the man so she'd rented all of his horses, seven days a week, from dawn to dusk for a month, and let the kids ride for free, telling him, 'My dad'll pay you when he next comes over.'

I told the man I had just three thousand dollars. 'That'll do!' he said.

I'd only been on St Lucia for about four hours and the eight thousand dollars was gone. But, it was worth every penny: Amy was so happy that we could help those people.

We had a lovely supper together, just the two of us. Amy had started to put some weight back on and she was looking very well. My only concern was that she drank a lot that evening, and while she wasn't drunk, when we said goodnight she was well on the way.

A couple of days later I flew home. Shortly after I'd got back, Raye and I went to a preliminary hearing of Amy's Prince's Trust Ball common-assault charge. The prosecution's case seemed weak, but our concern was more about Amy's volatility. After the hearing, our barrister told me that when Amy was in court she had to be respectful or the judge might find against her. When I told Amy what he had said, she replied, 'Don't worry, Dad. I'll show respect and behave myself. You know I can do it if I want to.'

That made me worry more, especially because she sounded as if she had been drinking.

Amy arrived home on 13 July, and when we talked about the impending court case, it was clear she was quite nervous. All she had to do was tell the truth, be respectful and courteous, I said, and, with a bit of luck, justice would prevail.

The night before the hearing, having learned long ago that you could never get Amy anywhere on time, I arranged for Amy and me to stay at the Crowne Plaza Hotel in Buckingham Gate, central London, to ensure we wouldn't be late the following day at nearby Westminster Magistrates' Court. Despite all of my planning, we were still late.

Amy was quite nervous as the court heard burlesque dancer Sherene Flash claim that Amy had hit her forcefully in the right eye after she had asked for a photograph while backstage at the Prince's Trust ball. Amy told the court that she had felt intimidated and scared by Flash when she leaned over and put her arm around her and denied punching her in the face. Amy said, 'I pushed her up, like away. I wanted her away from me. It was more like an indication of "Leave me alone, I'm scared of you." I meant to just get her away from me. I was scared. I thought, people are mad these days, people are just rude and mad, or people can't handle their drink. I didn't know what she was doing. She lunged at me and put her arm around me. She was just drunk. I think it was just intimidating. Suddenly out of nowhere she's got her arm round me, her face next to mine, and there's a camera in front of me. I think she was being overly friendly but that was intimidating. I was scared. I'm not Mickey Mouse, I'm a human being.'

The next day Amy was found not guilty and, delivering his verdict, District Judge Timothy Workman said, 'Having heard the evidence from all the witnesses, I cannot be sure that this was not an accident. The charge is dismissed and the defendant discharged.'

As this was all unfolding, there was the usual deluge of stories about Amy in the press. On 19 July the *News of the World* published a story saying Blake wanted £6 million in the divorce settlement. The *Sun* followed up by publishing a two-part story by Blake. In the first part it was just the usual stuff: how Blake saved Amy's life – nothing new, just Blake bigging himself up. However, in the second part he claimed that Amy had stolen cocaine from Kate Moss – I felt sure that Kate Moss wouldn't be happy reading that.

I went to Focus 12 again, on 22 July, and Jazz and Richard filmed me in a parents' meeting. I was beginning to learn just how difficult it was to get help for addiction if you couldn't afford to pay for it.

Jane and I went to Spain for a few days, and when we arrived back in England, in early August, Amy looked good and wasn't drinking, although I'd heard lots of stories of her getting out of control while I was away. I went to see her at Hadley Wood and found her on her exercise bike; I felt tired just watching her. She told me she hadn't been drinking for the previous few days and felt better for it. And while Blake had been calling her a lot, she hadn't spoken to him. I immediately called Brian Spiro and asked him to write to Blake's solicitor and get him to stop Blake calling Amy. This stage of her recovery was nothing if not fragile, and if one thing seemed certain to derail it, it was Blake.

Blake stayed in the picture, continuously trying to contact Amy and even getting her to agree to meet him at the Hawley Arms in Camden, where he failed to show up. In mid-August there was a story in the *News of the World* that Blake had said Amy wanted to get back with him. They ran a headline that must have taken them less than a second to come up with, 'Back to Blake'. I called Amy, on some pretext, then brought up the subject of her getting back with Blake. She didn't want to talk about it and I couldn't get a straight answer. The next day, it was much the same.

'One minute you don't want to talk to Blake,' I said to her, 'and the next minute you're arranging to meet him. Just tell me what you want to do.'

She was smart and knew exactly what I was worried about. 'Dad, I'll never take drugs again, if that's what you're thinking,' she said, laughing.

Amy was true to her word when it came to drugs. But her drinking was still a constant worry to me. In late August, she joined the Specials on stage at the V Festival in Chelmsford, Essex, and sang a couple of songs with them. She looked and sounded great, and as far as I could tell, there was no drink on the stage. After the show Amy said she had enjoyed herself and stayed sober throughout.

The following Monday, I met American Blake, who had been with Amy at the V Festival. Apparently one of her former drug-dealers had spoken to her there but, true to her word, she hadn't done any business with him. I told him that didn't surprise me but wondered whether Amy had been drinking over that weekend. He said she hadn't touched a drop before her performance, but afterwards she'd 'had a skinful', as he put it.

*   *   *

Amy knew that I had sung semi-professionally throughout my twenties. After I got married, and the kids came along, I did fewer and fewer gigs. But I always intended to go back to it and Amy was always encouraging me to do it. She said a number of times that I should make an album. So when Tony Hiller, a hugely successful songwriter and producer, approached me with the same idea, Amy said, 'Go for it, Dad.' Her input was invaluable to me on all aspects of my singing. In the same way that my mum had been Amy's biggest fan, it seemed to me that Amy was *my* biggest fan.

She and I went together to Tony's flat one hot summer's evening to discuss the album and Amy spotted a shelf full of Ivor Novello awards.

'How many have you got, Tony?' she asked. Six, he said. 'Aaah, I've only got three.' Amy was never one to boast, but she was always proud of her Ivor Novello awards.

When we'd finished, I took her to Reubens kosher restaurant where I ate a lot, as usual, and so did she, which pleased me. We talked briefly about her divorce, which was due to become absolute on 28 August, but when I saw she was getting upset I changed the subject. She was distracted, though, and I could see she wasn't really listening to me.

'Dad,' she interrupted. 'Blake rang today and wanted me to meet him in a hotel room. I didn't go,' she added hurriedly, as she saw my expression darken, 'because I didn't like something about the phone call. It didn't sound right to me, a set-up or something, and I told him I weren't going.'

I had to ask her: 'What made you smell a rat?'

'I don't know, Dad,' she said. I reckoned she did, but she wasn't going to tell me. While I was pleased that she had not only declined to meet Blake but told me about it, I was certain she still harboured strong feelings for him.

I was right.

When Blake had been released from prison, it had been under a licence that was conditional on him not leaving Sheffield. But he had been coming to London often to see his new girlfriend. Amy was unaware of this, until eventually Blake told her what he'd been doing. I suspect this was only because the newspapers had got hold of the story and he wanted to tell her before she read about it.

Around this time my friend Dr Phil Rich, a clinical psychologist and behavioural therapist who also deals with alcohol-dependent patients, was over from America on holiday. On 8 September I was with him when I got a call from Andrew. He told me that Blake was at the house in Hadley Wood. Phil and I jumped into my taxi and drove straight over.

We arrived at around ten thirty a.m. Amy was in the kitchen wearing just a T-shirt and a pair of knickers. The security guys were used to her walking around like this and took no notice of it, but Amy was shocked to see me and started shouting, 'Oh, no, oh, no ...'

'Where is he? Where's Blake?' I asked.

'No, Dad, no, Dad,' she kept shouting.

'He's upstairs in bed,' Andrew told me.

As I was climbing the stairs, Amy grabbed one of my legs and I ended up dragging her with me as she kept shouting, 'No, Dad, no, Dad ... Don't hit him, Dad.'

I managed to get upstairs, with Amy in tow, and sure enough, there he was, lying in Amy's bed. I got hold of him and said, 'Get out of bed and fuck off!'

Behind me, I heard Amy still shouting, 'No, Dad, no, Dad, no, Dad.'

Blake got up. 'Amy doesn't want me to go.'

'I don't care what Amy wants. *Get out!*' I yelled.

Amy was still shouting, and I told her it had nothing to do with her. I actually wanted Blake to hit me so that I could legitimately lay into him. I tried to provoke him: 'You and your family are scum,' I said, thinking that surely he'd hit me if I said that.

But he didn't. I have to hand it to him: he was as cool as a cucumber. I don't know if drugs had made him that way, but in any event, he fronted me out.

Instead he said, 'Can I have a shower?'

'No,' I said. 'Just get out now, because if you don't there's going to be trouble.'

I stood there while he got dressed, with Amy still shouting at me. He went downstairs, followed by Amy and me, and as he opened the front door, where there was a step leading down to the porch, he turned. 'How am I going to get to the station?'

'Fucking *walk*,' I said.

'But it's a mile away.'

'Too bad!'

Then he had the cheek to turn to Andrew and ask him, 'Can you give me a lift to the station, mate?'

With that, I gave him a lift all right: I kicked him right up the backside, as hard as I could, and he fell over the step. Amy wanted to go to him but I stopped her and slammed the door.

It was a hell of scene, but it didn't take Amy long to calm down. After about ten minutes it was like nothing had happened. Amy relaxed and we had a good talk. Finally when we'd got the events out of our system, she said, 'Dad, let's go to the East End.'

I was still burning over what had happened and now she wanted to go to the East End! 'Amy, you're really putting me through the mincer today,' I said. 'I can't handle it.'

She came over and gave me a big hug. How could I refuse her after that?

'Come on,' she said. 'We'll go and see where Nan and Pop Alec grew up and all that.'

She went upstairs to get dressed, and after a while I followed to see if she was all right. I heard her on the phone to one of her friends saying, 'Yeah, my dad threw Blake out and kicked him up the arse … My dad done his nut, it was fantastic.'

She was boasting about what I had done and seemed pleased that I'd done it. I crept downstairs, and when Amy finally appeared, she, Phil and I headed off to the East End.

About halfway there Amy started sweating, panting and shaking. Phil knew straight away what it was: 'She's going into alcohol withdrawal. You need to get her a drink, which will stave off the craving.'

'Are you kidding?' I asked.

'She needs a small amount of alcohol and that will do the trick.'

Amy was in a bad way, and I was in no position to argue, so I stopped the cab and bought her a miniature bottle of vodka. She drank it and, sure enough, it worked.

We went to Albert Gardens, had a walk round the park in the middle of the square, then went to the Ocean Estate, just around the corner, which was where Phil's grandparents had lived. We went back to Albert Gardens, and by now the news had spread that Amy was there and quite a lot of people were around. Amy signed autographs and posed for pictures. I leaned back on the cab and watched her, happy with her fans. 'I love people seeing Amy like this,' I said to Phil. 'They normally only get to see her in the papers and she's not like that. This is great.'

Amy looked at me then and smiled; she was pointing out to the people around her where our family, her grandparents, had lived in Albert Gardens. 'They were at number thirty-one, my uncle Percy at number thirteen ...' Then she blew me an extravagant kiss. She was on top form and there were no signs of withdrawal. What had started out as a traumatic day was turning out well after all. It was becoming a day to remember for the right reasons.

*   *   *

As Amy's twenty-sixth birthday approached, the situation with alcohol seemed to be turning. She'd had more sober than drunk days over recent weeks, enough that we started to have a lot more confidence in what she was capable of. Especially after she told Raye she wanted to be able to return to the US, to work with her producers, and then 'Who knows? Maybe do a few gigs over there.' Raye took her to an appointment at the US Embassy, which included a blood test, more in hope than expectation. The appointment went well and he said we'd get a decision within a fortnight. Generally Amy was keeping relatively quiet, playing guitar in her room and for the most part staying away from drink.

On 9 September 2009 John Reid told me that their offices had received a letter from Blake's solicitors with some incredible news. At the end of August, we'd served Georgette with our notice of court proceedings regarding her alleged copyright infringement of Amy's letters. Blake was now offering to drop all claims against Amy – but only if we agreed to drop our case for copyright infringement against Georgette. When I spoke to Amy about the settlement, she was all for it.

The deal with Blake was finalised towards the end of September. He agreed not to make any claim on Amy and we agreed not to pursue our case against Georgette. Pity for him he didn't know that, prior to his offer, we'd been going to offer him £250,000 in a full and final divorce settlement. In the end, he got nothing. My diary sums him up: 'He's a mug.' On 5 October, I told Amy that our solicitors had confirmed her divorce from Blake was now final. She told me two-thirds of her was happy about it, the other third wasn't. I never managed to get her to explain exactly what she meant, but I assumed it was because he'd recently rented a flat in Sheffield with the money he'd made selling stories to the press.

Though we all hoped Blake was now behind us, I had no illusions that things were going to be totally better. Around her birthday, Amy had a stretch of drinking days. Finally she checked herself into the London Clinic to dry out. She was going to be there for three days, but the next day a *Sun* journalist told me they'd heard Amy was in the London Clinic because she had overdosed on drugs. I soon put him straight.

While Amy was in the London Clinic, she had gynaecological tests carried out, and the results showed pre-cancerous cells in her cervix. It sounded worse than it was, and we were told that it was relatively simple for it to be kept in check. She had been reassured that it wouldn't stop her having children.

When I saw Amy in hospital later on, she told me she was thinking about having her breasts enlarged and had discussed it with a doctor that afternoon. Tyler was there, too, and told me that while they'd been on St Lucia, Amy had gone on about this a few times, constantly comparing herself to some of the other girls on the beach. While I don't approve of plastic surgery *per se*, I didn't mind Amy having this done: after I'd heard Tyler's stories, I felt it might boost her self-esteem and put an end to her doubts, something I always believed stemmed from her drug use and break-up with Blake. Amy had her breast implant procedure at the London Clinic on 8 October. Afterwards she looked great and her confidence increased as I'd expected.

Unfortunately Raye had to pass on the news that Amy's US visa had been refused again. Blood-test results had revealed too much alcohol and cannabis in her system. I decided not to discuss this with her until after her appearance on *Strictly Come Dancing*, which was scheduled for a couple of days later. She was performing in support of her protégeé Dionne Bromfield, who sang on the show with Amy backing her.

After the show, Amy said to veteran host Sir Bruce Forsyth, 'I used to be really scared of you because you were a baddie in *Bedknobs and Broomsticks*.' Sir Bruce had played the part of Swinburne, a petty criminal who carried a knife, in the 1971 film, which Amy had watched time and time again when she was a little girl. I am not sure whether Sir Bruce was flattered to be remembered by Amy as a knife-carrying petty criminal.

When I finally told Amy that she had failed the drug test for her US visa she was upset, but confessed, 'I'd had a bit to drink, Dad, and I had some people over. They were smoking and we were up all night.'

On Sunday, 25 October, Amy hosted a birthday party for her brother Alex at the Hadley Wood house, which sadly did not end well. Just as the party was getting going, Amy – who had had too much to drink – asked everybody to leave. Amy and Alex had a row and I said to Amy, 'This is getting boring now. You may be fed up of hearing me banging on, but I tell you, it's boring and repetitive for Alex, and your mum, and Jane, and me, to have to go through the same things with you now that you're drinking so much.'

Amy apologized to Alex for ruining his party. When Alex had left, Amy told me she had got drunk because she was upset that her US visa application had been declined. I told her it was of her own making and if she really wanted a US visa she needed to stop drinking and stop smoking cannabis.

On 26 October Amy attended the Q Awards at London's Grosvenor House Hotel. Unfortunately this was not her finest hour either. The organizers had booked a suite for her at the hotel to ensure she wouldn't be late arriving. Despite that, she was late, and when she was due to present the Most Inspirational Artist award with reggae singer Don Letts, she was nowhere to be seen. Just as Don Letts presented the award to the Specials, Amy arrived drunk. She pushed her way through the audience and clambered on stage midway through the Specials' acceptance speech. When they had finished, Amy grabbed a microphone and said, 'I know you've been to these awards a million times but give it up for the Specials,' which brought only muted applause from the crowd. She continued to make a nuisance of herself throughout the evening and heckled veteran Led Zeppelin vocalist Robert Plant during his acceptance speech. As I say, not a good evening.

The next day I was interviewed on *This Morning*, a TV breakfast show, about the previous night's events. 'Amy has been healthy for the last year,' I said. 'There is no total recovery. It's a recovery. It's a slow, gradual recovery. If you look back to where we were a year ago, you know we're on a different planet. We're in a different space and a different time and Amy is a different person. We all are. We're all recovering.'

The next few days brought a series of ins-and-outs between the London Clinic and the pubs of Camden. I felt they might as well have installed revolving doors at the Clinic. Each time I saw her when she hadn't had a drink, I congratulated her, as I'd learned was the right thing to do. I tried to be as positive with her as I could. We discussed her going back to the London Clinic, but Amy felt that she was okay dealing with the alcohol problem at Hadley Wood.

But Amy carried on drinking and developed a severe cold. In her drunken state, she took too much Night Nurse and became ill. Andrew took her to the London Clinic in the early hours of 16 November, where she was admitted again. By the time I got there, Amy was completely out of it and looked terrible, although Dr Glynne assured me that it wasn't serious. As I have already mentioned, Amy's powers of recovery were amazing, but though she felt a lot better the next day, this time she wanted to stay at the London Clinic for a few more days.

I went to see Amy the following day and she looked very well. She was a great kid and I'd have done anything for her but sometimes she made me do things for her that I found hard.

'Dad, I need some underwear,' she said.

'Okay. I'll go to Marks & Spencer and get you some,' I said.

'No, Dad, not Marks. Go to Agent Provocateur.'

The fancy lingerie shop? I gulped. 'Are you kidding? I can't go in there.'

Suffice to say, Amy had her way and I went to Agent Provocateur in Soho, which I found a bit awkward to say the least. I would have been embarrassed saying, 'I want to buy some knickers for my daughter,' so I said they were for my wife.

Amy was delighted with my purchases, but it was a mistake to tell her how embarrassed I had been. She loved the idea of making me squirm and really knew how to wind me up; she'd done it many times over the years and this time my usual response – 'Don't ask me to do this, Amy, ask your girlfriends' – had got me nowhere. The next day she sent me back to buy her a baby-doll nightie.

Amy was great with the nurses and patients at the London Clinic. She'd make it her business to get to know people. I'd go in and she'd say, 'That's Dave over there. He's had an operation on his back ... Susan's been in here for six weeks but she's going home tomorrow,' and things like that. Amy knew all the nurses' life stories. She had a brilliant memory when she was sober, and remembered all of their likes and dislikes, the names of their kids and their favourite music. In fact, once Amy had learned a name or a date, she never forgot it. She had a fantastic way with people and the nurses and patients loved her. A number of patients who were in the hospital at the same time as Amy contacted me after she had passed away to tell me how much she had cheered them up.

While Amy was in the London Clinic, she decided to have a tattoo of the Ace of Spades removed from her finger. She'd had it done when she was with Alex Clare, and Blake had never liked it. The *News of the World* decided that she was having it removed because she and Blake had got back together; they ran a story that Amy and Blake had got engaged and were due to marry early in 2010. I didn't respond to it, but when I next saw Amy I confronted her about it. Amy and Blake weren't engaged, but I thought the paper was probably right that Blake was behind her decision to have the tattoo removed. She wouldn't confirm or deny it, which convinced me that I was right.

Then she told me she wanted to have a nose job – she said she wanted it made smaller, that she hated its shape and that she couldn't bear to look at herself in the mirror. I went mad. I understood the reasons behind her wanting the breast enlargement, but this was ridiculous. When I left I just felt miserable and depressed.

Amy left the London Clinic on 25 November, and the next day I went to see her at the Hadley Wood house. She told me she was lonely, depressed, wanted to be with Blake, and didn't want to live in Hadley Wood any more. I told her in no uncertain terms how her family felt about Blake, but I said I could do something about the house. If she wanted to move back to Camden, I'd look into it. Hearing Blake's name again demoralized me: I'd thought Amy was starting to move on, but had to admit that she still loved him.

I called Dr Romete later that afternoon and we talked for a long time about Amy's alcoholism. Once I'd understood a few things, I went online and searched out what I could find about Alcoholics Anonymous (AA) and other approaches to helping recovering alcoholics.

The following day Andrew drove Amy to see Blake in Sheffield. The next day Amy told Raye everything was over between her and Blake. Like Amy's mood, her relationship with Blake seemed to change daily and it was hard for me to keep up. One day she'd decide it was all over between them, the next she was talking to him on the phone for hours.

When I heard that they were supposedly back together, I could take no more. I drove straight over to Hadley Wood where Amy and I had a terrible row about it. It was one of the worst arguments we had ever had. I said horrible things, and regretted them the minute they were out of my mouth. I can hardly bear to write down the words I hurled at her.

'It's your choice,' I yelled. 'If you go with him, you risk losing your family.'

Of course, the truth was we'd have stuck by her whatever she decided, but at that point I saw this as a disastrous setback. In Amy's eyes, Blake could do no wrong, despite the numerous stories he was selling to the press around that time. She was determined to get back with him and there was very little any of us could do about it. Amy and I could never stay mad at each other for long, though, and we'd soon put the argument behind us. Sadly, we couldn't move beyond Blake so easily.

18

'I'LL CRY IF I WANT TO'

At the start of 2010 I was completely preoccupied by Amy's relationship with Blake – the trouble he brought, the drama he caused and the undeniable possibility that he would be in Amy's life for ever. The drama with Blake and Amy was continuing and all-consuming. I was so caught up in the day-to-day events, I couldn't see further than the end of my nose. 'I live in hope it will one day be over,' I wrote in my diary, for the umpteenth time, on 1 January. I realize now I didn't even have an inkling then as to what was around the corner. I hadn't even begun to contemplate what the outcome would be for us all when Amy finally managed to quit her addiction to Blake.

The new year began with good news, though: Amy called me on New Year's Day to wish me a happy new year and told me she hadn't had a single drink on New Year's Eve, even though she was celebrating with friends. The Librium she had just been prescribed was making her tired, but she seemed resolved to stay sober. 'Keep at it,' I told her. Surely it was worth feeling tired if it meant she didn't drink.

'Dad, I'm fed up at Hadley Wood,' she said. 'I don't wanna be here any more. It's boring. I want to be back in Camden – that's where I'm happy.'

'I understand, Amy, I'm working on it,' I told her. 'What about if I get you a suite at a hotel in the West End for now? The Langham do you?'

She'd always liked traditional West End hotels and the prospect cheered her up immediately. She didn't ask why I hadn't made any progress on finding her a new home, which I was glad about. I'd been deliberately taking my time because I wanted to keep her away from Camden for a bit longer, just until she was strong enough to resist temptation. I'd also been busy at AA meetings, talking to people about their experience of recovering from alcohol addiction, and I'd seen the rest of the family regularly to discuss how we could continue best to help Amy.

The situation with Blake seemed ominously reminiscent of how the previous year had ended – regular run-ins between them that would result in Amy claiming she wanted to work things out with him and could clean him up. There were headlines in the tabloids that she and Blake were going to remarry, that they were back on drugs. She kept going to Sheffield to see him, even though she always returned in a bad mood.

I had no idea where these reunions were heading, but she was seeing him a lot. With this in mind, I devised a new Blake strategy: I would arrange to meet him to see if we could resolve our differences.

I didn't want to, believe me, but, much more to the point, I didn't want to lose Amy. My pals were worried that I was exhausting myself dealing with her and her cycle of addictions – Blake, drugs, alcohol – but I reassured them that the only time I felt weary was when Amy and I were apart. When I was around Amy, I had the energy and drive to face all of her demons with her. Amy was pleased when I told her that I wanted to see Blake and said she would talk to him and arrange it. It never happened.

Shortly after this Amy had a big row with Blake on the phone; she said it was because he had had another girl with him when they spoke. She was depressed and clearly hungover, and later that day she decided she was going to Sheffield to see him. That troubled me: would Amy stay strong, or would she succumb to whatever it was in him that drew her?

I was woken at four the following morning by the phone.

'Is that Mitch?' the voice asked. 'You don't know me, but my name's Danny. I'm ringing cos someone's got to tell you. Amy's overdosed.'

I was half asleep and at first the words barely registered. Then the worst rushed into my head: had Blake given her more drugs, had she drunk too much, or had she had another seizure? I uttered the words no father ever wants to say: 'Is she dead?'

'No,' he answered. 'She's in the Royal Oak Hospital in Paddington.'

None of this made any sense: Andrew had called me earlier to confirm he and Amy were on their way to Sheffield. How could she be in a hospital in London? There isn't a Royal Oak Hospital in Paddington. As I started to wake up I realized that this call from Danny was probably a nasty prank: he obviously didn't know Amy was in Sheffield.

I was disgusted and shocked, but before I could try to gather my thoughts I called Amy's phone. There was no answer so I called Andrew, woke him up and told him to get Amy to call me straight away. Within a few minutes she was on the line, assuring me she was all right, nothing had happened and the call was bogus.

After that, I couldn't go back to bed so I went and sat downstairs and stared out of the window. I couldn't understand what would lead someone to make a call like that. What kind of person would do such a thing? The constant abuse in the press was bad enough, and I'd had my fill of anonymous texts and shit like that. Now this. As I sat there, I felt worse and worse till suddenly – and unusually for me – I lurched to my feet and had to rush to the bathroom, where I threw up.

A few hours later Amy called to tell me again that she was okay, and to check that I was too.

One night when she was drunk she told me, out of the blue, that Blake was back on heroin big-time: she had watched him do it when she was up in Sheffield. She must have sensed my anxiety because, unprompted, she added, 'Dad, you know I'll never take class-A drugs again.' I did know that. My biggest concern right now was that she stopped drinking.

In February Amy went to Jamaica to spend some time working with Salaam Remi in the recording studio. It was still early days for her in her writing for a third album; she was a fierce self-critic so it would take her a lot longer to come up with the songs for this album than it had for the first two. She tried out and discarded idea after idea. It gave me hope that maybe, just maybe, it wouldn't be long before Amy was away from Blake for good. At times like this, when she was working, he seemed to be the furthest thing from her mind.

While Amy was away I found a new house for her in Camden Square. She was keen to get back into Camden Town – this felt like Amy's true home in London and I'd found the perfect place: a lovely early-nineteenth-century house in its own grounds. It needed substantial work, as it was currently divided into six flats, so we were going to have to gut it. It had amazing potential for all of the things

Amy wanted: a gym, a recording studio, lots of bedrooms and a lovely garden. Without even seeing it she told me to buy it.

When she came back from Jamaica, I took her there for the first time. She absolutely loved it and began making plans for its interior renovation. The bad news was that the work would take a long time and the lease on the Hadley Wood house was about to expire: she needed somewhere else to live, and quick. She still owned the flat in Jeffrey's Place, but she didn't want to go there, as it brought back bad memories. So, at the beginning of March, knowing that Amy wanted to be close to the centre of London, I found her a very nice flat to rent in Bryanston Square in the West End.

Along with her sessions with Salaam Remi, she had also started working with Mark Ronson again in London. In mid-March, Jane and I took her to lunch at Reubens restaurant, where we all ate ourselves silly. I was so pleased she was back working on what she did best, and it was fabulous for us to be talking about that instead of dancing around her problems. Amy said that the song ideas for the new album were progressing further than they had in Jamaica, although there were no completed tracks. In typical Amy fashion, she wouldn't talk to me much about her music because the work wasn't complete.

'You're going to have to wait, Dad,' she said. 'But I can tell you I've been working on the sixties-girl-group sound with Mark. I still like that. And a few other things. And in Jamaica I got into reggae again, so me and Salaam did a bit of stuff with that too.'

A day or so later Amy insisted I went on a spending spree with her in Selfridges.

She hadn't had a drink for three days, and revealed that she wanted to go on an intensive driving course – God help us, I thought. When we'd finished shopping, I did something a bit cheeky. I knew she wouldn't wear half the things she'd bought – we'd been down this road before – so, without her knowing, I took a lot back. Previously Amy would never have noticed the missing clothes, but she phoned me straight away.

'Dad, did I leave a Selfridges bag in your cab yesterday?' she asked. 'I've got stuff missing.' I pleaded ignorance but I think she knew what I'd done because she made me take her back to Selfridges to buy exactly the same things again. I was pleased she'd noticed that the clothes were missing.

At the end of March Amy started recording a track for the Quincy Jones seventy-fifth birthday celebration album *Q: Soul Bossa Nostra*. Amy had first met Quincy at the Nelson Mandela gig and they had stayed in touch. Over the following three days Amy recorded 'It's My Party', a track I knew well, which had originally been a big hit for Lesley Gore in 1963. Quincy had produced the original and he is credited for discovering Lesley Gore. It was a great honour that he had asked Amy to record the song. On the final day of the recording, I met Amy at Love 4 Music recording studios in Islington, north London.

Music had started to play a bigger role in Amy's life again, but she was not without her setbacks. A few days before this, she had started drinking seriously again. Raye and I tried to talk to her about it, but she wouldn't listen and only wanted to talk about Blake and the fact that he was on methadone. But when I turned up at Love 4 Music I was taken by surprise: Amy was ready to talk about her problems. She told me she was going to get her act together and wanted to book into the London Clinic to get the alcohol out of her system; just as importantly, she told me she was through with Blake. She thought it would be easier to break up with him face to face so she was going up to Sheffield the next day with Neville, one of the security boys.

Neville drove Amy up to Sheffield, but instead of coming back the same day, she stayed in Sheffield overnight. I worried and thought I'd have to go up there to collect her myself. In the end Amy returned the following day and told me it was over with Blake. But my initial delight disappeared when I heard how badly he had taken it: he was really upset and had resorted to drugs while Amy was with him, although she had tried to persuade him not to. The one positive was that I was sure Amy hadn't taken anything.

Straight away I arranged for her to be admitted to the London Clinic to deal with her alcoholism. Everything seemed to be going so well – but a week later she left the clinic, went to a local pub and got drunk. This was the problem: until she admitted she was an alcoholic she would carry on fooling herself that she could deal with it alone. She'd been drinking for so long now it was second nature to her. She returned to the clinic at three o'clock in the morning, singing and shouting. Once again, she was using it as a hotel. It was a different problem, but we were falling back into the same cycle.

Of course it wasn't over. A few days later Blake turned up in London, Amy dropped all her other plans and got drunk again. I wanted so much to stop her, but I knew from the expert advice I'd received that the only person who could stop Amy drinking was Amy. So I never ordered her to stop, just told her what the outcome might be if she didn't, and was as supportive as I could be in helping her to give up, picking up the pieces each time she lapsed.

'This is only going to end up one way, and it won't be good,' I told Amy. She was meant to have returned to the London Clinic, but she said she didn't want to be there any more.

The next day Amy fell over in her flat because she was drunk, badly bruising her eye and cheek. When I went to see her at about seven o'clock, she was going on about how she must be with Blake but couldn't because he wouldn't give up drugs, and that she wanted to persuade him to get help with his addiction. I told her she was wasting her time and should think about getting help for her alcoholism, rather than worrying about Blake. But I felt my words were futile: whatever I said to her she'd ignore it if it wasn't what she wanted to do at the time. I just had to find, somehow, the strength to face it day after day.

After a few days, I managed to convince Amy to go back into the London Clinic. The plan was that she'd spend four or five days sobering up before going to the Caribbean for a holiday, but after a couple of days she decided she didn't want to go away: she wanted to concentrate on getting Blake clean. She felt safe at the Clinic, she told me. It was like a haven to her, the only place where she could be helped. She wanted to stay.

The following day I was doing a gig at the Hay Hill Gallery in Mayfair and Dr Glynne had agreed that Amy could leave the hospital to attend. It was a great evening, and Amy and I did an impromptu duet – it felt really special, me and my daughter onstage together, doing what we both loved, and the audience loved it. At the end of our last song, I looked across at Amy and saw tears on her cheeks. 'What's the matter?' I asked.

'Oh, Dad, I love it when you sing,' she said, laughing at herself. 'It makes me so happy I cry.'

Amy returned to the London Clinic, but a few nights later she went to a party with her friend Violetta and got drunk. For reasons that are unclear, Amy and Violetta stayed at the Jeffrey's Place flat that night, and the following day the security guys called me to say that Blake was there. By the time I arrived, he had gone, probably scared of what I might say to him. But Amy was drunk and tearful over Blake arriving out of the blue. She'd had no idea that he was in London but somehow or other he had managed to track her down.

I was dismayed that Blake had been there, but it seemed his actions stemmed from desperation. Perhaps if Amy could keep him at a distance for long enough, he'd finally move on.

Amy had returned to the London Clinic, and when I went to visit her there I heard some really encouraging news. She told me that one afternoon a few weeks previously she had met a guy who was gorgeous and she'd really liked him. They had arranged to go out on a date the following week. Not wanting to make a big deal of it, I didn't ask too many questions, but she told me his name was Reg.

It was only later that Amy told me the full story of how she had met film director Reg Traviss. His parents ran a pub on Devonshire Street, near Bryanston Square, and Reg had been sitting outside it one afternoon, having a cigarette, when Amy and Andrew passed him. Amy cast Reg a look and walked on; Reg knew who she was but didn't return her look as, he told me later, he didn't want to make her feel uncomfortable. Amy glanced over her shoulder for a second look at Reg, then went on up Devonshire Street.

About fifteen minutes later Reg was in the pub with some friends when Amy and Andrew walked in. Reg didn't know it at the time, but Amy had been visiting the pub quite regularly over the past few months and had also been working out at the same gym as Reg's mother and brother. She went over to talk to Reg's brother. Reg walked casually up to the bar and Amy, bold as brass, came up to him and said, 'I like your shoes.' They were retro tan loafers, which Amy would have been into, but I think now that he could have been wearing football boots and she'd have gone over to start a conversation.

Over the following weeks, Amy went to the pub several times and chatted with Reg. It was a convenient place for them to meet, as they both lived within walking distance, and it's not one of those pubs with loud music where everyone's getting drunk. It's a nice, quiet, traditional pub where you're as likely to see customers drinking coffee and eating a sandwich as you are to see them with a pint of beer.

One day Reg wasn't there so Amy left her number with a note for him to call her, which he did. Reg couldn't be more different from Blake. He's a film director but, with his immaculate greased-back hair and stylish retro clothes, he looks like a 1950s American movie star. Amy thought he had the look of my father Alec and his brothers; perhaps that was the initial attraction.

The night before her first date with Reg I saw Amy – she looked great and was very excited to be going out with him. Initially I was careful not to read too much into it. Of course I was desperate for her to move on from Blake, but I didn't want to blow anything out of proportion. Blake hadn't stopped calling her all the time, but she had told him that they should see other people as their relationship was over. Not only was Amy going on a first date with a new guy, she was seeing Blake off.

Amy's first date with Reg had gone well and they planned to see each other again, but when Amy had got home that night Blake called her and they had a row. I couldn't have wished for a better reaction from Amy. Blake had told her he was taking heroin intravenously, but instead of getting drawn into it, she had told him that, though she felt very sorry for him, she wouldn't consider reconciliation. I felt relieved and proud that she was staying so strong.

I can't say that Reg was the sole reason why Amy was able to dismiss Blake, but I think he had a lot to do with it. When I first met Reg a few weeks after he and Amy had started going out, I could see why she liked him. He was everything Blake wasn't, and his warm, quiet and polite manner was appealing. He also seemed to have a fair grasp on how to deal with things relating to Blake. Reg understood that Amy would need to talk about him and was happy for her to do so. Things weren't going well for Blake so he was bugging Amy; he was living in Sheffield, but whenever he needed help, whether it was money or a shoulder to cry on, he called Amy. Reg was tremendously supportive and patient with this.

On one occasion Blake wanted to come to London to meet Amy. She was unsure whether she should see him or not, and when she asked Reg for his advice, he suggested that she meet Blake to put the whole thing to rest. Amy asked Reg to go with her, and while he didn't really want to, he said he would. He thought the meeting might be easier if he wasn't there and was concerned that Blake and Amy might feel inhibited in saying what they needed to say in front of him. After several discussions, Amy told Reg that Blake wanted to meet him. Ultimately, it didn't matter. When Amy and Reg went to the meeting, Blake didn't show up.

In the end, Reg helped to put Blake out of Amy's mind once and for all. Being with Reg changed her whole perspective on Blake. As she told me, she'd finally realized just how immature he was. She thought he saw her more as his mother than his ex-wife. Even so, the time had come for her to cut herself loose from him. She changed her phone number and the contact petered out. The last time they spoke Blake asked Amy to send him a postal order for two hundred pounds. Reg suggested she agreed only on the understanding that she never heard from him again and, as far as Reg and I know, she never did.

I'd spent so much time and energy worrying about Blake and his influence on Amy. I'd blamed him for her drug problems. I'd been looking forward to this moment for so long and it had finally arrived. Strangely I felt nothing, perhaps because I had her drinking to worry about – and, unlike her drug addiction, there was no one I could blame for that.

There's no question that Reg was a stabilizing influence in Amy's life, and I know they talked about getting married. I also know that if Amy had become pregnant, and Reg told me she'd thought she was on two occasions, they would have got married straight away – it might have saved her life.

*   *   *

With Blake out of the picture, and Reg in Amy's life, it felt like we had turned another corner in her recovery. Amy looked much stronger in herself and she was determined to get better, but she was still drinking heavily. In many ways I felt she was moving beyond help.

On 11 May Amy was meant to meet Lucian Grainge at Universal to discuss progress on her recordings and how close they might be to a new album, but she was too drunk to go. By the middle of May she was back in the London Clinic. When she got there she had been vomiting all day, and Dr Glynne called me to say that he was shocked by Amy's appearance. She claimed she had a virus and that was why she'd been vomiting, but I told her, quite simply, that I didn't believe her and knew it was drink related. We argued.

'I've lost patience with you,' I told Amy. 'When you were high on drugs I couldn't tell you anything because you wouldn't have heard me, you wouldn't have listened, but you can bloody well hear me now. I am sick and tired of the same thing every day. Will you be drunk or won't you? You need to stop lying to yourself and everyone around you. You need to listen to your doctors.' And I left.

Amy called me later to apologize and, as she was sober, we had a reasonable discussion about her drinking. But by now I thought that talking was a waste of time: she was beyond the point at which she could help herself, and I just didn't know what to do next.

Amy stayed at the London Clinic for a week. During that time she didn't drink and she didn't leave the hospital. But the next week, back at home, she seemed out of control again: some days she was drunk and other days she was sober. It was impossible to know which Amy I would find when I rang. Reg's presence moderated her drinking, but when he wasn't with her she drank a lot more. Added to which, alcoholics are crafty about their drinking, I'd learned, and if they want you to think they're not drinking, or drinking less than they are, they'll find a way. Amy continued to drink every day until 10 June, when she was once again admitted to the London Clinic.

'Did they stamp your loyalty card?' I asked. I was so fed up I had to make a sarcastic remark, but in truth I was angry.

I kept thinking she'd reached rock bottom, but time and again she proved me wrong. This was different from when she'd been taking class-A drugs. Drugs were illegal, expensive and required privacy. Alcohol was freely available, and she could drink wherever and whenever she liked, mostly without public criticism. As a consequence, her lack of inhibition about drinking was yet another problem – it was moving beyond serious, and if she carried on, her illness might end up killing us both.

For ten days after she'd left the Clinic, Amy remained dry, but I felt a lapse was probably around the corner.

On 20 June, I played a gig at Pizza on the Park, one of London's top jazz venues. I had the honour of being the last act ever to perform on the stage there because, sadly, after thirty years the place closed. The venue was packed for my performance. A lot of my friends and family were there that night, including Amy with Reg. Amy looked fabulous and, at the end of the night, joined me for three duets, much to the delight of the audience. It was a wonderful evening that went down a storm and, to top it off, Amy remained sober throughout.

On 1 July, Amy, Jane, Reg and I went to see Tony Bennett perform at the Royal Albert Hall in Knightsbridge. He was absolutely fantastic. We went backstage after the show to congratulate him and all agreed that he was not only a superb performer but also a lovely guy.

The next night Amy and I went to see Tony Bennett again, this time at the Roundhouse in Camden Town. The previous evening, I had told him that Amy and I were going to his second show and he asked us to have dinner with him afterwards. I was really looking forward to it. He was due on stage at eight forty-five so I went to pick Amy up from Bryanston Square at seven to ensure that we wouldn't be late – I knew my daughter when it came to getting ready. Amy said she still wasn't drinking, but after she took her medication her whole persona seemed to change: she just kept messing about and wouldn't get ready. I was going mad at her and we ended up not leaving the flat until nine fifteen – by which time I suspect she had had a drink.

When we arrived Tony Bennett was already onstage singing, and as we walked in everyone was turning round to look at Amy. As if that wasn't bad enough, while we were walking to our seats, Amy started clapping and wolf-whistling. 'Be quiet, Amy,' I told her. It was very embarrassing.

Finally we sat down, but Amy continued to be disruptive: she was standing up in the middle of the songs, and clapping or whistling at inappropriate moments. 'If you don't sit down and keep quiet, I'm going to leave,' I told her. But she wouldn't, so I left.

'You're just trying to spoil my fun,' Amy shouted after me, drawing yet more attention to herself.

After the show Amy went backstage again and Tony Bennett asked her where I was. She told him the truth: we'd had an argument and I had left. I'm not sure she told him what it was about, though. I was so angry with Amy that night: I knew it was the drink that made her behave that way, but while it wouldn't have mattered as much in a loud club, it had been neither appropriate nor acceptable that evening.

About a week later Amy called me with a lovely surprise. She'd had a session with her band at a rehearsal room, the first for some time. 'Listen to this, Dad. I've written some songs and we bashed something out today.'

She played bits of a couple of songs down the phone to me on the MP3 player she'd used to record them. I couldn't make much out, apart from an upbeat reggae sound. I told her they sounded great, as I knew how much my approval meant to her at that time. It wasn't clear to me why my opinion mattered so much then, when it didn't at other times, I just tried to fulfil her need. She went on to tell me she had had a few drinks the previous night but had not got drunk and had had no alcohol at all that day.

'You're doing great, Amy. Well done.' I said.

'Yeah, thanks, Dad,' she replied.

*   *   *

At the beginning of August, Amy's drinking was still a big problem but I needed a break. With Reg on the scene, and Amy channelling her obsessive nature into their relationship, I felt I could now devote some time to my lovely wife and to looking after myself a bit. Jane and I went on holiday to Spain.

While I was away I heard lots of stories about Amy's drunken behaviour; the press were having a field day. On 3 August a journalist contacted Raye to say he'd seen Amy drunk in Soho at ten in the morning. The next day I got a call to say Amy had run away from a cab drunk and not paid her fare. Two days later there was a report in the *Sun* that Amy had insulted the King of the Zulus, with photos of her falling asleep in Reg's lap in the middle of a speech he had made to open a Zulu restaurant.

While Jane and I were in Spain I became very ill. When we arrived back I was taken straight to hospital. I had developed Septicaemia and felt terrible. I had an MRI scan, which revealed I needed to have my gall bladder removed; the scan also showed that I had Mirizzi syndrome, a rare complication that meant it couldn't be dealt with using keyhole surgery and that I would have to have a full-blown operation, but this couldn't happen until the Septicaemia had been dealt with. Throughout my nine days in hospital, Amy and Alex came to see me every day; they were there from first thing in the morning to late in the evening. I don't know if it was my being ill, or Reg's talk with her after her behaviour at the Zulu restaurant, but Amy had been sober for nearly two weeks, which cheered me up immensely.

The following week, she was drinking again. Alex and his girlfriend Riva had recently got engaged and were having a party at the end of August to celebrate; I hoped I'd be well enough to attend, and put off my operation until after the event, but I was worried how Amy might be at the party. I spoke to her about it and she promised me that she would stop drinking four days beforehand and not drink at the party. She really wanted to be there. I told her I didn't believe she could do it.

On the day of the engagement party, Amy agreed to meet me so I could assess the state of her sobriety. She knew that if I detected she had been drinking, I wouldn't let her go. I saw her in the afternoon and she hadn't had a drink, so I told her she could be there.

When she arrived, she was a little tipsy; she wasn't drunk, but she'd definitely had something to drink. She told me she'd had to have a drink to stave off alcohol withdrawal, but she wouldn't have anything at the party. She was as good as her word, but when she got up to sing, she wasn't very good, and I heard people muttering that she was drunk. I was too weak from my time in hospital to respond as I normally would, but I was disappointed with her behaviour.

Not long afterwards I went back into the London Clinic to prepare for my operation the following day. I was very nervous, but I was reassured by the doctors that I had nothing to worry about. In the end, they were right and the operation was a success. I was in hospital for eleven days and, once again, Amy came to see me every day while I was there. Never once did I think she had been drinking, even when the tabloids tried to stir it up again by printing stories about Reg two-timing her. The mistake the papers made was to suggest he had done this on a date when, in fact, he and Amy had been at home together. She dealt with it in a way that gave me real optimism about her recovery. She was still drinking, but I thought she was staying dry for longer periods every time.

When I saw her at the end of September she looked marvellous. And for once she was concerned about me and all of the weight I'd lost during my illness.

'I've beaten booze, Dad,' she told me proudly. But it wasn't that simple. We'd been there before with the drugs. I knew she had to take it one day at a time and try not to put herself in situations that might trigger her drinking. I told her I'd met someone at an AA meeting when I was looking into ways of helping her, and he'd introduced himself as an alcoholic but hadn't touched a drop in thirty years. 'It's something you're going to have to watch for ever, Amy.'

'You worry too much, Dad,' she told me. 'I'll be fine.'

In early October I had another gig at a club in the City. Amy said she'd liked to come and watch me rehearse. I arranged to pick her up, but when I got to her flat that afternoon, she was drunk and hadn't slept. She insisted she wanted to accompany me anyway and I reluctantly let her do so. However, that meant we were a bit late, so Amy stayed for the gig as my rehearsal overran. When I started my first number, Amy jumped up on to the stage and stood right next to me the whole time I sang. I did my five songs, then let her do two, which were very good. I told her afterwards that she shouldn't have got up onstage with me, but she couldn't understand why: she'd thought she was supporting me. I'd found it a bit unnerving, to have her just standing there. I told her she wouldn't have done it, had she been sober; it had looked unprofessional. We had to agree to disagree.

The following month I was out of London for a few days doing some gigs. While I was away Amy didn't drink, and each time I spoke to her, I felt more positive about her recovery. I knew she would drink again, but it was beginning to seem that she had a real desire to beat her alcoholism, which she now openly acknowledged. I had learned that was a hugely important step on the road to recovery. I was proud of her. I knew it was tough, but we were making progress, even if it was slow.

After I returned, Amy went to Barbados to work with Salaam Remi for the next week. She had good and bad days with her drinking. According to her security, she was drinking, but she wasn't getting roaring drunk and upsetting people. Unfortunately little recording got done.

When she'd finished in Barbados, she flew to St Lucia where she drank much more. When she called me on 4 December to wish me a happy birthday she sounded sober, so I asked about her drinking.

'I'm doing my best, Dad,' she said. 'Some days it's just so hard...'

There was a long silence. I knew if I let her go on down that road we'd both end up crying, so I changed the subject. We talked about the work being done on the Camden Square house, her new recordings, my gigs, her mosquito bites, my operation scar, Alex and Riva, Reg, Jane and a million other things. We were on the phone for more than two hours, which was a lovely birthday present. Only once more during the call did she come close to breaking down, but she pulled herself back from the brink.

About a week later, she came home and continued to drink. I didn't let her attend my sixtieth birthday party as she had been drunk during the day. Finally she and I had a terrible row when I went to see her at Bryanston Square. It was ten in the morning and she was already drunk. I reminded her that she was due to go to Russia for some gigs the next day and that she wouldn't be capable of flying if she didn't resolve to stop drinking, at least until then. I went back to Bryanston Square later and Amy was so drunk that she couldn't speak. I called Dr Romete, who examined her and suggested I take her to the London Clinic, which I did. She wasn't admitted, and after about three hours I took her home. By that time Amy was sober and determined to go to Russia.

Shockingly she made it to Russia, and two days later, Raye called me to say the gig had been fantastic and that Amy had been 'absolutely brilliant'. She'd also managed to keep her drinking in check, even though, it being Russia, everybody had tried to give her vodka shots. When I spoke to her she was physically very tired but still mentally exhilarated from the trip.

When they returned, Raye and I had a chat. We were both encouraged that she had managed not to drink before going onstage – that had been her usual method of dealing with stage fright. Performing live was always going to be an important part of her career, so Raye and I were thrilled that she'd found a way to cope without a drink.

On Christmas Day, Jane and I popped in to see Amy at Bryanston Square before we set off for Jane's mum's home and Christmas lunch. Amy had been invited, but she felt, as she was detoxing, the temptation to drink might be too great and decided to stay at home. She didn't drink over the Christmas period, which she was very proud of. I was proud too. It was an amazing achievement, especially since she'd been with friends who were drinking.

On New Year's Eve Amy called me with more good news: she still hadn't had a drink and she and Reg had been talking about getting married. I was delighted. It felt like a perfect end to the year. I knew we weren't out of the woods yet, but Amy had definitely improved and things were going in the right direction. I'd never believed that she would be rid of Blake, but here she was, talking about marriage with Reg. As the year closed, it was hard not to feel that things were moving in the right direction.

'I feel that overall 2010 was a better year than 2009 and a much, much better year than 2007 and 2008 had been,' I wrote in my last diary entry. 'There's a lot to look forward to in 2011.'

19

'BODY AND SOUL'

Cheered by her success in Russia, Amy spent the first days of 2011 rehearsing for her forthcoming trip to Brazil. On 4 January she called to say, 'I'm ready for my gigs – and I've been sober all year, ha ha.' I couldn't imagine Amy getting on a plane without there being some last-minute drama, but for once there wasn't one and she actually got to the airport in good time.

The next day she rang to say she had arrived safely and to tell me how beautiful Brazil was. The first show was on 8 January and I spoke to Raye before the show: Amy hadn't touched a drop since they had been in Brazil. I hoped she wouldn't need a drink before she got onstage that night and, to my delight, Raye confirmed that she had stuck to water throughout. The show had been fantastic and Amy had performed like the star the audience had been expecting. The press reviews of Amy's first Brazilian show, at the Summer Soul Festival in Florianópolis, were sensational.

While Amy didn't sing any new original songs, she did perform two new covers that she was thinking of including on her third album. As with her lyric books, she squirrelled away notes about any new song she was told about or heard and liked, and she was happy to sing a cover as long as she liked the song and could put her own spin on it. The two she chose here were Little Anthony and the Imperials numbers 'I'm On The Outside Looking In' and 'Boulevard Of Broken Dreams'. The latter was the one written for the 1934 film *Moulin Rouge* and made popular by Tony Bennett, not the Green Day hit from 2004.

Amy did five shows in Brazil, the last on 16 January. I spoke to her after her performance, which she said had gone very, very well. She also told me, proudly, that she still hadn't had a drink and that it was more than two weeks since she had had any alcohol. I was extremely pleased when I heard that, and said to Jane, 'I didn't think she could do it, if I'm honest. I didn't want to tell her or say anything to her before, because it's no good her thinking I've still got doubts about how long she can keep it up, but I didn't think she'd make it this far.' Still, I couldn't bring myself to tell everyone I felt optimistic because I knew I couldn't take any more disappointment.

When Amy got back to the UK, we talked on the phone for more than an hour, with her telling me all about Brazil. She was completely sober and reiterated her desire to stay that way. I had been to see the Camden Square house and all of the work had been completed. It looked great and we discussed when she might move in. The next day I saw Amy and she looked great – she had even put on some weight while she was away. She told me, apologetically, that she had had one or two drinks the previous evening. I didn't berate her: it was only to be expected. I reminded her that it was similar to when she was quitting drugs. Then she had lapsed on numerous occasions. Sadly, I knew a lot about the habits of addicts now. It was only natural to lapse in the process of getting clean.

Frustratingly there were always risks alongside the relapses. One morning I had an early call from American Blake, who was in the US. He had been talking to Amy on Skype when she'd had a seizure. I immediately called security at the Langham hotel, where Amy was still staying, and they rushed to her room. When they got there she was fine and, like most people who have this horrible experience, had no recollection of the seizure. I told Amy I was coming over, but she tried to persuade me that it was unnecessary: she felt okay, and she was going to sleep. I drove over anyway. When I arrived Amy was asleep and I woke her up. She didn't look very well so I took her to the London Clinic, where she was admitted for observation, though she had not been drinking.

I'd thought for a long time that it was risky for Amy to detox without medical supervision and after her latest seizure she agreed. The next day I saw Dr Romete, who said that Amy's detox could lead to seizures, which she was prone to anyway. I asked her to try to come up with a plan for Amy to detox with medical supervision.

In the morning Amy felt a lot better. I put this down to her being in her 'safe place', the London Clinic, where she wanted to stay for now. Over the next week, she continued to do well there and I saw her almost every day. When she was discharged, I picked her up and went with her to Selfridges to buy some essentials for the Camden Square house, which she moved into that day. Her security guys had moved in a week earlier.

I parked the cab outside the house, and Amy marched up the steps to the front door, leaving me to struggle with the shopping. She ran from room to room, telling me which bag to plonk where, and was as excited as I'd seen her for ages. 'Put that one there to go down to the gym, Dad,' she called over her shoulder.

Next to the gym was her studio. She'd had her kitchen put in on the ground floor, looking out over the front, and it had a lovely retro feel, black and white with a black table. I followed Amy into the lounge, which was huge. At one end there was a gaudy 1960s-style jukebox, which Amy had ordered specially.

'Oh, good,' I said, teasing her. 'When I'm fed up with you I can go and kick your jukebox, can't I?'

Amy ran over to it – the thing was on casters and it rolled into the corner when she threw herself across it to protect it from me. 'No, Dad, no.' She laughed.

We wandered round the rest of the house together, and when we came out of her studio I noticed she was clutching the guitar we'd bought in Spain what seemed a lifetime ago. I was pleased to see it: maybe she was going to start writing seriously again. When it came time for me to leave, she threw her arms around me and said, 'Thanks for getting me the house, Dad.'

I rang her a couple of days later, and when she answered I could hear she was still strumming her guitar, the phone cradled in her shoulder. She sounded different, in a good way. 'I know you didn't really want me back in Camden, Dad,' she said, 'I know you thought it was the wrong place for me, but I gotta tell you, I feel like I belong here.'

I was going to defend myself but she continued, 'Thanks again for sorting this out for me, Dad. I'll call you later because I'm working.'

It was the same over the next few days: she was always too busy to chat for long, which was great. I hadn't seen her focus like that since those days in Spain when she'd locked herself away and written a lot of *Back to Black*. Creating music – her greatest passion – seemed to be doing her more good than anything else we'd all tried.

However, one day in early February, I went to Camden Square at lunchtime and found that Amy had already had quite a lot to drink. She wasn't drunk, but if she'd had another couple of drinks, she would have been. 'Let's have a cup of tea,' I said, and brought it to her in the lounge. I really wanted to tell her off, but I knew that would be wrong right now. Instead, I said, 'Don't worry, these things happen.'

'I never went to bed last night, Dad,' she replied, 'and when I finished working I couldn't sleep and needed something to help me wind down.'

'Maybe you can go to sleep now, darling,' I said. I covered her up on the couch, told Anthony, the security guy, to keep an eye on her and left. I wrote in my diary: 'Are we back to square one or is this just a blip? She didn't seem to show any remorse for her drinking today. We've come so far we *mustn't* fall at the last hurdle.'

Despite setbacks like this, it seemed to me that the pattern of her drinking had changed. She was putting her work first and her periods of abstention were longer. Of course she'd have lapses, but overall she seemed to be pulling things together.

As Amy prepared to fly to Dubai for a gig, she told me that, once again, she had stayed dry for it. It didn't last. After the gig Raye texted that it hadn't been great. Technical problems had led to Amy's earpiece not working, meaning she couldn't hear herself sing. Other technical problems meant that some of the crowd, especially people at the back, couldn't hear very well, and after three songs some of the audience had left. If that wasn't bad enough, Raye also told me that Amy had had quite a few drinks before she went on. 'What a disaster,' I wrote in my diary that night. 'Just when I thought that work would get her through the drinking, this happens. Technical problems or not, she can't go onstage drunk.'

Surprisingly, when Amy returned from Dubai, she seemed more or less okay, despite the disappointment of the show and the setback with her drinking. Before long, she'd had four non-drinking days. Riva had been going to see her every day and Amy's friend, Naomi, had moved in. Amy, Riva and Naomi got on very well together. Tyler told me that Amy had said she was sick of being drunk and wanted to stop drinking altogether. When I saw her next she reiterated it to me. I knew that she meant it; I also knew that there were likely to be more lapses before she finally stopped drinking.

Nonetheless, now that Naomi lived with Amy, and Riva went there every day, I began to feel cautiously optimistic about Amy stopping drinking. Naomi and Riva both reported, on 2 March, that Amy hadn't had a drink for six days. I had seen for myself that she hadn't been drinking, but Naomi and Riva set my mind at rest.

The following day Raye took Amy to the US Embassy for her interview about getting a US visa. Afterwards he told me it had gone well and he was optimistic this time that a visa would be granted.

When I saw Amy she opened up to me about Reg: they were not seeing each other for the time being and she was really upset about it. We spoke for at least an hour about their relationship, and although it was far from over between them, I understood how she felt about not seeing him. Reg had been working very hard and had been away a lot, shooting a film on location in Scarborough, North Yorkshire.

'I tell you what,' I said to her, 'this is what you should do. When he's back, sit down with him and tell him exactly how you feel.'

'He knows I love him, Dad,' Amy interrupted. 'I keep asking him to move in.'

'So what's the problem? That's great.' I was pleased for them both.

'He won't, Dad. He doesn't want people to think he's a sponger.'

Unlike Blake, I thought, but didn't say.

'But I don't care, Dad,' she carried on, 'because he's not, you know that.'

'I do. We all like Reg. He's a great bloke. You've got to keep at it with him, and you'll get there, darling,' I said.

On a more positive note, Amy hadn't been drinking, although I worried that, with Reg still away, she might start again. She didn't – well, not that day.

Looking back, 6 March seemed like another turning-point for Amy. Riva called me from Camden Square to say that Amy was drunk and self-harming. Jane and I immediately drove to the house. When we arrived Amy wasn't very drunk, but she had cut herself. She said it was a delayed reaction to not seeing Reg and a response to something that had happened with Blake. My heart sank, but as soon as I'd heard she'd cut herself, I'd known his name would crop up. A week or so earlier he had been arrested by Leeds Police and charged with burglary and possessing a firearm. Amy was convinced it was related to drugs.

Riva talked about trying to get Amy sectioned, but I told her that we had to let this play itself out. We had been unable to get Amy sectioned when she had been a thousand times worse than she was now, so I knew it would be a non-starter. I stayed with Amy for the rest of the day and when she'd sobered up we had a long talk.

She told me some of what had happened the previous night, but it wasn't what I'd expected. 'When I was in the pub toilets, some girl came up to me,' she said. 'She asked me if I'd come and say hello to her friend who was a big fan and that. I went to the table and sat down and she was in a wheelchair. I talked with her for a while, and I asked her to be honest. Was she finding it tough to get by? I knew she was so I ended up giving her all the money I had on me. It was nearly a hundred pounds. She didn't want to take it but I told her she'd got to. I insisted. That left me with nothing to pay my bar bill.'

'That's a lovely story, Amy, and it was very kind of you,' I said. 'D'you remember when you met that disabled kid in Nice airport?'

'Nice?' She looked puzzled. 'Oh, yeah, the mum said she was scared to come over in case I hit her. Ha ha ha. I was doing that then, wasn't I?'

'You weren't doing too well then, no, but the mum got in touch with me after and said you were great with her daughter. You spent an hour talking with her and she was thrilled. You're a good girl, Amy.'

She sighed. 'Dad, seeing that girl last night made me realize how lucky I am. I really, really am fed up with all this,' she added. 'I've decided I'm done with drinking and I mean it this time.'

I took it with a pinch of salt – I'd heard it so many times before, first with drugs and then with alcohol – but I can't deny that part of me still clung to the hope that this might be the start of the final stretch in Amy's recovery.

For the next few days she stayed away from drink, and when Raye came over to see her she still hadn't had any. She had an important decision to make: Tony Bennett had arranged to sing with her on his second album of duets, and Amy was due to choose the song that morning. Tony had given Raye five or six for her to pick from. Amy chose 'Body And Soul', her reason being, 'My dad loves it.'

I was very flattered. 'That's great,' I said. 'Do you know the words?'

'Of course I know the words, Dad.' She laughed. 'I'm your daughter. You've been singing "Body And Soul" to me for twenty-seven years.'

That was true. I'd belted it out in the car when I'd picked her up from school loads of times.

I was pleased when Amy told me her non-drinking was continuing and we spoke about her flat in Jeffrey's Place. Naomi had lived there for a while, but now that she was with Amy, it was empty. It had fallen into disrepair and looked dilapidated. Jane and I were still living in Kent, and Amy said that, during her recovery, she would be happier if we lived closer to her. She suggested that we get the flat fixed up and that Jane and I could stay there, for at least part of the week. I thought that was a great idea, and when I ran it past Jane, so did she.

*   *   *

April began badly. Amy's drinking lasted just a day, but it was enough to depress me. She seemed to recover fairly quickly, but she was angry with herself. She told me that things were getting better with Reg, but she still didn't see him as much as she'd like to. Reg's work ethic meant that when he was working on a project he totally threw himself into it, often losing track of time. One evening he'd told Amy that he was going to pick her up at ten to go out for dinner. Amy was dressed and waiting, at what she said was ten (but, knowing her, was probably more like eleven), when Reg phoned to say he was still working and was going to be about an hour late. According to Amy, he didn't arrive until two.

'You need to try and understand how Reg is with his work,' I told Amy.

'I know, Dad,' she replied. 'I'll give it a go.'

The next morning Amy called to say she wasn't feeling well. Dr Romete was with her, recommending that she be admitted to the London Clinic as her detox might be causing her to feel ill. I went there about an hour later. Amy wasn't too bad that day, and I stayed with her, chatting, until eleven thirty p.m. The next day she was tetchy as alcohol withdrawal had really kicked in. I was learning these were temporary mood swings, and by 11 April it seemed that she had won the battle. She was well enough to leave the London Clinic for a short time and went to her gym at the Camden Square house. On doctor's orders, she was back at the hospital by eight thirty that evening. The next day Amy told me she couldn't stay in the London Clinic for ever and checked out. I agreed with her and drove her home.

I went to Camden Square on 15 April where Chris, a fairly new member of the security team, told me that Amy had woken up at four a.m. and drunk a bottle of wine. She'd woken again at eight and drunk another. When I arrived at ten thirty she was totally out of it and at midday she was still asleep. When I went back again at seven she was awake and acted as if nothing had happened. This led to a big argument and I left feeling frustrated and angry.

The next day was worse. I arrived at Camden Square mid-morning and found Amy collapsed on the kitchen floor. I got her upstairs and into bed. She was ready to go out and get more booze, but she couldn't even stand up. She did lots of shouting and swearing, and I was just as bad. I didn't know what to do: Amy was determined to get more drink, but in that state, God knows what might have happened to her if she'd got out. Fortunately it wasn't long before she fell asleep, and she remained asleep until the following morning. I told Chris that, in future, if he could do it without Amy seeing, he should water down her drinks. It seemed an unlikely trick to work, but anything that might make her drink less must help.

The next morning when I arrived at Camden Square, Amy was sitting in the garden sipping a latte. Considering the amount of alcohol she had consumed, she looked remarkably well. Neither of us brought up her behaviour of the previous day – I didn't have the energy for another argument – so we had an unusually awkward conversation, both dancing round the subject.

'Did I tell you? Me and Jane are going to Tenerife again next month,' I said to her.

'Oh, that's good, Dad,' she replied. 'Oh, yeah, Anthony's had to call the air-con people. It's on the blink again. Must be nice in the cab when it's warm like this with the air-con.'

'Oh, it is. I'm taking the cab in for a service on Friday.'

I got up and walked to the end of the garden and looked back at the house, jingling the change in my pocket. It was fabulous. Everything Amy had had done made it very special, the first proper grown-up house she'd owned. I called to her, 'The place looks great from here, doesn't it? A real home for you.'

'Yeah, I know, Dad. I love it so much, I can't see me ever moving out.'

It was time for me to go. As I was leaving, Amy stopped me. 'Dad, sorry about yesterday.'

'It's okay,' I said. 'It's just part of getting better.'

'Aaaah, thanks, Dad,' she said. She got up and ran over to give me a big hug, in the inimitable Amy fashion.

On 21 April Amy told me again that she was through with drinking. I'd heard it all before, and was fully prepared that, after two or three days, she'd start again, but at least she was still acknowledging she had a problem: six months or a year previously she wouldn't accept it and insisted she could stop whenever she wanted to. So, in reality, Amy's statement didn't mean she was going to stop drinking: it meant that she was beginning another period of abstinence, which, every time, I hoped would last longer than it had previously.

Over the next few weeks Amy did really well. Dr Romete was seeing her regularly, and kept telling me how pleased she was with her progress. Amy was a bit miserable and moody, but she was determined to maintain her sobriety.

Then on 11 May she was readmitted to the London Clinic. She wasn't very well and blood tests showed her potassium and glucose levels were high. She was told that this might result in heart problems, which frightened her. Dr Romete felt it might relate to how Amy had been detoxing. She was put on a drip to stabilize any immediate problems, and by the following day she felt a lot better. After another blood test, where the results were normal, Amy was discharged.

She abstained for a while and things looked good. I rang Camden Square one Saturday evening to see how she was doing and Reg answered. Before he passed me over, he said he wanted to tell me they'd just got back from a fabulous day out in the West End. They'd been strolling about after lunch and gone into a bar in Kingly Street where a house band was playing. The two of them had sat down and when the band were about to start their second set, Amy had, on the spur of the moment, called, 'D'you fancy having a female vocalist with you?'

They immediately invited her up and she sang a whole bunch of songs with them. That was like the good old days, when she'd been so happy to entertain her fans in that way.

I flew to LA two days later, but as soon as I arrived at the hotel, I got a call to say that Amy was drinking again. She had been off alcohol for more than three weeks and I had no idea what had caused her to start again. Everything was going well with Reg, she had started writing songs again, she'd put on all of the weight she'd lost and was looking really good. I really couldn't fathom it, but I reckoned that this was probably the longest spell she'd had of not drinking and I was encouraged by that. The longer between the lapses, the more progress she was making, or so I thought.

On 17 May Raye called: Amy had been rushed to the London Clinic because, after drinking all night, they had been unable to wake her. She'd come round now, and seemed to be responsive, but she was being kept in the hospital for overnight observation. The following day she discharged herself and went home to Camden Square.

A few days later I arrived back in London and went straight to see Amy at Camden Square. She was drunk. Dr Romete was there and told me that she could no longer be Amy's doctor as whatever she said to Amy wasn't going to stop her drinking. She handed me a letter to give to Amy that set out all of her medical problems, along with the events of the previous couple of days. The letter said Amy was in immediate danger of death; it said she had been in a coma on 17 May, and less than twenty-four hours later, against medical advice, she had discharged herself from the London Clinic.

The letter was blunt, matter-of-fact and incredibly shocking. We all knew Amy's life was in danger, but seeing those words spelled out on paper somehow made it much more real and terrifying. I was shaking and tasted bile at the back of my throat. I felt worse than I'd ever felt. It was pointless showing the letter to Amy when she was drunk, so I didn't bother. The next day she was still drunk and all of my hopes for her recovery from alcoholism were dashed.

And so it continued. On 22 May Andrew called me to say that Amy had got up at ten o'clock, drunk half a bottle of wine and gone back to sleep for the rest of the day.

*   *   *

By 24 May Amy was drinking all the time. Riva suggested that we try to persuade Amy to go to rehab at the Priory in Southgate, north London. I thought it was a waste of time, but I said I'd give it a go. Riva and I spent the whole of the next morning trying to get Amy to agree to going into rehab; we even arranged for Dr Brenner from the Priory to come and see her at Camden Square. Amy was very rude to Dr Brenner, but he was used to that and persisted. It wasn't easy, but in the end the three of us managed to persuade her to go.

We got her to the Priory at about two o'clock but she wanted to leave immediately. I stayed with her for a couple of hours and she gradually acclimatized herself to the place and seemed a lot calmer. I knew things were looking up when she asked me to go out and get her some KFC.

Within a couple of days Amy's stay at the Priory had made all the headlines. At first she was desperate to get out, but little by little she seemed more relaxed and agreed she was happy to stay until the end of the month. She was looking much better in herself and, once again, told me how much she wanted to stop drinking.

'I realize that just saying it isn't going to make it happen, though, Dad.' She was making a great effort to see her problems clearly. 'I didn't think it would be this difficult. I thought that once I'd quit drugs I could beat anything, but stopping drinking is a lot, lot harder than I'd thought.'

'You know, darling, if anyone can do it you can,' I said. 'You've done it once before and so you can do it again. You can be strong enough. You can do it.' I meant every word.

On 31 May Amy checked out of the Priory. She looked marvellous and agreed to return as an outpatient. When I spoke to Andrew later that night he confirmed that Amy hadn't had anything to drink. But when I saw her the next day she got really angry with me for having made her go into the clinic. I was convinced she was looking for an excuse to have a drink. We had a bit of a row before we made up and I left, but I found out later from Andrew that Amy didn't drink that day, so my fears had been unfounded. I asked him if she had been playing her guitar much, or using the studio; he said she hadn't been near the studio but he'd heard her playing up in her room.

I met Raye a few days later and told him that, while she was playing again, I didn't think she was writing much. He wasn't surprised, and said it seemed the album was still some way off. He wasn't sure if she was well enough to tour either. Amy had told us both how much she wanted to get back to live work and she was confident that she would be well enough to perform. There was no denying that the Priory had been of great help to her: Raye and I both felt she was showing signs of beating her alcoholism. Still, we agreed to proceed slowly before finally confirming the Eastern European tour.

Amy continued not to drink for the next week, and when I saw her at Camden Square on 9 June, she was buzzing with excitement about her forthcoming gigs and there was no sign of alcohol withdrawal. We talked about Reg and Blake. She told me that she loved Reg but couldn't help feeling sorry for Blake and wanting to help him.

'Of course that's your choice, Amy,' I said. She knew I didn't approve of her even talking to Blake, let alone helping him.

'Yeah, but, Dad, I couldn't not help him, could I?'

I would never have helped him, he was a bad lot. But that was Amy: she found good in everybody, even Blake.

Three days later she did a gig for friends and family at the 100 Club on Oxford Street in the West End. It was a 'rehearsal' gig for her Eastern European tour later that month. She still wasn't drinking and, apart from a slight sore throat, was in fantastic form. Her band started, playing a few songs without her, then Dionne did a couple of numbers, then Amy arrived on stage. She knew everyone in the audience personally and came on to rapturous applause and cheering. I knew how nervous she had been feeling before the show and I was worried she might have a drink to calm her down, but she didn't. And once she started singing the nerves disappeared.

She was great. She was laughing and joking with the audience, talking to individuals, and poking a bit of fun at me and others in the family. There was a lot of back and forth with the band. At one point Amy looked at the set list, then turned to Dale. 'Oh, we're not doing that now, are we? I don't want to do that one now, I want to do it later. What shall we do instead?'

Dale laughed and said, 'Let's do "Valerie",' and Amy hopped over to him and said, so that we could all hear, 'No, I'm not doing "Valerie" tonight, what else?'

The whole band laughed. She seemed really relaxed. Her throat was hurting, though, and she asked if anybody happened to have any honey with them. Five minutes later a bottle of honey arrived on the stage. Because she was with friends and family, she said, 'I'm just going into my dressing room to take some honey quickly. In the meantime, my dad'll sing a few songs for you.'

I nearly fainted. I love singing and I'll do it at the drop of a hat, but I really wasn't prepared – this was Amy's big moment and I'd been totally absorbed in it. But I got onto the stage and told the audience to talk among themselves while I spoke to Amy's pianist to see what songs from my repertoire he could play without music. We quickly sorted some out and, by the time I was halfway through the first song, Amy was standing in the audience cheering and whistling. I assumed that I would finish the song and she would come back onstage. But she shouted, 'You carry on, Dad,' and I sang a few more.

After that, Amy was back and, to everyone's delight, said to Dale, 'Right, let's start with "Valerie",' and she carried on where she'd left off, mixing laughter with her brilliant music. When she performed 'Rehab', she singled me out from the audience as she sang right at me, 'My daddy says I'm fine.' I cracked up, along with everybody else. We all had a wonderful time, watching and listening to her that night. It felt more like a party than a gig, and Amy was definitely back to her best.

Later, in her dressing room, her caring side showed once again. 'How's your glandular fever?' she said to my friend Paul's daughter.

She hadn't seen Katie for about a year – I couldn't believe she'd remembered. I'd seen Katie many times, but had totally forgotten she'd been ill.

*   *   *

Amy stayed dry for another five days, and I was feeling very positive about her Eastern European tour. But on 17 June, the day before she was due to fly to Serbia, I knew something was wrong the minute I arrived in Camden Square. 'I don't want to do the tour, Dad,' she said, after a short time.

I was surprised. It had been planned since the start of 2011 and it was definitely something that Amy had wanted to do. Raye and I had had our reservations about it but had kept faith with Amy's desire to play to her fans in Eastern Europe.

She had been saying for ages how bored she was and my response had been, 'Get out there and do what you do best – make music. Do a tour or go back into the studio.'

And for the last few months, when Amy hadn't been drinking, she had got very involved with the arrangements. She always played an integral part in establishing the look of her live gigs, getting heavily involved with her band's clothes, the production, the lights, just about everything. Right from *Back to Black* she had had a very clear idea of how she wanted her three backing singers to look onstage. Because she was so into fifties/sixties style she'd once made Raye go into the costume department at the BBC to hire three baby blue dinner suits for them. She named the trio the Nights Before and, at her final gigs, decided she wanted them to wear peach-coloured suits.

But now she was saying she wanted to cancel the tour. I couldn't understand what had changed and she couldn't explain it to me. All I could get out of her was that she didn't want to do it – and whether it was to do with stage fright, or the fear that she'd return to drinking, I never could get out of her.

By the next day Amy had changed her mind again and wanted to do the tour. I was still apprehensive that she might back out or start drinking, but I spoke to her before she got on the plane and she sounded fine. Raye agreed to give me a running commentary, so over the next forty-eight hours I got constant calls and texts: 'She's in the hotel room', 'She's in the car', 'She's at the venue', 'She's on the stage...'

Then, at two forty-five a.m. on 19 June, Raye phoned to say that the gig had been a complete shambles.

Amy had been in a funny mood in the car on the way there. She wasn't drunk, but she had been agitated in her hotel room and wanted a drink; so Raye had allowed her one glass of wine to calm her down. Amy would often ask people to give her drinks once she was on stage. But that didn't happen in Belgrade: she was drunk before she got onstage. Neither Raye nor Tyler, who were both with her that day, have any idea how she'd got drunk but she must have smuggled some alcohol into the gig, or got someone to do it for her.

So, that night in Belgrade Amy went onstage drunk, and it showed. Her performance was disastrous and much of the audience were booing. She couldn't remember what city she was in, or the lyrics of her songs, or even the names of her band members. Throughout, Raye was trying to pull her off the stage, but she wouldn't leave. She stayed for ninety minutes. Her gigs normally lasted seventy-five. It was the worst ever.

They left the gig and went straight to the airport. All the way, Amy was demanding a drink in the car, but Raye wouldn't let her have one. On the plane she asked Raye if it was the worst gig she had ever done.

'Yep,' Raye replied. 'It's right up there with Birmingham.' He told her off for letting everybody down. But Amy didn't like what she was hearing, and argued back, then went off and sulked at the back of the plane.

The next gig was in Istanbul, and when they arrived Amy apologized to everyone.

'This stops here,' Raye said. 'You can't go out and work like this. It's ridiculous. If you don't want to do these gigs, then we don't do them. But these are a nice run of shows. We're going to places that we haven't been to before, playing in front of people that haven't seen you before, people that really want to see you. You went onstage and done that. Why? What was the problem?'

Amy gave him the Amy shrug. She said she didn't know the answer.

Raye cancelled all the remaining gigs.

I wondered why she couldn't say anything to anyone, including me, about this. Did she feel she was letting everyone down if she told me that quitting drinking was harder than she'd thought, even after everything we'd been through together? Did she still want to try and deal with everything on her own? Did she not know that whatever she needed from me I'd have given her?

Amy knew she didn't have to do those gigs if she didn't want to: Raye had told her so over and over again. But Amy loved being with her band and she had really wanted to do that tour. And Raye had thought that going ahead with it might help get her creative juices flowing again. Amy often said that she was bored singing the same old songs. 'Write some new ones, then,' we'd replied.

I'm not sure that it was actually boredom, though. I think it was only the *Back to Black* songs that she didn't want to sing. 'Wake Up Alone', 'Unholy War' and 'Back to Black' seemed to be the hardest for her. They reminded her of Blake, and a time in her life that, understandably, she wanted to forget. Raye thought singing those songs triggered memories of the drug spiral she had been in and that that was one reason why she would drink so much before she performed.

I don't know if that was the case or not, but Raye had worked closely with Amy's musical director, Dale Davis, to make sure the *Back to Black* songs were interspersed with covers and songs from

Frank. They didn't want to have a build-up of songs that reminded Amy of that hellish time. Dale would present the set list to her and, as she trusted him implicitly, she never queried it. This seemed to be working, so we know the songs weren't to blame for Amy's behaviour that night in Belgrade.

Everything was fine with Reg, so we know it wasn't that. And Blake was a thing of the past. So, what had caused this lapse? We only found out later that Amy had suffered from the worst case of stage fright she had ever had.

At the time I despaired, thinking Amy was going back to drinking regularly. We had no understanding of what was going on. 'My daughter needs help and we are all helpless,' I wrote that night.

But I was absolutely wrong. Amy didn't drink again until a couple of days before she passed away.

20

'GIVE ME A CUDDLE, DAD'

Over the next few days I had a lot of tweets blaming me for Amy's performance in Belgrade. 'How could you let her go on like that?' her fans asked. 'You should have known this would happen.'

No one knew what Amy had been through during the preceding months. No one knew she hadn't touched a drop for weeks before the Belgrade gig. Neither did they know how much her music was helping her at this time. A lot of people blamed me, and a lot of people blamed Amy's management, but I knew that Raye wasn't to blame. Amy had definitely wanted to do the tour and the comments were incredibly hurtful.

On 20 June, two days after the Belgrade gig, Reg flew to Istanbul to meet Amy. Once he was there, she seemed a lot better: she was calmer and able to think rationally about the future again. She didn't want to do any more live work until she got her stage fright under control, and she decided she'd rather spend her time working in her home studio, with her next album still some way off. I knew that *Back to Black* had come about when she'd felt she had a coherent whole, based on the girl-group sound she loved. I don't think she ever found the same guiding inspiration to bring together the ideas she had for a new album.

On 22 June Amy came home. She looked much better, but I was being careful what I said to her and it was Amy who brought up the Belgrade gig. She told me how disappointed she'd been with herself once she'd sobered up. She didn't like what alcoholism was doing to her, or to her family and Reg. She felt terrible about letting everyone down. And then she told me all about her stage fright. She hadn't felt up to the tour, and for hours before the first gig she'd been shaking with nerves. She'd thought that a couple of drinks might help, but they didn't, so she'd had some more.

'All the time I was drinking, Dad, I was thinking how much I hate this,' she said. 'I really, really want to stop. I really don't want to go through all this shit again. Every time something happens. You believe me, don't you?'

'Of course I do,' I told her. 'But I can't make these things stop. You're always going to be around alcohol, and in situations where you're going to want to drink again. You've got to find the will to stop it yourself.' All I could do was encourage her. I knew she hated what kept happening, but I had no way of knowing how long it would be before she took to drink again.

That day was a bit strange. Amy and I spent an hour or two together and, after we'd talked about Belgrade, she was very reflective. She spoke a lot about my mum, which we often did, and then, which was unusual, she wanted to watch some clips of her live performances on YouTube. 'Do you think I'm good, Dad?' she asked, after we'd watched a bit.

'Of course you are,' I said. 'You know you are.'

Then she asked, 'Dad, do you think I'm beautiful?'

'I think you're the most beautiful girl in the world,' I replied, 'but you're asking the wrong person. I'm your father.'

Until then, she had never, as far as I knew, watched herself like that – she wasn't very interested in looking back – and it was the first time I could remember when she'd taken time to study herself in that way. It wasn't so much about her self-image – I knew she'd had problems with that in the past, but she seemed over those now; this time she was coolly examining her own performance, and seeing what made her special.

'Just give me a cuddle, Dad,' she said, and we sat together for about an hour, me holding her in my arms. It was lovely, a very special moment, but at the time I didn't attach any importance to it. It would be easy to think that she had some sort of premonition, but I don't really believe that. I think it was just a lovely moment.

*　　*　　*

The next day I saw Amy again. Mostly we talked about the work she needed to do for her new album. I had a sneaky scout around the house for alcohol, but there was none. I saw Amy most days over the following two weeks, and on the days I didn't see her I spoke to her on the phone. Gradually our conversations stopped featuring the word 'alcohol' and I was content that, for the time being, she had stopped drinking.

On Sunday, 10 July, Jane and I had a lovely day with Amy at Camden Square. We had lunch and then just whiled away the time, talking and listening to music. Amy had done an impromptu DJ set at one of the local pubs that week and she was really into her record collection. It was a normal family Sunday.

The next day Amy called to say she was going to a local bar to play pool. I was concerned: for Amy, playing pool in a bar was synonymous with drinking. I phoned Andrew, the security guy, immediately and told him to call me the minute she had a drink. But he didn't call. He didn't need to. As soon as they'd arrived Amy had gone to the bar and told the owner, 'Do not sell me alcohol under any circumstances.' That night I wrote in my diary, 'I'm very proud of Amy. This is very positive.'

On 14 July we spent the day together again. Amy had searched the Internet and found some dance remixes of 'Please Be Kind', one of the songs on my album. We listened to them together – Amy thought they were pretty good – and jokingly said, 'I tell you what, Dad, I'll take these down with me next time I do some DJing and before you know it you'll be number one in the dance charts.'

'What – you going to do this regularly, then? Hope they're paying you,' I joked.

'Oh, shut up! I love doing it, Dad. I feel like I can do anything I want here in Camden. It's like my playground. But when I've had enough I can come home here where it's all peace and quiet and I feel safe.'

I was flying to New York on 22 July for some gigs, so the day before I left I went to Camden Square to say goodbye to Amy – this was when she showed me the photos she'd found. She told me she was going to see Dionne perform at the iTunes Festival at the Roundhouse in Camden that night; I told her to wish Dionne good luck from me. When we spoke the next day, she told me she'd had a great time at the Roundhouse: Dionne had invited her on to the stage and she had danced while Dionne sang.

Sadly, that was Amy's last public appearance.

On Saturday, 23 July 2011, my darling daughter Amy passed away.

21

FAREWELL,
CAMDEN TOWN

I arrived back at Heathrow airport on the morning of Sunday, 24 July. My friend Hayden picked me up and drove me to his house in north London where Jane was waiting for me. We cried and cried until it seemed there were no tears left.

We went to Janis's house not far away and we all cried some more. Alex and Riva were already there and people continued to arrive throughout the day. I was in a daze and I don't really remember much of what went on. Things were happening around me and I felt removed from the scene, as if I was watching a movie.

I kept asking myself, how could this have happened?

I had seen Amy the day before I flew to New York and she was fine. Janis, Richard and Reg had seen her the next day and she was fine. And she was still fine later that night – although, according to Andrew, she was 'tipsy'. When Andrew checked on her a bit later, she was singing and playing drums in her room. He had checked on her again in the morning and thought she was asleep. Then he checked a few hours later and realized she wasn't asleep. Immediately he had raised the alarm.

A lot of people believe that Amy's life was in turmoil during her last eighteen months. But nothing could be further from the truth. Yes, she had lapses back into alcoholism, but those lapses had been gradually getting further and further apart. There was no doubt in those around her that her life was going in the right direction. I always equated Amy's neatness, or lack of it, to how well-ordered her mind was at any particular time. During those last eighteen months the clothes in her wardrobes were neat and tidy, her books and CDs were organized alphabetically and her sketchbooks numbered.

I knew that Amy couldn't have died from a drug overdose, as she had been drug-free since 2008. But although she had been so brave and had fought so hard in her recovery from alcoholism, I knew she must have lapsed once again. I thought that Amy hadn't had a drink for three weeks. But she had actually started drinking at Dionne's Roundhouse gig the previous Wednesday. I didn't know that at the time.

The following morning Janis, Jane, Richard Collins (Janis's fiancé), Raye, Reg and I went to St Pancras mortuary to officially identify Amy. Alex couldn't bring himself to go, which I fully understood. When we arrived there were loads of paps outside the court, but they were all very respectful. We were shown into a room and saw Amy behind a window. She looked very, very peaceful, as if she was just asleep, which in a way made it a lot harder. She looked lovely. There was a slight red blotchiness to her skin, which was why, at the time, I thought she might have had a seizure: she looked as she had done when she had had seizures in the past.

Eventually the others left Janis and me to say goodbye to Amy by ourselves. We were with her for about fifteen minutes. We put our hands on the glass partition and spoke to her. We told her that Mummy and Daddy were with her and that we would always love her.

I can't express what it was like. It was the worst feeling in the world.

Then we went to Camden Square, where we were joined by Alex and Riva. The police were still investigating the possibility of foul play, so we weren't allowed inside the house. But hundreds of fans were there and they had turned the square into a shrine. We gathered together and looked at the tributes left at the edge of the police cordons. I thanked the reporters and fans for coming, and shook hands with many of them, fighting back the tears. There were drinks and cigarettes, some beautiful notes and lovely artwork, soft toys, flowers and candles. It was very touching and comforting to know how much Amy was loved. Eventually I broke down and couldn't stop crying.

After that we went back to Janis's house where our friends and other members of the family were waiting. I told them what had come into my mind during the bleak hours over the Atlantic as I'd flown home. 'I started thinking of a Foundation,' I said. 'Amy's Foundation. So that disadvantaged young people dealing with addiction, ill health or homelessness can be supported.'

I hadn't thought much more than that but the idea was out there now. Gradually others started adding to it, and it grew.

The post-mortem examination was inconclusive. The Metropolitan Police said, 'It did not establish a formal cause of death,' and that they were awaiting the results of further toxicology tests, which were not expected for two to four weeks. In the meantime, the police treated Amy's death as unexplained.

An inquest was opened and adjourned until 26 October to allow us to make the funeral arrangements.

In the Jewish tradition a funeral must take place at the earliest opportunity and, since the coroner had released the body, the funeral could take place the following day, 26 July. Certain branches of Judaism do not permit cremation, but my mother had been cremated and we thought that was what Amy would have wanted for herself when she was to be reunited with her Nan Cynthia. There was so much to do and my marvellous friends rallied round us to ensure that everything that had to be done was done, in time for the service and cremation. I started to write Amy's eulogy.

*   *   *

Amy was cremated at the Golders Green Crematorium in north London on 26 July 2011, a service just for family and friends, in the same hall we had used for my mother's funeral in May 2006. Following the service, we filed outside into the gardens, leaving Amy's security boys to look after Amy in death as they had done in life. They emerged ten minutes later and I knew that it was over.

We then went on to the Schindler Hall in Southgate, north London, for the beginning of the *shiva*, the Jewish period of mourning: each evening, for the following three days, hundreds of family and friends came to pay their respects and join us in prayer. The *shiva* eases the pain just a little bit. My dear friends wouldn't leave my side during the days that followed, which was a great comfort to me.

Before the cremation, there had been a service for Amy in the prayer hall at the Edgwarebury Jewish cemetery in north London. When we'd arrived at the cemetery that morning, I was still in a daze and felt that it wasn't really happening. I just couldn't take it in. The service was by invitation only and there must have been five hundred people inside the hall, and at least another five hundred outside. We said prayers in English and Hebrew, and ended the service with a recording of Carole King's 'So Far Away' – Amy's favourite song.

Before that, I read my eulogy, most of which had been written the day before. I had deliberately left gaps, where I didn't need the written word to know what I wanted to say:

> Family and friends. We are here to celebrate the life of our darling daughter Amy. I could say that Amy was the most iconic singer of the twenty-first century. I could say that Amy has sold over 22 million CDs, I could say that Tony Bennett said that Amy was the greatest singer since Ella Fitzgerald. But what I will say is that Amy Winehouse was the greatest daughter, family member and friend that anyone could wish for. My friends and Janis's friends were Amy's friends.

I told the congregation the stories I've written here about Amy's youth, about her games and how she would play up; I told them about the times she'd spent at her various schools, the friends she'd made then and later within the music industry.

> Amy's friends were lifelong and deep. Tyler, Naomi, Jevan, Catriona, Chantelle, John and Kelly, Nicky Shymansky, Lucian Grainge, all at Metropolis and 19 Management and, of course, Raye Cosbert, Selena and Petra. Raye is more than Amy's manager: he is our brother and our guide. Amy's boys – Andrew, Anthony, Neville and Chris – are family to us. I would trust my life to them. Their care and patience over the years have been outstanding.

I wanted to explain to people what we knew about Amy's last days, as there had been lots of incorrect speculation in the papers that I wanted to address.

Recently Amy had found love with her new boy Reg and he had helped her deal with many of her problems; she was looking forward to their future together. She was happier than we had seen her in a long while ... really happy.

Three years ago she conquered her drug dependency and she was really trying hard to deal with her alcohol problems. She had just had three weeks of abstinence and was really very content with her life.

She had been told by her doctor, Christina Romete, that drinking and then abstaining was perhaps worse than carrying on drinking, as it screws up your electrolytes and can bring on seizures, which could result in death.

Sadly, Amy was prone to these seizures.

But let me stress that Amy was not depressed ... I had seen her on the Thursday before I went to New York, and Janis, Richard and Reg saw Amy on the Friday. She was on top form.

That night Amy was in her room playing her drums and singing. As it was getting late, Andrew told her to quieten down. She did so and Andrew heard her walking around for some time later.

He then went to check her and thought she was asleep on the bed. Several hours later he checked on her again and realized she hadn't moved in that time. She had gone.

So that was it. We are all left here bereft and stunned. Janis's and my baby has gone. She was the light of all of our lives and will, together with Alex and Riva, remain the light of our lives.

I wanted to say something about the special talent my daughter had been blessed with. I spoke about how she'd done what she'd told Sylvia Young she wanted to do all those years ago. As a family we wanted people to continue to find their troubles eased by Amy's voice.

Amy's last gig was at the 100 Club. Her voice was good but her wit and timing were perfect. Everyone enjoyed themselves … most of all Amy. She had a terrific generosity of spirit, which always shone through.

Her legacy will remain.

Reg and Tyler, Janis and Richard, Alex and Riva, Janey and I will somehow have to find a way to continue without Amy. It will be hard. But we have you lot to support us … and together we will get through this.

I told them a little about my mother and Amy, and then I continued:

Richard recently showed me an old school book of Amy's from 1995. This was from just after Janis and I divorced … Amy drew a heart and split it into sections of things that she loved the best. She wrote: Alex, her mum, and me, her dad. This was just after I had left the house … she wrote that she missed me.

I had never seen this before.

In the last entry in the school book she wrote: 'I love to live … and I live to love.' She was just twelve years old.

Good night, my angel, sleep tight.

Mummy and Daddy love you so much.

EPILOGUE

Amy's passing was and is unbearable. Our lives have changed for ever and will never be the same again.

On Friday, 29 July 2011, Janis and Richard, Alex, Reg, Tyler, Jane and I were allowed into her house in Camden Square to remove some of Amy's personal things. Among them we took her beloved guitar for safekeeping.

We were greeted again by mourning fans. Around the square layers of floral tributes, photographs and messages were still growing. I tried to show the fans my appreciation for their support and love for Amy by handing out some of her T-shirts. I put on a brave face, and even managed a small smile as I watched their reactions.

On Saturday, 30 July, the immediate family and some close friends attended Finchley Reform Synagogue for a Sabbath morning service, which included some special prayers for Amy.

It was the end of the worst week of my life.

Over the next few weeks and months, four things were going to consume my time: setting up Amy's Foundation; waiting for the result of the inquest into Amy's death; dealing with Amy's musical legacy; and, happily, attending my son's wedding.

Among the multitudes of cards and letters sent to us, Jane and I received three scrapbooks in the post from a young lady called Florence, who was in her twenties and had learning difficulties. The scrapbooks were full of newspaper cuttings and pictures of Amy, accompanied by Florence's comments. For example, if there was a picture of Amy coming out of a pub, Florence had written, 'No Amy, no pub, no pub.' If there was a picture of Amy smoking, Florence had put, 'No smoking, no smoking Amy, no smoking.' We were so moved that this young lady wanted us to have her beloved collection that we decided to go and see her. We wanted to give the scrapbooks back to Florence, and for her to continue adding to them, because Amy's story isn't over. Through the work of Amy's Foundation, Florence will have many more cuttings to add to her collection. About that, I am determined.

Jane and I went to see Florence again some months later, taking with us one of Amy's bowling shirts. It was being with her that made me think that maybe some good could come out of our tragedy.

*   *   *

I realize that in times of bereavement your mind can play tricks on you. I was looking for answers and signs, and there were a number of spooky incidents in the days and weeks after Amy's passing. They could be interpreted as nothing more than coincidences, with logical explanations, but I found them comforting: they made me feel that Amy was close.

It had started at the service for Amy at Edgwarebury Lane. As I began reading the eulogy, a black butterfly came into the prayer hall.

I had my head down, because I was reading, but I could hear people muttering and thought that the paparazzi had got in. The butterfly landed on Kelly Osbourne's shoulder, then flew around me. I believe that it was sign from above to show Amy's loved ones she was now at peace. She was with us in spirit and I believe that she was present at her own funeral in the form of that black butterfly.

The next strange thing happened at my sister Melody's house a few nights later. A very small blackbird, which isn't a common sight at night, flew into the house and landed on Jane's foot. It was so tame and quite happy sitting there. We took it out into the garden and gently threw it into the air, where it circled and came back. We threw it into the air again and again, but each time it circled and landed next to us. Eventually we gave it some milk and bread and it spent the rest of the evening with us.

The next incidents took place in Jamaica. About three months prior to Amy's passing, Jane and I had arranged to go to the wedding of the son of a friend. We were due to leave on 6 August. As the day approached I didn't want to go: the image of Amy in the mortuary wouldn't leave me. Jane pointed out that it might do us good to get away – it might help me to shake myself free of that picture. In the end I agreed with her. When we arrived at our hotel, though, my head was still all over the place. I felt very miserable; I couldn't be bothered to unpack and went out onto the balcony, where I was greeted by a bird and a butterfly, pirouetting around each other, as if they had been waiting for me.

Early each morning Jane and I went for a quiet walk on the mostly deserted beach. Every day we'd walk, talk and cry. And every day we were followed by a butterfly. We stopped, the butterfly stopped, we walked on and the butterfly continued following us. We tested it and started to walk back the way we had come and the butterfly came with us. We sat down on a sun bed and the butterfly joined us. It really was quite amazing.

I had been praying to my mum for Amy to give me a sign, just give me something, and I really felt that those prayers were being answered. I asked myself, when do you ever see a butterfly come into a hall full of people? When do you ever see a blackbird hop into a room full of people and keep coming back? When do you ever see a bird and a butterfly dancing together? When do you see a butterfly keeping pace with you while you're walking and stopping when you stop?

I decided that I was going to name the company that would handle the Foundation business 'Bird & Butterfly' and that a bird and a butterfly would form the logo for Amy's Foundation.

Working on Foundation business helped keep my mind off my pain. But as the days passed, things got harder rather than easier. More and more the enormity of what had happened struck me. I missed Amy so much and there was nothing I could do about that. I found myself sending her a text: 'When are you coming home?'

I can't help myself: my heart is broken.

A couple of months after Amy's death I had another of those odd moments when a message from Amy seemed to come to me. Trenton Harrison-Lewis, my manager, told me he'd seen Amy the Wednesday before she had passed away. She was at the Roundhouse to watch Dionne Bromfield perform and she'd gone up to Trenton, patted his stomach and said, 'Look after my dad.'

That was odd. Had she had a premonition that something was going to happen to her?

*   *   *

There had to be an inquest into Amy's death and, as part of that process, Janis, Jane and I went to see the coroner, who told us that no trace of drugs had been found in Amy's blood. I'd been going on about Amy not having taken drugs for about three years but there were still a lot of people who didn't believe me. Toxicology reports later confirmed that Amy's system had not contained any illegal drugs at the time of her death. The alcohol levels found in Amy's blood, however, were very, very, high: 416 mg of alcohol per 100 ml of blood. The pathologist who conducted her post-mortem examination said 350 mg of alcohol per 100 ml of blood was considered a fatal level.

On 26 October we attended the Coroner's Court, where the St Pancras coroner, Suzanne Greenway, said, 'The unintended consequence of Winehouse drinking so much alcohol was her sudden and unexpected death.' Dr Romete told the inquest that Amy had said she did not know if she was going to stop drinking but 'she did not want to die'. The coroner's verdict was misadventure.

I did feel a sense of closure after hearing the verdict. But now that feeling of closure has gone because at the end of January 2012 the legitimacy of the inquest's verdict was questioned. We were told by the Coroner's Court that Suzanne Greenway resigned in November 2011, amid allegations that she was unqualified to do the job. Rules stipulate that she could be appointed only if she had worked as a registered English solicitor for five years; she had been registered for only two and a half. She was also required to have five years' experience as a 'qualified medical practitioner', but there were allegations that she was only qualified as a nurse in her home country, Australia. She had been appointed to the role of assistant deputy coroner by her husband, Inner North London coroner Dr Andrew Scott Reid, who was quoted as saying, 'In November it became apparent I'd made an error in the appointment process. While I am confident that all of the inquests handled were done so correctly, I apologize if this matter causes distress.'

Suzanne Greenway was responsible for approximately thirty inquests, all of which, including Amy's, could now be declared illegal. We were told that this will only happen if verdicts are challenged in the High Court. At the time of writing we are still awaiting the result of an investigation.

*　　*　　*

'Body And Soul', the duet recorded by Amy and Tony Bennett, was released on 14 September 2011, Amy's twenty-eighth birthday; all the proceeds went to Amy's Foundation. Amy's performance on that record was honoured on 12 February 2012 when she was posthumously awarded the Grammy for Best Pop Duo/Group Performance with Tony Bennett. Janis and I accepted the award on her behalf.

Meanwhile Amy's third album, *Lioness: Hidden Treasures*, was released. It wasn't the planned follow-up to *Back to Black* as only two songs, 'Between the Cheats' and 'Like Smoke', had been completed prior to Amy passing away. The album is a compilation of recordings from before the release of *Frank* to the songs that Amy was working on in 2011. If my darling daughter had lived, she would have released many great albums, I know, but as she'd had no idea her life was going to end so early and so abruptly, she hadn't left behind enough finished recordings to make a complete album in the way that *Back to Black* and *Frank* are complete.

We had given producers Salaam Remi and Mark Ronson our consent to compile the album and they worked together on it. Salaam said, 'It makes no sense for these songs to be sitting on a hard drive, withering away.' We were very pleased with the final result, which was why we, Amy's family, endorsed its release.

After Amy passed away, Jane and I spent a lot of time with Reg. I guess being with him made me feel close to Amy. Reg talked about the times he had spent with her and we laughed a lot because we focused on Amy's brilliant sense of humour and wit; he, too, had found her very sharp. There was no crying. I knew Reg, like all of us, was missing Amy so much and suffering terribly. On Valentine's Day 2012, Reg took flowers for Amy to her house in Camden Square; her cat, Katie, now lives with him.

I was reminded recently of a regular conversation I used to have with Amy. She loved joking with me about a movie about my life, in which Amy was the casting director. She decided that Ray Winstone would be perfect to play me. I would counter that by saying George Clooney would be a better choice. Amy said Reg could play the part of my dad as a young man because he looked like him; Jane would be played by Helen Hunt, and my mum by Elizabeth Taylor, who was still alive at the time. We both knew it was never going to happen but we loved the game.

Amy never said whom she would cast as herself.

* * *

Hearing Amy's music – even if we just walk past an open window and hear it playing inside somewhere – is still difficult for me. One evening Jane and I were passing a bar where they were playing 'Rehab', and I heard the line, 'My daddy thinks I'm fine'. I wrote in my diary, 'This is so hard. I don't know how much more of it I can take. Amy's everywhere I go, but she's not here. I need some comfort, but there is none.'

But Amy and my mother Cynthia are together now. Amy believed, and I believe, that love conquers all. Even death.

* * *

Thank you for allowing me to share with you the story of Amy's all too short life. Writing this book has brought it all back to me: reading my diaries, remembering the good times, the bad times and the very worst time of all, when Amy passed away. It's easy to forget that Amy was only a young woman when she died, as so much had happened in those years, and so many people had been touched by her life and her music. I sometimes think that perhaps I should have handled some situations differently, but that's me. For my own sake, and that of Amy's family, I decided not to look back and regret, because nothing good would come of that. I always did my best for Amy but sometimes I couldn't cope and hindsight can be very cruel.

Amy will be in my heart and mind for ever. I miss her so much that sometimes it physically hurts. Her legacy is already having a positive effect on many young people's lives and, as I have said, I will be spending the rest of my life working for Amy's Foundation. Together with my family, my dear friends and the many, many other people helping us, we will ensure that Amy is never forgotten.

Amy was a great girl with a huge heart. Please keep her in yours.

A NOTE ON THE AMY WINEHOUSE FOUNDATION

One major factor helping me through the months after Amy's death was creating the Foundation that carries her name.

Many people have helped in all sorts of ways to ensure that the Amy Winehouse Foundation was established, is funded, properly run and able to give financial support to those organizations most in keeping with our aims. They are too many to name here, but among those I worked closely with in establishing the Foundation were my lawyers and accountants, Universal Records, the Outside Organization and Comic Relief, who, through their US arm America Gives Back, are assisting with the collection of donations in the US.

So many individuals found ways to offer their support for the Foundation. Matt Goss asked me if I would open for him at the Royal Albert Hall, my fee to go to Amy's Foundation: Amy's passing had resonated with him as his little sister Carolyn died in 1988 when a drunk-driver crashed into her car. John Taylor, of Duran Duran, wanted to offer more than just financial support, and proposed setting up our own juvenile rehabilitation facility; it may take time for this to come about, but his strong interest in the Foundation's planned work was a real boost to me. Robbie Williams's mother, Jan, who helps to run Robbie's charity, Give It Sum (also administered by Comic Relief), met us to discuss working in partnership together.

Individually, some amazing donations came in. Michael Bublé made a generous donation. When Tony Bennett and his record label, Sony, told us they were donating $100,000, my breath was taken away – what an incredible thing for them to do. Amy's fans from all over the world made donations, which, however modest, have brought us the greatest pleasure of all, affirming to those who work for the Foundation and who have supported it that Amy's life and work will always be treasured.

As well as the income that Amy's music generated for the Foundation, other organizations collected money for us. Fred Perry decided, with our support, that they would go ahead with Amy's autumn 2011 and spring 2012 collections, with all Amy's commission paid to the Foundation. Most of the work on the collections had been done when Amy was living at Bryanston Square and it always amazed me how brilliantly she could transfer what was in her mind to paper. I guess it was just another of her many creative talents.

By October 2011 Fred Perry reported that sales of Amy's collection were 40 per cent up on the same time the previous year.

In November the dress that Amy wore on the cover of *Back to Black* was sold by Kerry Taylor Auctions at La Galleria in Pall Mall, London. Created by the Thai-based designer Disaya, it had been loaned to Amy for the photo-shoot in 2006, after which it was carefully stored in Disaya's archive. Following Amy's passing, Disaya decided that the dress should be sold and the money raised would be donated to Amy's Foundation. Sotheby's had valued the dress at £10–20,000; it was sold for £43,200 to the Museo de la Moda fashion museum in Chile. I couldn't believe it. What a huge amount of money for the Foundation. The sound of a hammer going down can be very cathartic, and we are all truly grateful to Disaya, who was with me at the sale.

The Foundation has provided hundreds of thousands of pounds to a variety of projects, both in the UK and elsewhere, including hospices and other organizations devoted to terminally and chronically ill children and young adults, such as Chestnut Tree House near Arundel, the Little Havens Children's Hospice, Rayleigh, Essex, Hopes and Dreams charity in Essex, and the LauraLynn House in Dublin, Ireland's first children's hospice. I was so proud and pleased to be helping these kids in Amy's name.

Amy had told me she wanted to do something for some of the children on St Lucia – Janis is spearheading this project on behalf of the Foundation and is currently discussing a long-term project with the St Lucian government.

The Foundation is also supporting New Horizons Youth Centre, in Euston, London, by helping to fund its music work, designed to provide skills to young people, and their free food service for those unfortunately homeless.

With the Angelus Foundation, set up by author and broadcaster Maryon Stewart after losing her daughter, Hester, in 2009, after she had taken the 'legal' drug GBL, the Foundation is supporting efforts aimed at encouraging the government to introduce drug-awareness education into schools in the UK.

I had been speaking to MPs and to the government already on the issue of rehab centres for young addicts who wanted to quit. I had meetings with Keith Vaz MP, chairman of the Home Office select committee, and James Brokenshire MP, Home Office minister for crime and security. I learned that half of the government's budget to help people with addiction problems – some £200 million – was used to enable addicted offenders within the criminal justice system to receive treatment in a residential rehabilitation unit. This meant a convicted criminal was five times more likely to be offered residential rehab than a non-offender.

At a further meeting with some senior civil servants I was told they viewed residential rehabilitation as 'an expensive luxury'. Their solution was to treat people in the community where, for example, heroin addicts were given methadone; that, however, just produces methadone addicts, and methadone deaths are increasing as a result. Don't get me wrong, there is some very good work being done in the community, but there is a desperate need for some people to go into residential rehabilitation, which is lacking at the moment. After our meetings with government and other parliamentary officials, I felt that, certainly in the short term, I wouldn't be able to rely on the government to provide any of the help needed by people who were desperate for residential rehabilitation. I became even more determined to ensure that Amy's Foundation would help those people who needed our assistance.

One such organization working in this field is Focus 12, whom I'd first had contact with in September 2008 when I met their chief executive, Chip Somers. The Foundation was proud to provide a donation to Focus 12 of £30,000 towards a permanent full-time place for young people battling their addiction.

Focus 12 was important to me because just a week after Amy passed away I had a call from a friend of a friend who had little money and was desperately seeking help for her daughter. The young woman was an alcoholic, addicted to cocaine and cannabis, and suffered from an eating disorder. I called Chip and arranged for her to meet him at Bury St Edmunds the next day. She stayed at Focus 12 for six weeks and her family were very grateful. I was more than happy to pay for this myself, but Chip said that there would be no charge.

There are some truly wonderful caring people out there.

CREDITS

While every effort has been made to trace the owners of copyright material reproduced herein and secure permissions, the publishers would like to apologize for any omissions and will be pleased to incorporate missing acknowledgements in any future edition of this book.

Song lyrics
'In My Bed' – words and music by Amy Winehouse and Salaam Remi © 2003; reproduced by permission of EMI April Music Inc/ Salaam Remi Music Inc/ EMI Music Publishing Ltd, London W8 5SW

'What Is It About Men' – words and music by Amy Winehouse, Felix Howard, Paul Watson, Gordon Williams, Wilburn Cole, Donovan Jackson, Earl Smith, Luke Smith, Delroy Cooper © 2006; reproduced by permission of EMI Music Publishing Ltd, London W8 5SW

'Take The Box' – words and music by Amy Winehouse and Luke Smith © 2002; reproduced by permission of EMI Music Publishing Ltd, London W8 5SW

'Back To Black' – words and music by Amy Winehouse and Mark Ronson © 2006; reproduced by permission of EMI Music Publishing Ltd, London W8 5SW

'Rehab' – words and music by Amy Winehouse © 2006; reproduced by permission of EMI Music Publishing Ltd, London W8 5SW

Images

All images and notes provided © Mitch Winehouse except: Picture Section Two, p.1 © Alex Lake; p.2 top left © David Butler/Rex Features, top right and bottom © Press Association Images; p.3 top and bottom left © Press Association Images, bottom right © Getty Images; p.4 top © Richard Young, bottom © Opticphotos. com; p.5 © Opticphotos.com; p.6 top left and right © Opticphotos. com, bottom © Press Association Images; p.7 top © Paul Sassienie, bottom © Rex Features; p.8 © Denise Collins